# submerged

## A LIFETIME OF DIVING

by Mick Moriarty

**COMHAIRLE FÓ-THUINN**
Irish Underwater Council

78a Patrick Street, Dun Laoghaire,
Co. Dublin, Ireland

**Published by:**
**The Irish Underwater Council – Comhairle Fó-Thuinn(IUC/CFT)**
**78a Patrick Street, Dun Laoghaire, Co, Dublin, Ireland**

**Tel. 01 2844601    Fax. 01 2844602    E-mail: scubairl@indigo.ie**
**Website: http://www.scubaireland.com**

**Printed in Ireland by W&G Baird LTD**

**Typesetting and design by Bernard Kaye**

**Cover design by John Moriarty**

**Cover photo by Nigel Motyer**

**ISBN      0 948283 05 X (Paperback)**
**0 948283 04 1 (Hardback)**

# FOREWORD

This is not a 'Teach Yourself Diving' book. I have simply tried to write about my experiences and adventures of more than forty years of diving. It is based on the personal diaries and diving logbooks that I have maintained over the years, while in more recent times, I have also had, as the Archivist to CFT, access to a large range of records and documents. While trying to avoid being too technical, I felt that at times I could not avoid going into some detail for the benefit of the non-diving reader.

It is my own story, as I remember it. Of necessity, it is also the story of the early days of the Curragh Sub Aqua Club, the Army Sub Aqua Group and of CFT - The Irish Underwater Council, in all of which I have been deeply involved. While I have tried to avoid writing a historical account, a certain amount of history is necessary, if only to assist future researchers. If I have disappointed or hurt anyone by error or by omission, I am truly sorry, it was most certainly not intentional.

In September 1998, at the end of a hard day's diving, spent conducting Leading Diver examinations at Smerwick Harbour in West Kerry, Billy Nott and I made our way rapidly to the pub in Ballyferriter to wash away some of the salt. An elderly man, sitting comfortably at the bar, watched us rush in. He leaned over and said to me, "Aren't you a biteen old for this sort of thing", and turning to Billy, "And you too?" Perhaps he was right, and after a heavy day, I might agree with him. But the truth is that the magic has not yet faded, the desire to dive is still very strong, thank God, long may it continue.

In doing research for this book and musing over the events presented here, I can only marvel at the patience of my wife of 38 years, Anne Cosgrove. I have to thank her most humbly for her support and above all, her tolerance of my obsession.

Dublin, 2000

# THE SEA

*Fount of all life, master of the planet,*

*Source of all we are, without her we die,*

*Playful sands, warm bountiful pools,*

*Giver of all good, on her we rely*

*Shimmering, glistening, murmuring,*

*Restless, tumbling  - millions of years,*

*Seeking, searching, pushing, filling,*

*Lapping on shores, cliffs, rocks and piers*

*Destroyer of man, bringer of grief,*

*Taker of life, maker of sorrow,*

*Thundering, roaring, frightening,*

*No human power can narrow*

*Moana*

**submerged**

# Contents

# ACKNOWLEDGMENTS

In the research and preparation of this book, I wish to acknowledge the help and advice of Mick O' Farrell, Des Branigan, Dr John de Courcy Ireland and the many divers and former divers who helped me to clarify certain dates or incidents. In particular, I wish to thank my wife Anne and daughter Niamh for their assistance and encouragement, John for his design of the cover and other helpful suggestions and Daragh for untangling the many computer problems that I incurred over the period.

I wish to express my sincere thanks to Gearoid Murphy and the Executive of CFT for their practical support in publishing this book. My special thanks to Bernard Kaye for his great work in preparing the end product, and finally, I wish to pay a special tribute to my editor Ruth Hyland for her great patience and perseverance.

The views and opinions expressed are my own and are not necessarily those of Comhairle Fó-Thuinn - the Irish Underwater Council.

All photographs were taken by the author unless otherwise stated. In the interests of brevity, I have adhered to the standard English usage of 'he', 'his', and 'him' as referring to both men and women.

# CHAPTER 1
## *"In the beginning —"*

On a warm afternoon in late summer 1957 at Lough Owel, Mullingar, something happened which was destined to affect my life in a most unexpected and radical way. It is not often that a person can look back over a span of more than 40 years and identify a precise event that changed the direction of his or her life. But my first snorkelling experience proved to be one of those occasions, lightning struck at me out of a clear blue sky, scoring a direct hit.

Carefully following instructions, I pulled on two blue rubber flippers (nowadays they are called fins). Each had a soft shoe-type moulding but they still felt big and awkward on my feet. Then I put on the oval-shaped facemask that covered both my eyes and nose. Next I threaded the metal breathing tube under the headband of the mask to keep it in place, and gripped the blue rubber mouthpiece in my mouth in a manner similar to the way a boxer or a football player holds his gum shield. It all felt very strange and slightly uncomfortable, I could smell rubber from the mask and taste it in my mouth. I was now only able to breathe through my mouth. Just to be sure, I held on with one hand to the concrete side of the ramp that stretched from the shore out to the diving platform and with great care, I eased my face slowly into the calm warm water of the lake.

Any worries I had were immediately forgotten. I could see! I found that I was looking at my feet; they were very large and seemed quite close to me, as if my legs had become shorter. Suddenly the world that I had known for 26 years, a world that ended at the surface of the water, was gone. I was in a new and strange place, bathed in a brown-gold light from the late afternoon sun. The slanting rays threw mysterious shadows along the bottom of the lake behind the bigger stones and the pillars that supported the ramp. I inspected the support pillars and then looked out towards the darkness of the deeper water beyond. I was able to see for about fifteen feet in any direction around me.

Forgetting my over-water surroundings, I let go of the ramp and allowed the water to support me as I drifted slowly along, mesmerised by the flood of sensations I was experiencing. I felt as if I was flying, or more correctly gliding. This sensation was intensified as I moved outwards towards the deeper water around the diving platform. I was weightless, free from the strains of gravity, and I found that with one or two kicks of the flippers, I would move forward with speed and ease. By now, I had forgotten that I was

1

Lough Owel, Co. Westmeath, where it all started!

breathing through a narrow metal tube. It had already become an automatic process, pushed to the back of my consciousness by the joy of gliding along, supported by the upward pressure of the water.

The lake bottom was littered with large and small gold-coloured rocks and there was very little weed, just some short dark green strands in clumps here and there. The bottom sloped gently for a short distance and then it dropped more steeply into the depths beyond the platform. The dark gloomy depths looked threatening and unattractive so I turned back into the shallows. Looking around in fascination, I saw a small shoal of perch passing across my front, paying little or no attention to me. I followed them for a while as best I could, using gentle free-style kicks of the fins to drive me along. I could see beautiful, glowing colours on their sides and noticed that they were craftily camouflaged, being darker on top than on their sides or underneath. This colour scheme was designed to make them less visible to predatory birds. Their colours seemed to change and glisten in the low sunlight as they twisted and turned. I noticed that they all moved and turned in unison to some invisible signal. The smaller fish sometimes were taken by surprise and had to scurry to catch up with the larger ones. Occasionally, a flash of bright silver would catch my eye as a fish would suddenly turn on its side to eat something, the sunlight reflecting from its silver flank. Not being a fisherman, I knew very little about fish, so this experience was quite a revelation to me. I was viewing the fish in their own element, going about their daily business, and it was so much more interesting than watching bored fish in a tank.

2

Out of the corner of my eye I noticed movement! I turned in time to see a string of small bubbles coming up from underneath a stone. I glided over to investigate and turned the stone over quickly but was disappointed that there was nothing beneath it. I realised then that the bubbles had been probably created by the decomposition of vegetation, and not by some small aquatic animal. I turned over some more stones just to be sure, but did not notice anything of interest other than to note the difference in the colour and appearance of the underside of the stones. The undersides were clear of minute organic growth and were whitish in colour. I was surprised by the fact that stones that would seem quite unremarkable when seen on dry land took on mysterious characteristics that warranted closer attention when seen underwater.

Then I turned my attention to the other swimmers passing around me. From this new point of view, they appeared to be thrashing around in the water, as if they were fighting for their lives. They looked so awkward and appeared to be burning so up much energy in the effort to stay afloat and to move. I felt far superior in my new-found world and in the knowledge that they were oblivious to the marvels that lay so close beneath them. By comparison with their wild, frantic, thrashing, I was drifting along, expending little or no energy, and feeling very comfortable in a manner that I had never experienced before. I felt like a bird soaring over rocks and gullys, and I found it enthralling.

I continued to move around in the shallows for an hour or so, until fatigue and the chill drove me from the water. It was with great reluctance that I handed back the mask, snorkel and flippers to Dr Trevor Winckworth, a fellow-member of the Mullingar Swimming Club. He was watching me with a smile on his face, aware of the impact that this unexpected experience had had on me. Trevor had recently received the equipment from a friend of his, Val Hynes, who brought it in from the United States. Val himself had been a keen swimmer in his day, a graduate of Blackrock College, Dublin, and prominent in Bray Cove Swimming Club.

\*   \*   \*   \*   \*   \*   \*   \*

From an early age I was fascinated with water. I have vivid memories of bathing in the small sandy coves, or fishing for crabs from a pier wall, at Courtmacsherry in County Cork. When our family moved to Listowel I spent hours each August cavorting in the breakers on the beach at Ballybunion, the Men's Beach that is, us males were not allowed on the Ladies Beach. I took my very first strokes in the pool in the Black Rocks there and remember being used as a 'patient' while someone was being put through her life-saving tests.

After my father, Tomás, a 'Cigire Scoile' was transferred to Ennis, Co. Clare, I took every opportunity to swim in the river Fergus at Ennis, at a place know as the Turret. In those early years all swimmers had been aware of the threat posed by water, and the need for anyone who indulged in water sport of any sort to be profoundly careful. Any mistake or miscalculation in or on the water had the potential to be fatal. We were all very conscious of not swimming after taking a meal, or when swimming in cold water after heavy exercise.

In Dublin, Cork, or Belfast, the swimming galas were held in the small corporation indoor heated pools, or public baths, as they were called then. Others took place in the larger open-air unheated venues such as those in Blackrock or Clontarf in Dublin, the Pickie Pool in Bangor, or in the Victoria Pool in Cork. Elsewhere in Ireland, the swimming galas took place in a variety of locations such as lakes, rivers or canals. In Clare, galas were held in the Fergus at the Turret, or in the canal basin in Scariff, the sea in Kilkee Bay, off the White Strand at Milltown Malbay, in the Shannon at Killaloe, the graving docks in Limerick or in the harbour at Liscannor - whenever the tide was in.

At the annual gala held at the Turret, the premier event was a race called the Fergus Swim that was always keenly contested. The course, of about 600 yards, started in the Claureen, a small tributary of the Fergus. The riverbank along the route of the race - before the meeting of the Claureen and the Fergus - was heavily draped in places with overhanging trees and long reeds. Swimmers from Cork, like Frank O'Donovan or others like Dan Brilly or Billy Dooley from Limerick, would complain about this race. They always maintained that the Ennis swimmers would get out of the water at discreet places - where the judges could not see them - run along the bank for a while, and then jump back in again. It was completely untrue of course, it was only their way of explaining why outsiders rarely, if ever, managed to win this particular race!

Swimmers were always aware of the unseen dangers that lurked beneath them in these locations, especially the rivers and the canals. Apart altogether from barbed wire, old bicycles, dead dogs, (even then people used the nearest open water in which to dump their rubbish), other half-formed horrors hung around the fringes of the swimmer's mind. Passing over or through some sea or river weed, it might well be the feelers of some dreaded marine monster trying to pull one under, clutching at you all way to your toes, definitely an unsettling experience. The modern swimmers in their heated swimming pools and centrally-heated dressing rooms, complete with showers, toilets, hair dryers, and soft drinks dispensers are ignorant of the terrors of the open water, cosseted as they are in their clear, warm, and obstacle-free pools.

A strong element of competition existed amongst all us young people as to who could go deepest, who could stay down the longest, or who could find and bring up an object thrown into the water. We were experts at 'funny' dives, or at tricks on and under the water. Ernan Barron, one of the elders of the Ennis Swimming Club, was the leader in this area and had us imitating him or trying to best him. There was always a great curiosity amongst us about the bottom of the river and what it looked like, and how many or what kinds of fish were under us as we swam along. All we could go on were brief and blurred glimpses, snatched when the water was clear enough, a rare event in itself. For me, the wonderful world of Cousteau and his millions of followers were still in the future, waiting to be discovered.

*    *    *    *    *    *    *    *

On that late summer's evening at Lough Owel, I had been given an unexpected and astonishing introduction to the strange and enthralling water world - which up to now had been so dim, threatening, mysterious, and out-of-focus. It was quite literally an eye-opener! Archimedes must have felt a bit like this as he watched the water pouring over the side of his bath, too distracted to wonder what the wife, or his slave, or both, would say about the mess. Stout and breathless Cortez must have felt such emotions when he stared out at the Pacific, not just from the climb up the hill, laden down as he was by all that body armour, but also as a result of the excitement that he must have felt at seeing a new ocean.

As I dressed and drove back to barracks, I talked excitedly about my wonderful and unexpected experience. The more I talked about it, the more I realised that the underwater world was the new direction for which I had been waiting for quite some time. I was coming to the end of my competitive swimming career and felt very much in need of a new activity, a new purpose, preferably connected with water. The dreaded golf was staring me in the face, a fate that I regarded as considerably worse than death. I had been a follower of the Mullingar Rugby Club in the 1950s, and occasionally I even took part in training sessions with the team. I could well have become a 'reserve' player on the bench if I had wished. I had never played rugby up to this - and as it turned out, I never did.

I was certain that I had found my future activity. I had 'seen the light', a term borrowed from another source and used by Shane O'Connor a year later in the Curragh swimming pool. That was how he described yet another 'goggler' coming out of the Curragh pool with that special look in the eye, that glow of surprise, that reluctance to leave the water, which indicated that he or she was 'hooked'. He or she had 'seen the light'. However, despite the impact of my first look beneath the surface, another visit to the bottom of Lough Owel might not have been repeated, were it not for the fact that I was at that time a member of a book club. Each month the club sent me a book, sometimes of my choice, sometimes not. Shortly after my introduction to the under-lake world, a fortunate, and in retrospect, a fateful coincidence occurred.

A book called 'The Silent World' - written by Jacques-Yves Cousteau and Frederic Dumas - arrived in the post. The book recounted the story of the development of the first practical aqualung in France and the application of this simple but effective device during the war years and afterwards. The story had a huge impact on me and I must have read it several times in the first few months after receiving it. 'The Silent World' became my bible, and Cousteau became my hero, living the kind of life and experiencing the kind of adventures that I have ever since been longing to imitate. This was before TV was widespread in Ireland, when we eagerly gathered at the Officers Mess in Ceannt Baracks to watch another episode of the excellent series of underwater films on BBC TV by Hans Hass. We were not deterred in the slightest by the grainy black and white reception and poor sound.

I was determined to get my own equipment, but it was not a straightforward matter. Diving equipment was not yet readily available as the sports shop as we know it today had not yet been invented. One had to go to the drapers for shorts, socks, shirts, and so on, and to the shoe shop for football boots or 'gym shoes'. What I did not know then was that two diving clubs already existed in Ireland, one in Belfast, the other in Dublin. It was some time before I found out about them, however. I eventually heard that there was a shop in Dublin that sold some diving equipment and after a while I traced Geoffrey Hammond to his shop in Parliament Street, where I bought my very first mask, snorkel and flippers. The snorkel was made of metal, with a blue rubber mouthpiece; the mask was of blue rubber with a 'toughened' oval-shaped glass, and both were manufactured by Typhoon in England. The blue flippers were called 'Rondine' and were made by Cressi in Italy.

Geoffrey turned out to be the Chairman of the Irish Sub Aqua Club, and his advice was very helpful. Later, when any of our new divers would be buying an item from him, he would invariably state that it was an excellent piece of equipment - he could thoroughly recommend it as he always used it himself. He referred to so many items of equipment in this way that at our weekly meetings in the Curragh we built up a collective mind-picture of poor Geoffrey, so laden down by all that diving equipment that he would have needed a crane to get in and out of the water! In the dealings we had with Geoffrey, he was always full of helpful hints and advice. Members of his Club gave a diving demonstration at an Army Swimming gala in July 1958 at the Curragh Camp.

\* \* \* \* \* \* \* \*

It is unlikely that any items of diving equipment were ever treated with such loving care and attention as my new acquisitions. They were passed from hand to hand in wonder and carefully washed out and dried after every use. They were also kept out of the hot (Irish!) sun in strict accordance with the manufacturer's instructions. The flippers were designed to give the wearer greatly increased power in the water when used in the manner of a free-style kick. The mask gives the diver the ability to see without distortion in the water, because there is an air space between his eyes and the water. Finally the breathing tube, or snorkel, enables the diver to breathe through his mouth without having to lift his head. The combination of all three can enable the user, with the minimum of instruction, to enjoy hours of relaxed pleasure in the sea.

Thus equipped with the basics, I passed many happy hours at Lough Owel and perfected my 'duck dive'. This manoeuvre is more correctly called a 'surface dive' and it is an essential next step in learning to become a skilled snorkel diver. I found that it was not necessary to carry any weights in order to get down. Without a protective suit, a diver's body was only marginally buoyant and it was quite easy to fin downwards.

To execute a surface dive, you take a deep breath, bending quickly at the waist and pointing your head down, as if you intend to do a handstand on the bottom. As part of the same motion, you bring your legs vertically upwards and out of the water. The weight of your body then helps to thrust you down, so that you slide easily and gracefully towards the bottom. You can then remain underwater only for as long as you can hold your breath. When the need for a breath becomes impossible to ignore, you dash for the surface. Once there, it is necessary to blow the water out of the snorkel tube, (because it had would have filled as you went down), and only then are you free to inhale deeply once more.

It became obvious to me at an early stage that it was necessary to gauge my ability to remain under the water very carefully. I had to ensure that I had enough 'puff' remaining in my lungs to clear the snorkel when I returned to the surface. Otherwise I would make an undignified arrival at the surface, gasping and coughing, probably snatching the mask from my face in a desperate desire for air. If no one was watching, it was not too bad, but in front of an audience, it was very much 'infra-dig', or in the idiom of the time, 'non-U'. The experienced snorkel diver should never let himself down like this - it left him open to embarrassing comment. In practice, it rapidly became an instinctive reaction, and I could normally surface with grace and dignity. As with all exercises, repetition improved my performance. In a short time, I found that my ability to stay on the bottom had increased impressively, while my ability to fin at speed and for long distance on the surface had improved dramatically. I was becoming an accomplished 'snorkel diver', a term to be used later on.

During these late summer months in Mullingar, I was reading and dreaming of the exploits of Cousteau, while at the same time struggling with the practicalities of purchasing an aqualung. Cousteau coined the term 'aqualung' to describe the complete assembly of a steel air cylinder, a demand valve, and a harness with which to strap the apparatus to one's back. The twin-hose, single-stage demand valves of the time had the function of reducing the high-pressure air contained in the cylinder and supplying it to the diver 'on demand' at just above ambient water pressure. Cousteau subsequently patented the name 'Aqualung' when his company went into mass production of diving equipment.

Extremely simple and reliable, this device enabled the diver to breathe easily underwater at depth. But like all things in this world, there was a price to pay. The cost of an aqualung was well beyond the monthly salary of a single lieutenant, so I spent many of my waking hours scheming and plotting as to how to raise the necessary funds. Other members of Mullingar Swimming Club such as Brud Corcoran and Dr Trevor Winckworth had also become interested in the underwater world. We spent many hours discussing ways of raising the price of two aqualungs, the minimum number we felt we needed in order to start exploring the lake. We considered holding flag days, or collecting in front of the churches, or even appealing to swimming and other clubs in the area for grants. Eventually, we had to face the awful but obvious solution, we had no option but to form a diving club.

Now, at this time in Mullingar, I was an active member of the swimming club, the tennis club and the musical society. I had taken up processing my own photographs, and I was a follower of the rugby team. I was also on my unit rifle shooting team, which entailed spending long hours in the spring and early summer on the rifle range at the lake near Athlone. I was barrack welfare officer to boot, which meant organising functions in barracks for the soldiers. The prospect of becoming involved in yet another organisation was not something that I could look forward to with relish, and yet it appeared to be the only way forward.

But while all these discussions were taking place, and while we were about to commit ourselves to starting a club in Mullingar, fate, in the unlikely guise of the Director of Artillery, Col. D.J. McLoughlin, stepped in. Completely out of the blue, I was transferred to Magee Barracks in Kildare to become an instructor in gunnery at the Artillery School. That was it, I had to leave all my friends in Mullingar, the beautiful lake, and in particular, the plans we had for starting a diving club. It was with great regret that I packed my Morris Minor 'banger' for the move to the Curragh. It was the place from which I had been so glad to escape five years before, having spent two gruelling years in the Cadet School. Was this to be the end of the brief diving adventure? It seemed so.

But what I did not know, and could not have foreseen, was that I had just set a match to a fuse, an underwater one to be sure. The fuse sparkled and smoked along the road under the Morris Minor as it trundled through Edenderry and Rathdangan to Magee Barracks in Kildare. This fuse eventually ignited the rocket that launched me into a series of adventures, friendships and life-experiences that have continued to this very day.

# CHAPTER 2
# The New Club

The Curragh Training Camp, as it was inappropriately titled, is not a camp at all but a large complex of mainly red-brick permanent buildings. With some modern additions, it stretches for a couple of miles across the Curragh Plains. Magee Barracks, Kildare, now closed, was the centre for artillery training for the Corps and it opened up many new and fascinating activities to keep me busy for quite some months. However, like all new things in life, the novelty eased somewhat after a while and I was able to turn my attention to the swimming pool in the Camp. It was built by the Corps of Engineers during the war years for training soldiers in water-crossing techniques. For this reason it was built to an unconventional design and dimension - 40 yards long - featuring huge sliding doors at one end and on one side to facilitate the introduction of large boats and rafts. As part of their training, all recruits were required to swim one length of the pool dressed in full combat equipment and carrying their rifles. The water was heated, but not the dressing rooms. Not only did the building lack central heating, but the roof ended on metal posts a good six inches above the supporting walls. The result in summer was a very pleasant fresh-air atmosphere, and the pool was well used. However, in winter the attendance dropped off noticeably. It was easily the biggest indoor swimming pool in Ireland at the time, and those of us who were able to use it regularly were the envy of swimmers in other parts of the country.

I took to using my fins, mask and snorkel there, and I spent many hours inspecting the bottom of the pool, to the extent that even today I can close my eyes and hear the distinctive throb of the water circulation pump. The hours I spent in and under the water were to stand to me later on when I became a spearfisherman, a sport that required considerable breath holding ability, but that was still some time in the future. My activities attracted much attention, and I became accustomed to losing much of my own practice time to provide others with 'a go'. Most people, especially the good swimmers, reacted favourably, if not with outright enthusiasm, to the experience. So much so, that it was often difficult to recover my property before the end of the swim session. Fairly quickly, some of the regulars had made the pilgrimage to Geoffrey Hammond in Parliament Street, Dublin, to buy their own basics. This considerably eased the strain on my overworked diving gear. In motoring terms, the fins would have passed the 100,000 mile mark, while the snorkel was definitely in need of a re-bore!

On Thursday, the 15th of May 1958, four people met in the small lecture room - part of an annex to the old gymnasium - and decided to form a club to be called the Curragh Sub Aqua Club, (CSAC). It was the third diving club to be formed on the island of Ireland after Belfast Branch, British Sub Aqua Club and the Irish Sub Aqua Club in Dublin. The object of the Club was 'to further the sport of diving and, if required, to render assistance to the Military and Civil authorities'. The Patron was to be the Officer Commanding the Curragh Training Camp, the HQ was to be at the Swimming Pool and the colours were to be red and yellow. The logo was a leaping orca (killer whale), a member of the dolphin group of mammals.

Present at the inaugural meeting were myself, Lieut. Mick McDonough, Lieut. Mick O'Farrell and Austin O'Donnell. We decided on a provisional committee until an AGM could be held in the Autumn. Mick McDonough agreed to become the Chairman, because he was the senior officer present, and military protocol had to be respected after all. I took the duties of Diving and Training officer, because I was reckoned to have the greatest experience of diving at that stage. Austin took on the job of Treasurer, mainly because none of us military types wanted to have anything to do with money, conditioned as we were by six-monthly audits of messes, the menace of courts of enquiry, and so on. We felt that he knew more about handling money than any of us because he worked with his dad in their grocery shop on O'Higgins Road. Finally, Mick O'Farrell was designated as Equipment Officer, even though we had no club equipment whatsoever at that stage. Mick nearly fell from his chair laughing at the mere idea - he thought that this was going to be an easy job. However, we quickly got our own back on him by deciding to have an outing to Dunmore East at the forthcoming long weekend. He was to be in charge of the 'equipment', i.e. the Army two-man tents - known to us as 'bivvies', the cooking and eating utensils, and the blankets. These were all to be 'borrowed' from the stores of his own unit, the 3rd Infantry Battalion. This made him cross. He didn't like the idea of having to sign for these expensive items and to take responsibility for their safe return.

Annual subscriptions were set at one guinea for men and 10 shillings and sixpence for ladies, should we ever happen to attract any. It was to have been one pound for the men, but the horsey types amongst us, i.e. all the others, insisted that it sounded 'posh' to use guineas. After all we were on the Curragh, the home of the horse industry, where all dealings in horses was carried out in guineas. Unfortunately, there are no minutes of this meeting in existence, but even if there were, the minutes could not have recorded the hilarity of the occasion, the jokes that were flying, and the regular peals of laughter.

Thus, the club started in an atmosphere of laughter, merriment, and general good humour, a condition that has continued to characterise the Club down through the years, and has contributed in no small way to its success.

The week leading up to departure for Dunmore east was filled with frantic phone calls - not an easy matter in those remote low-tech days. The phones were of the wind-up type, and there were only five or six in each Barracks, where the Barracks exchanges were manned by civilian operators, usually ex-soldiers. The calls were about such vital matters as food, where to 'bivvy', i.e. where to set up our tents, what to bring in the shape of personal kit, money, etc. I was providing the transport, being the only one with a car, so that at least was not a problem. At this time we were all, bar Mick O'Farrell, busy making our own spears, in case we had to defend ourselves against the monsters of the deep. Now here was truly unsophisticated apparatus. Some time previously, I purchased a new wooden brush handle in O'Donnell's shop in the Curragh Camp and acquired a six-inch nail and some bailing wire in Magee Barracks. I cut a groove into the side of the handle at one end and beat the large nail into it, the point of the nail protruding beyond the handle for about three inches. I then wound a length of bailing wire as tightly as possible around the handle and the nail, in order to keep it in place. The result was laughable, but it served its purpose, and Austin and Mick McDonough quickly made their own versions.

I should state here that Mick McDonough was known to one and all as 'The Mighty', probably because he was an instructor in the Army School of Physical Culture, as well as being a very fine all-round athlete. Mick O'Farrell, a Cadet classmate of mine, was known as 'The Tiger' because he was, well, a bit wild, although he too was an excellent athlete, especially with the javelin. Having nicknames helped us to cope with a situation in which 75% of the membership of the new club were called Mick. In those days, when our group was being introduced to strangers, it must have sounded a bit like the (very much later) Monty Python TV sketch wherein all the Australian males are called Bruce: "I'd like you to meet Bruce, and this is Bruce, and over here we have Bruce"! In our case, it was a great relief that we had an Austin amongst all the Micks, otherwise we could not have been taken seriously. Not that we expected anyone to take us seriously. Most people would say things like "you mean you go under the water for fun - you must be mad". Our standard reply was that "you don't have to be mad to go diving, but it helps"!

On Friday afternoon, 10th of July 1958, I drove in to the Curragh from Kildare and collected Mick O'Farrell, the two 'bivvies' and some cooking equipment in the 3rd Battalion. We strapped the tents and the cooking equipment on the roof rack, and drove to Austin's shop, where we picked up Austin and Mick McDonough. We managed to wedge a Kosangas cylinder in between the tents, jammed some food in the boot, and headed off towards Waterford. The car was overloaded, but we were not in a hurry and we sang as we went along. At this particular time, the 'Dam Busters March' by Billy Cotton was very popular, and we were singing this at the tops of our voices, doing all the bit parts, such as the voices on the aircraft intercom, the aircraft engine sounds, and the sound of the anti-aircraft explosions.

Coming down the long winding descent into Castlecomer, the inevitable happened. As we went around a particularly tight bend, the roof-rack decided that it had had enough, so it slid back and down off the roof and came to rest in the middle of the road. It didn't skip and hop like the bouncing bomb about which we had been singing, nor did it spread into its component parts across the road. It simply remained in one neat pile in the middle of the road, right at a tricky bend. When I got out of the car, having pulled in at a safe place, I was greeted by the sight of Mick McDonough doing a handstand on the roof rack, something he was good at, of course. Traffic was fortunately very light in those days, so we got Mick down off the roof-rack and had it back on the car before any tragedy could strike.

As we settled back into the car and continued more cautiously down into Castlecomer, someone said he could smell gas. This required immediate action, so we pulled up at the nearest pub, where we borrowed some sealing wax. Then the 'The Mighty' and the 'The Tiger' placed the gas cylinder on the counter-top, and solemnly proceeded to rotate it slowly, sniffing for gas, holding a lighted match, ready to drip sealing wax on the leak! By now, Austin and I had moved out to the car, just in case. There was no leak of course, otherwise the Curragh Sub Aqua Club might well have come to an abrupt end there and then, as well as a goodly portion of Castlecomer! After holding a prolonged EGM in the pub, we continued on our way, arriving without further incident into Dunmore East around dusk.

Mick O'Farrell was from Dungarvan, so he knew the area. Following his lead, we pitched our tents on a small grassy hill to the south of, and overlooking, the harbour. As soon as possible after pitching the tents and sorting ourselves out, we retired to the Haven Hotel to hold another meeting. It was fortunately very easy to contact all the members for an EGM - we constituted the entire 100% membership of our new club after all - and anyway we were very thirsty. What we didn't realise until the following morning was that our campsite overlooked the local convent. During the night, the poor nuns had been subjected to our drunken screams and witticisms, such as "Banzai, Amelican Almy

Number 10, Japanese Almy No 1", and other even less palatable expressions, as well as a few more choruses of the Dam Busters March. The convent no longer exists; the nuns have left and it became first a hotel and later on a hostel. It is quite possible that the nuns felt that they could not have lived with the dreadful prospect of yet another CSAC outing to Dunmore. So they probably accepted the very first offer they received for their property. In retrospect, perhaps CSAC should have claimed some of the profits made by the developers, as we must have contributed to the departure of the nuns.

It was close to midday on Saturday before we felt able to approach the sea. I had no knowledge of the suitability of the coastline for diving, so I chose the easy option. We went down the slipway in the village, and prepared for the historic moment. As we did not possess diving suits, we put on our army long-johns, and as many other pullovers and shorts as we had with us. (A small word here is necessary about Army long-johns. All members of the Forces were issued with these instruments of torture on entry to the Forces, but only the masochists could love them. They were probably the forerunners of brillo pads or the coarsest sandpaper. Fortunately today they are no longer on issue). The Mighty was the first into the water, as befits the Chairman, and he had only been in for about thirty seconds when he screamed that he had just seen an enormous crab. This speeded up our entry, by which time he had skewered an unfortunate and distinctly average crab, waving it about in triumph at the end of his homemade spear.

As it happened, a short time before the weekend, I had become the proud owner of a real speargun. Made in Italy, the Folgore speargun had belonged to a flying officer in the Air Corps called Shane Gray, who had lived part of his earlier life in Libya, and who had some experience as a spearfisherman. It was the first manufactured speargun that I had seen, and it cost me the huge sum of £5. The Folgore as the name suggested, could be dismantled and folded up for travelling. It was powered by a long internal spring and to load it, you had to press the spear back down the barrel against the resistance of the spring until the notch on the spear engaged on the sear of the trigger. It had a grip, trigger, and a trigger guard like a pistol, and it was fairly well balanced at the grip. You sighted along the barrel and released the spear by pressing the trigger. The spear was attached to the gun by a light line, so that the spear, and hopefully the fish, could be recovered. The Folgore had a range of about two or three metres, so it was necessary to use stealth to get as near as possible to the fish. At this time, because of my lack of experience, the advantage lay very much with the fish. At Dunmore East, I was using it in the sea for the first time and I surprised myself by bagging an unfortunate and very small wrasse that happened to be passing across my front.

The founder members of CSAC at Dunmore East, July 1958.
From left: Mick McDonough, Mick O'Farrell, Austin O'Donnell and the author.

Each day we got into the water at a different place, having to suffer the considerable torture of putting on our very damp and odorous 'protective' clothing. Early on the second day, both the 'Mighty' and the 'Tiger' decided that the cold sea was not quite up to the standards of the Curragh Pool, and they found compelling reasons to be elsewhere. To be fair to them, as practising, and very good, athletes, it was not the kind of exercise likely to help them in their competitions. That left Austin and me to continue our exploration of the shallows along the foreshore around Dunmore East. We also spent long hours in the pub trying to restore our lost body heat.

We soon came to realise that the sight of all the long johns and pullovers drying out on top of the knoll made our 'bivvy' area look rather like a Chinese laundry, and that it was probably time to withdraw and re-group in the Curragh. Locally, the nights must have been a little quieter with the 50% fall in our numbers, but even so, the likely reaction of the nuns to our continued occupation of the high ground would surely have led to confrontation between ourselves and the Church. As the Church was very powerful in those days, a swift transfer to Fort Leenane in north Donegal might well have been in store for me! Austin was safe enough though, being a mere 'civvy', - or to use the vernacular of the club at that time - 'a f—- g civvy'! So we packed up and left. Austin and I certainly enjoyed ourselves and we even managed to bring back all the stores that were on charge to the errant Equipment Officer.

The weekend was adjudged to have been a great success, even if 50% of the membership failed to last the course. There was a surprise postscript to the weekend, for me anyway. Just a short time before the weekend, I had been appointed as Aide de Camp (ADC) to Colonel Tony Lawlor, Officer Commanding the Curragh Training Camp. My new duties were varied and interesting, certainly very different from those at the Artillery School. I was his 'go-for', and in addition to the normal domestic chores, this job involved a lot of formality and protocol, because he had to receive visiting ambassadors and other VIPs from time to time. It was also very exciting when he went on his inspections of Barracks, as I was on the safer side of his wrath. I'd moved from Magee Barracks into the Officers Mess in Ceannt Barracks, to be nearer to my place of work. On the return from Dunmore East late on the Monday night of the long weekend, I went straight to bed, exhausted from the driving, diving, and from all the special EGMs.

The inevitable happened, I slept out! It fortunately falls to very few young, eager and ambitious officers to be woken up by the Command Adjutant himself. The Command Adjutant was, and still is, God Almighty to all young officers. He is to be avoided at all costs, or to be approached with great caution, and then only when absolutely necessary. Comdt. Tom O'Hanlon was gazing sternly down at me. He spoke tersely, "The Command OC requires your presence immediately, if not sooner"! Even as a Cadet, I had probably never moved more smartly, and I was quickly ushered into the presence of the great man. He sat and glowered up at me with his penetrating green eyes in silence for a few moments. This gaze put me in mind of his reputation as a ruthless member of the old IRA in Mayo during the War of Independence, and I started to look out for signs that he was reaching for his trusty 45.

However, being the gentleman that he was behind all the outward crustiness, he relaxed, smiled and asked me to carry out some chore for him. Both officers were very good about it and the subject never arose again. They probably put it down to this mad new diving thing, but no doubt they started to compile a special file on my behaviour, in anticipation of my inevitable collapse.

All through that first year we gradually started to gain more members. As well as the founder members, the list of members for 1958 finally read more or less in the order in which they joined the Club:- Joe Leech, Niall Callinan, Shane O'Connor and later on, his new wife Betty, Jim Motherway, Brendan O'Flynn, Liam Lunney, Larry Bradley, Teresa Bradley, Ronnie Gallagher, Con Crean, Phil Douglas, Ultan Lyons, Conal Bradley, Jenny Simcox, Fintan and Adrian Mullowney, Billy Graham, Jimmy Flynn, Pat Doody, Cora Brennan, Eileen Noonan, Veronica Conlon and Johnny King. As well as the above, we gained some members in Limerick - Ronnie Hurley, Johnny Ryan, Adrian Clancy, Dermot Fitzgerald, Ray Doyle, and Eoin Geary. A year later, on the 8th of July 1960, the Limerick members all left to form their own diving club in Killaloe. We were assured that this had nothing to do with the fact that Eoin Geary's collar bone was broken during a 'rugby match' on the beach at Duncannon, Co Wexford, while on a CSAC diving weekend at the Hook.

All these individuals contributed in significant and varied ways to the progress of the Club, but of special significance was Shane O'Connor, who had started off in the pool one evening by borrowing my mask and snorkel and one flipper - the other being on loan to somebody else. For years afterwards Shane would describe his very first experience, and how, because he was using only one flipper, he kept going around in circles in the water, like a ship with one propeller out of action. He was totally engrossed in the experience, only to be brought back to reality when he bumped his head sharply against the handrail. He 'had seen the light' with a vengeance - and probably some stars as well - and he still talks about that first experience with great affection. Shane became a vital and seminal figure in the early development of the Club. Later on, as diving developed in Ireland, he became the first President of Comhairle Fo Thuinn, CFT – The Irish Underwater Council, the new national organisation.

In the early days of the club, we had a lot of trouble describing exactly what it was that we were or what it was that we did. Diving was such a new sport that many people had great misconceptions about it. We were described as 'frogmen', 'deep-sea divers' or worse, 'sub aqua divers', a ridiculous term. We were also being confused with the spring and high-board divers. Some people seemed to struggle with a mental picture of us, wearing strange clothes and carrying awkward equipment, trying to do forward somersaults in the tuck position from the high board. "No, no", we'd say, gritting our teeth, "we're divers, we're free divers, we go diving under the sea, we're free to roam around underwater, not attached to a support vessel overhead. We do not have great big copper pots on our heads, we don't wear large lead boots, and we don't have to struggle with giant squid who try to cut our air hoses. We're 'divers' and we call what we do 'diving'."

The 'sub aqua' in the title came into common usage following the formation of the British Sub Aqua Club in 1954 in London, and as a result, nearly all the early clubs here used 'Sub Aqua' in their titles. However, some clubs like Aquamarine Divers or Dalkey

During All-Army Week in the Curragh Camp, 1963, at the CSAC stand: Captains Shane O'Connor and Jimmy Flynn.

Scubadivers were amongst the early exceptions to this practice. In other countries of the world, clubs are called by much more prosaic or appropriate names, such as the 'Fin-twisters' Diving Club, 'The Boston Bottom Scratchers', 'The Miami Gogglers', 'Vanquatics' of Vancouver, and so on. In recent years in Ireland, new clubs with names such as 'Alpha Dive' have appeared. The problem of giving our new activity a suitable 'job description' was a worldwide one. In their own inimitable style, and having a great passion for capitals and abbreviations, the Americans started to describe themselves as 'scuba divers'. SCUBA stands for 'Self-Contained Underwater Breathing Apparatus'. Can you imagine chatting up an attractive member of the opposite sex and telling him or her that you are "a self-contained underwater breathing apparatus diver"! It is a term I dislike, although I must also admit that it sums up pretty well what it is that we are and what it is that we do. I would much prefer to be known as a 'Free Diver', although today we would best be described as 'sports divers'.

Because of our newfound hobby, some members of the Club had taken to reading about diving on the coral reefs of the Caribbean and the Red Sea and dreaming of what it would be like. On our frequent diving weekends at the Hook Lighthouse, some of us would go into the old graveyard at Churchtown, which is close to the Lighthouse. There we would solemnly stand around the grave of a seaman on which had been placed a large and very weather-beaten piece of coral that he had presumably brought back from one of his voyages.

When some of us were down at Hook Head in 1959, we mentioned the subject of coral to the lighthouse keeper, Eugene O'Sullivan, and said that we had been wondering if it was to be found in Irish waters. "Yerra", said Eugene, "I know a lake over near Clifden that is full of the stuff". He stated that his son Albert had taken it in "lumps as big as turnips". Eugene was a Corkman, as Jim Motherway reminded us! Without further ado, Shane O'Connor, Jim and myself decided to make an expedition to Clifden, Co Galway on the very next weekend, and we headed off in great excitement in my VW, another in a long line of 'bangers'.

On the Ordnance Survey half-inch map, Sheet 10, the lake is called 'The Salt Lake', but it is known to locals as 'The Monk's Lake' as the remains of a monastery can be seen nearby. Situated outside Clifden on the road to Ballyconneely, it is quite a small fresh-water lake and is separated from the sea by a weir, which was located almost directly under the road bridge. At high tide, the seawater pours in, resulting in a mix of fresh and seawater in the lake. It creates a very unusual biological mixture, much like Lough Hyne in West Cork.

We changed beside the car and picked our way over the grass to the lakeshore. Shane and I were in our dry suits, while Jim had only the protection of some pullovers. We were very excited at the prospect of seeing real corals for the first time. We were snorkelling of course - none of us owned aqualungs at this time. We were in for a few surprises as we entered the water. The water was quite cold, but when we dived down, we passed into a layer of water that was noticeably warmer. We had just encountered our first halocline. A halocline is a condition to be found in mid-water where there are layers of cold and warm water, distinctly separated one from the other. It is usually found where there is a mixture of fresh and seawater. The seawater, being both heavier and warmer, lies below the fresh water. It was so well defined in this lake that it was possible to see the boundary between the layers as well as feel it.

The lake seemed to be about 20 feet deep, and it quickly became obvious to us that we were not seeing coral. At first sight of the sloping rock faces, I was reminded of a pretty garden, there appeared to be a profusion of white and pink 'flowers' growing on the rocks. However, as we approached the 'flowers', some of them would suddenly withdraw into the shelters of the 'tubes' in which they were living. Other flower-like animals, anemones, would not react unless tickled, whereupon they slowly retracted into themselves. The tube-livers cautiously emerged again after we had moved away. The tubes were twisted and intertwined in large clumps, rather like deranged organ pipes.

We removed some large clusters of the 'organ pipes' and placed them on the grass after the dive. While we changed back into our clothes, cursing Eugene O'Sullivan for having raised our hopes, we were astonished to see the poor animals struggling out of the tubes, driven out by the hot sun. We didn't find any corals, of course. What we saw was a type of worm, annelid, that lives in tubes in large colonies. They feed by putting out coloured tendrils to catch the passing microscopic food. 42 years later, I still have a small piece of the empty calcium tubes in my back garden.

There are corals in Irish waters, but not in the form of the colourful reefs as seen in the tropics. The only true coral that a diver can see is the Devonshire cup coral. It is a small oval coral, about 2cm across, and can be found in profusion in relatively shallow water on the southwest and west coasts. It is called a 'cup' coral, because it is shaped not unlike a small, shallow cup, with fluted edges. There is also a soft coral called gorgonia, which is usually white in colour. It looks for all the world like a small shrub that has lost its leaves. It can be seen in much the same conditions and locations as the cup coral. Both cup corals and gorgonias are fairly common in the South and Southwest waters, but do not appear be found in the Irish Sea.

Today, we know of the coral reefs that lie in very deep water, (300m or more), off the west and northwest coasts, as announced recently in 'Technology Ireland'. These reefs had actually been discovered in 1869 during a research cruise sponsored by the Royal Irish Academy and the Royal Dublin Society, but had been forgotten until now.

# CHAPTER 3
# THE EARLY DAYS

The new Club began to advertise for members in the Curragh Bulletin, the military newsletter of the Curragh Camp, and also in the Leinster Leader, the provincial paper based in Naas, Co. Kildare. A youthful Chris Glennon was the reporter most often given the task of reporting on us for the Leader. Members met at the Curragh Pool at 9 o'clock every Monday evening, and spent an hour or so practising our techniques. The only proviso for our use of the pool was that a lifesaving instructor had to be present. Of course we had several of these within our ranks, so that was never a problem. Our activities were regarded as being part of training for the military members, who formed the greater part of the membership at that time.

I made contact with some members of the Irish Sub Aqua Club (ISAC) in Dublin, and they could not have been more helpful. I was able to get advice on how the Club should be structured, what officers we needed, the types of equipment to buy and where to buy it, and what books to read. They offered to come down to the Curragh pool to give us a demonstration, an offer that I eagerly accepted. Tony Bishop, Cedric Bowmer, Hugh Quigley, Brian Pim and others travelled to the Curragh for a very informative demonstration of diving at the All-Army Gala in the Swimming Pool on 1st July 1958. The Secretary of ISAC gave me copies of their application for membership forms and membership cards. We were very impressed with the assistance of the divers of the Irish Sub Aqua Club. So much so, that later on, as our club developed, we in turn went out of our way to help other new emerging clubs such as those in Galway and Mullingar. This practice, whereby an established club undertook to assist an emerging club, became an operational principal following the formation of Comhairle Fo-Thuinn, The Irish Underwater Council, in 1963. It was a very practical means of support and it usually worked to the advantage of both clubs.

Because diving was a novel activity, offering a new form of adventure, many were attracted, but just as it is today, few persevered. When it came to the crunch, getting into cold water and staying underneath for 15 or twenty minutes without the benefit of a diving suit required a lot of enthusiasm. For many potential members, the rewards were just not sufficient, and only about one in every ten would complete the training. It is a problem that persists to this day, many people surrender at an early stage, even during the pool-training phase, when they find that the reality is quite some distance from the dream.

\*   \*   \*   \*   \*   \*   \*   \*

Mick McDonough and Jim Motherway at Hook Head, Aug 59, preparing to dive.

The author and Mick McDonough at Greystones preparing to go spearfishing, July 1958.

With members of the Irish Sub Aqua Club at Greystones, Jul 58. From the left, standing: Cedric Bowmer, the author, Mike Suchard, Paddy Hughes, Rory Breslin. Kneeling: Anthony Bishop, Brian Pim.

One day, while I was in my little office beside that of the Command OC at Command HQ, I received a most important letter from an Army friend in Cork. It included a cutting from the Cork Examiner, the front page, no less. It was completely filled with photographs of a group of divers from the Belfast Branch of the British Sub Aqua. They had been spending the previous week 'exploring the deeps' along the Cork coast, and 'De Paper' had given them a front-page spread.

I was thunderstruck and spent most of that day on the phone, telling everyone about this wondrous event. I resolved to make contact with members of the Belfast club as soon as possible. Some names were mentioned in the write-up, so I wrote to one Derek Nelson and had a response within the week. He told me all about his club and said that it was imperative that we have a get-together as soon as possible. When I heard that they were planning to go to Carraroe in Connemara for a weekend in August 1958, I proposed that we meet up with them in Galway and move on together from there. So we decided to bring a quantity of 'bivvies' and some cooking equipment with us to cater for approximately 26 divers, 13 from each club.

To this day, I remember the last instructions I received on the phone from this still 'unmet' Derek Nelson in Belfast. We were to search the pubs along the western side of the Square in Galway anytime after seven on the Friday evening. We were to look out for a group of shabbily dressed and heavily bearded, (the male members of the group that is), student-types speaking in strong Northern accents. On the 6th of August 1958, we set out from the Curragh Camp in great excitement with Austin in his father's estate car carrying the bulk of the camping equipment. Apart from Shane O'Connor colliding with a sheep, and me getting a puncture, we arrived into the centre of Galway in good order. It says a lot for the anticipation of both groups that we found the bearded wonders - perfect strangers - in only the second pub that we inspected. Our common interest ensured that we became firm friends on the spot, admittedly with the help of a considerable consumption of the 'black stuff'. Our new acquaintances were Colin McMurtry, Derek Nelson, Margot Sydney-Smith, Alistair Gilmour, Maureen McGladdery, Hugh Hennessy, Gerry Crangle, Hilda Maguire, Peter Paice, Michael Clarke, and Maurice Megahey.

I had a reputation at that time for being relatively abstemious, so it fell to me to organise where we were going to stay for the night. After we were put out of the pub, not an easy task for the owners, we discovered that it was raining heavily. There was a distinct lack of enthusiasm for setting up tents at that late hour of night. Then I had a potentially disastrous, (for my career, that is), idea. I said to my new-found friends, "I know what we can do, we will go up to the barracks and look for beds for the night".

This was greeted with great enthusiasm. So we drove up to the main gate of Mellowes Barracks, home of the 1st Infantry Battalion, the Irish-speaking unit, at Renmore. I asked everyone to be very quiet while I went inside to negotiate.

I was having some perfectly understandable difficulty in persuading the senior officer in the Officers Mess to allow us to stay, but he did eventually agree to go down to the gate with me to see the group for himself. When we got down to the main gate, I was horrified to see that, despite my warnings, some of the brand-new bosom buddies were practising Irish dancing on the road in the pouring rain. The sound of laughter and drunken singing was swelling out from inside the cars of the convoy, the largest of which carried Northern Ireland number plates. I knew there and then that all was lost. To be fair to the officer, he was quite apologetic in refusing us entry, and his decision probably saved my career and possibly his too! The sentry at the gate, no doubt, enjoyed it all. It must have helped him to pass a wet and boring night.

So we decided to go to the campsite out in Salthill, where we were supposed to have gone in the first place, but about 12 hours earlier. When the convoy of cars ground to a halt in the middle of the campsite at about 1.30am, the singing was at a crescendo. We were asked to leave immediately. We eventually ended up in the commonage behind the White Strand, where we set up the tents in the headlights of our cars. In the morning, there was a very confused departure for Carraroe, with divers from Belfast travelling in Curragh cars and vice versa. The confusion was so great that a brand-new member of the Curragh club, one Jim Motherway, a Lieutenant in the Signal Corps, being known to few of the group, was left behind. At Carraroe, we discovered that in the confusion, we had also forgotten many of the tents, so I had to borrow the Belfast minibus to drive back to Galway. We found Jim sitting on a folded up 'bivvy' and staring out to sea. He was quite good about it really. He said, "Once I saw that you had left some of the tents behind, I knew that you had to show up sooner or later". I collected Jim, and more importantly, all the property of the Minister, and we were back at Carraroe by lunchtime.

We watched in awe when the divers from Belfast began to unpack their diving cylinders and personal equipment and started to prepare for the water. Nobody in the Curragh club possessed any equipment like this, so it was a new and wonderful experience for us to be actually handling cylinders and discussing the merits of demand valves or diving suits. To this day, I can remember our surprise and delight when they started to arrange who was to dive with whom. We had expected to be shown the equipment and to be allowed to watch them while they went about their dives. But they had different ideas. They had come prepared and determined to bring each of us on our very first dives. This was an exceptionally generous offer because they had no means of refilling their cylinders once emptied. The nearest filling stations were in Dublin or in Belfast. They had not brought a portable compressor with them and indeed such items were not to be found in Ireland at that time.

I was told that I was to dive with Alistair Gilmour, a bearded university student, who promptly proceeded to kit me out with a cylinder and demand valve and to give me some instruction on how to handle myself underwater. The 20 cubic foot cylinders were what the Belfast divers called 'tadpoles'. These cylinders had previously been used in aircraft and were specially adapted for diving. Painted grey with black and white segments around the shoulders of the cylinders, they were filled with air to a working pressure of 1,800 pounds per square inch, approximately 120 bar. The demand valves were mostly the EsseGee (Siebe Gorman) Mistral twin-hose, single stage models, with some Siebe-Heinke twin hose two stage valves also. Siebe Gorman had been manufacturing Cousteau Gagnan demand valves in Britain under licence.

The mouthpiece on the earlier models of the Mistral valves had one peculiarity. If the diver took the mouthpiece out of his mouth while submerged the hoses would fill with water. To clear the water and to resume breathing, the diver to roll onto his left side, (the left side hose was the exhaust hose), and blow all the water out of the hose with what air he had retained in his lungs. This took some co-ordination and it was the cause of many a coughing fit under water, a potentially dangerous occurrence. The problem was corrected in later hoses by fitting non-return valves in the mouthpieces.

Alistair himself was clad in a very impressive green latex-rubber diving suit, and looked the epitome of the experienced diver. I was clad in a collection of my own and army pullovers and shorts. The tide was about halfway in as we struggled down over the rocks to the water's edge. The sea was calm, the sun was shining, and conditions were perfect, as befits one's very first aqualung dive. I have no recollection of the coldness of the water I was so engrossed with the new and much-longed-for experience. Alistair shepherded me out about 50 metres from the rocks, still on the surface and indicated that we would now submerge. Remembering his instructions, I duck-dived to the bottom, clearing my ears as I went. Because I had already spent so many hours snorkelling in the pool and in the sea before this, I was not nervous. The air came to me on demand and without any effort on my part, apart from a deep inhalation. The valve made a distinct, slightly metallic sound when I inhaled, while the air roared and bubbled behind my head each time I exhaled.

When we reached the sea floor, I started to look around me. We were in about 12 feet of water - in those days we measured depth in feet, not in metres. The bottom was covered in a white shingle-like substance that was not sand, being much more lumpy in texture, but it reflected the light very effectively. This made the water seem much brighter and clearer than it really was, providing a horizontal visibility of about 20 feet. I was informed afterwards that the shingle-like substance came from a form of calcifying seaweed.

We moved slowly along on the bottom, with Alistair peering into my eyes at frequent intervals to check that everything in there was calm and under control! It was a technique that I have employed on practically every dive afterwards, especially with beginners. It is very easy to judge the level of stability of a diver simply by looking into his or her eyes. "The eyes are the windows of the soul, - - ".

To this day I remember almost every detail of that first dive. I saw and admired a smallish lobster under a rock, for the first time being able to take my time and to look closely at one. He, in his turn, had a long and nervous look at me, coming out occasionally to have a better look and retreating hastily if I as much as twitched. I also saw a scallop for the first time, and went over for a better look. To my surprise, he suddenly took off in a wobbly and most ungainly flight, jet-propelled by dint of squirting water out of his shell. He was using the powerful muscles with which he closed his shell when an enemy starfish threatened. I burst into laughter and flooded my mask when I saw the poor fellow's pathetic attempts at swimming. After about five despairing bounds he fell back to the sand exhausted, having travelled about twelve feet.

This wonderful introduction to the sea ended after about fifteen minutes. Over the weekend, we all observed the meticulous care with which the Belfast divers recorded their dives. They carried hardback notebooks in which they wrote down every detail of every dive. It was a very sensible habit, one that I learned from them and have followed right through my diving career. Thanks to the generosity of the Belfast divers, we had been "blooded". We had inhaled and exhaled good Belfast air in the beautiful waters of Connemara near Carraroe. We wanted more, much more, and as soon as possible.

As a result of this weekend, a bond was forged between the two groups of divers that has lasted in a more subdued form to the present day. We dived together at many locations, both North and South of the border. We travelled to each other's club dinners and fund-raising events and stayed in each others homes on occasions over a very happy 15 years. Two of the leading lights in Belfast, Alastair Gilmour and Derek Nelson,

With members of the Belfast Branch of the British Sub Aqua Club at Clogherhead, Co.Louth, Sep 1958.
From the left: Foreground: Michael Clarke, Isobel Dobbin, the author.
At rear: Maureen McGladdery, Vernon Collier, Shane O'Connor, Derek Nelson, Brendan O'Flynn, Margot Sydney-Smith.

emigrated to Sydney, Australia a few years later. Colin McMurtry later went to teach in London while Margot Sydney-Smith moved to Zimbabwe, then Southern Rhodesia, to marry Basil Corlett. Before Margot left for Africa, she was elected as an Honorary Life Member of the Curragh Sub Aqua Club at the AGM of December 1964. This was in recognition of her long and friendly association with our club. In appreciation of this gesture, she donated a book called 'Exploring The Secrets of the Sea' by William J. Cromie to the Club Library.

It is a matter of great regret, but the unrest in Northern Ireland did eventually manage to create an artificial barrier between us that has not yet been fully restored. It will require a new generation of divers to fully heal the rift that has developed between the divers of CFT and the BSAC divers in Northern Ireland.

*     *     *     *     *     *     *     *

Having used aqualungs on a dive at Carraroe, courtesy of our friends from Belfast, we were determined to waste no more time. Once back in the Curragh Camp, a campaign of fund-raising was launched. We sold tickets for raffles and for concealed prize draws, this latter the brainchild of Larry Bradley from Newbridge. We also organised dances on Friday evenings in a wooden hut, built during the war years for use as a social centre for soldiers, their families and friends. It was located in McDermott Barracks, close to the centre of the Curragh Camp. We advertised in local shops and in the Curragh Bulletin, hired local musicians to play and we charged two shillings and sixpence at the door. The first dance was held on 14th October 1958. The band cost eight pounds and the spot prizes cost one pound, ten shillings. Sgt Hogan, the caretaker, and a woman who looked after the cloakroom were both given ten shillings, while a box of crystals cost two shillings and six pence. The crystals were essential to help the dancers to overcome the resistance of the bare wooden floor. We made a profit of six pounds, 13 shillings and nine pence on that first dance, and were very pleased with our efforts.

Over the next three months a series of dances were held at McDermott Hall, but eventually we found that the support, and the profit, began to fall away. So we moved to bigger things at the Town Hall in Newbridge, Co Kildare. There we organised our first major public dance on 28th of November, hiring Maurice Mulcahy and his Band. The profit for this, our first major venture into the entertainment business, was a satisfying twenty-seven pounds and one shilling. This was more like it. We held many more dances there during the winter and into the spring of 1959. Our fortunes were mixed, as we suffered some losses also. However, after about six months of effort, we eventually had amassed enough money to order two demand valves and two cylinders from Midland Diving Supplies in York. I can still remember the excitement when Shane O'Connor, Austin O'Donnell and I met in Shane's room in the Officers Mess to open the boxes. The demand valves were Siebe-Gorman Mistral twin-hose single-stage valves and they glistened and sparkled in the light as we passed them around with great care. The cylinders were the usual 20 cubic foot cylinders with a working pressure of 1,800 pounds per square inch (PSI). Thanks to Shane O'Connor harnesses were made from discarded army webbing material. Thus equipped we could finally call ourselves a real diving club. All we needed now was to get the cylinders filled at Industrial Gases in Bluebell, Inchicore, Dublin and we were in business. Serious training could now start at the swimming pool.

Those early Mistral valves had two other drawbacks, in addition to having non-return valves in the mouthpiece. One was the lack of provision for a take-off pressure gauge so that a diver could know how much air was in the cylinder before or during his dive. It was

At the Hook, June 1960. From the left: Jim Motherway, Shane O'Connor and the author.
Photo, Betty O'Connor

the practice at that time for a diver to continue until he felt that it was becoming more difficult to breathe, so he informed his buddy and they surfaced. The club purchased a 'dry' pressure gauge that was solemnly handed around between the divers prior to the dive. It was called a dry gauge because it could not be used under water. This was a very important item of equipment, because it was common practice for a cylinder of air to be shared between two divers. By prior arrangement, one diver finished early, the second diver checked the contents and then did his own short dive, finishing off the remaining air. It was not a very safe practice, but the dives were in shallow water and of short duration.

The second problem was that the valves were equipped with hexagonal bolts for clamping the valve to the cylinder pillar valve. To do this it was necessary to use a spanner. In the course of time, the nut became rounded because of the use of pliers or the wrong spanners.

Shane O'Connor came to our assistance by having small t-bars brazed onto the worn nuts, thus obviating spanners.

After the arrival of the aqualungs, Jim Motherway and I travelled down to Milltown Malbay, Co Clare, to give out Limerick members an introductory dive. We found a very large rock pool near Spanish Point that was about three metres deep. I had brought a length of light rope with me that I tied to the elbow of each diver as he submerged. The purpose of the rope was to ensure the safety of each diver should he get into difficulty, but more importantly, it enabled me to haul him back to the surface should he try to exceed his allotted five minutes under water. It was elementary but it provided Ronnie Hurley, Adie Roche, Dermot Fitzgerald, Eoin Geary and others with their first experience of the underwater scene.

*     *     *     *     *     *     *     *

Disaster struck our developing club in December 1960. Both Shane O'Connor and myself were informed that we were to travel to the breakaway province of Katanga, in the Belgian Congo, as members of the 34th Battalion in January 1961. This presented the committee with a major crisis, as we two had been the main movers and shakers up to this. How was the club going to manage without us, we would be missing for the best part of eight months? We were the ones with the greatest experience and knowledge at that time. However, as we always knew but might not have been willing to admit, in this life nobody is indispensable. Jimmy Flynn, who up to this had been the club 'morale officer' and Austin O'Donnell, (Treasurer), the Club's Clancy Brothers specialist and guitarist, held a little meeting and decided that there was no way out for them. They just would have to step forward and keep the show on the road.

So, in order not to appear foolish in front of the trainees, they organised a series of private training sessions for themselves during the days between club meetings so that they could demonstrate their abilities. In addition, Jimmy Flynn made another, and in retrospect, a most far-reaching and revolutionary decision. He decided that there had been too much emphasis on lengths of the pool, to much emphasis on fitness or the passing of tests, and not enough on the social side of the club. He introduced the dash to the nearest bar after the swimming pool session on Monday nights, and he also introduced a series of social outings that were not remotely connected with diving! The initial 'watering hole' was that of the Officers Mess in Ceannt Barracks, but as explained elsewhere, we were eventually required to move to the Winning Post in Newbridge. How aptly named was that pub! The scramble to get there before closing time must have generated terror and dismay amongst the regulars as forty thirsty, noisy divers descended on the pub to shatter their Monday night tranquillity.

While all this was going on, Shane and I were enjoying the sun in the Southern Hemisphere, having brought our fins, masks and snorkels with us of course, even though we were confined to snorkelling in the fine outdoor pool at the 'Stade' in Elizabethville. When we did eventually resume our Mondays nights in the Curragh pool in the autumn, it took us some time to get used to the new regime, even though we were the first to admit that the changes were very much for the better.

*     *     *     *     *     *     *     *

In 1963, Club member Padraig McSweeney, who worked in Kinsale Co. Cork, told us that there was a quantity of diving equipment for sale in a store in the town. Apparently, the American professional diver, John Light, who had been diving with a large team on the Lusitania during the summer months since 1960, had wound up his operations and departed suddenly for the United States. He left a considerable quantity of diving equipment behind in Kinsale, which was eventually put up for sale by locals. With Pat Mc Sweeney's help, the Club bought a large quantity of the equipment for £80. On the 2nd of December 1963, Johnny King, Shane O'Connor and Eric Gregan drove down to Kinsale in Johnny's truck and brought all the equipment back to the Curragh.

When we examined our purchase we were astounded at our good fortune. There were as many as fourteen diving cylinders, some of which were linked by manifolds into 'triples' and 'twins'. Most of the cylinders came complete with harnesses, and all made by US Divers. There were also a number of large underwater lights and underwater telephone sets, with many metres of waterproof cabling, and a small number of wet suits of an early type which were unlined in the inside. For a small Club such as ours, £80 was a considerable sum of money, but it was all recouped rapidly as the cylinders were sold on to the members. We dismantled the 'triples' and most of the 'twin' sets and sold the cylinders as 'singles'. I bought a 'twin' complete with harness, hardly able to believe my good luck. They served me well for a number of years. There is an interesting story associated these same 'twins'.

About that time an American called Don Sooey joined the Curragh Sub Aqua Club. He had served as a Marine Captain in Vietnam, and, after leaving the service, he and his wife 'Moose' came to Dublin where he studied medicine at Trinity College. He called her 'Moose' because she was taller and bigger than himself. While she did not dive, they both were great additions to the Club. They were very popular and participated fully in the social whirl. Don, an avid diver, announced one evening that he intended to dive on the Lusitania, which featured largely in the papers at the time. We didn't take notice, as diving to the Lusitania was considered well beyond the reach of amateur divers. It lay in 180 feet of water over which raced a strong tidal current. But Don was serious. He started doing preparatory training such as diving to 80 feet on his own at a large marker buoy some distance out from Bulloch Harbour.

He would hire a small boat and boatman, and when he dived he just sat on the bottom for as long as possible. Mutterings about decompression, the dangers of hypothermia and lone diving began to be heard. Diving on one's own was, and still is, a cardinal sin, as it is very dangerous to be without the close assistance of a companion under water. All attempts to discourage him failed, he was determined to go ahead. One day, he called to my house in Kilcullen and said that he wished to borrow my 'twins' as he was heading South for some diving. I reluctantly gave him my treasured cylinders and he took off. It was some days afterwards that we heard what took place.

When he arrived at Kinsale, he went around the fishing boat captains, trying to find one who would bring him out to dive on the Lusitania. Now, most of the fishermen knew quite a bit about the hazards of diving and the need for a major back-up team, having watched John Light in action over a couple of summers. They could see the foolishness of a lone diver attempting such a dive and they refused to take him out. However, he eventually persuaded a skipper to take him out to the wreck site, which was clearly buoyed. He subsequently described what happened on the dive.

As he went down the marker buoy line, well past the 100 foot, (33 metre) mark, he realised that he had lost his depth gauge, his compass and his diving watch. He was also getting seriously over-weight and had to hang on tightly to the shot-line to avoid plunging at increasing speed to the bottom. The sea floor eventually appeared below him but by now he was in a state of great confusion. As he described it to me afterwards, "I saw a brown wall very close by, only a few metres away. It was very dark. I let go of the line and swam over to touch the wall and returned immediately to the line. I was so over-weight that I had to fin furiously in a vertical attitude simply to prevent myself from falling the remaining few metres to the sea floor. At this stage I was more frightened than I had ever been before because I felt that I was going to die. I started hauling myself furiously up the line, completely forgetting that I should use my fins as well to assist my ascent. As I rose into shallower depths, the light improved and my narcosis disappeared. I then realised that I had not lost my instruments after all. With the collapse of the neoprene suit as the pressure increased, the straps, which had been quite tight at the surface before the start of the dive, had become too loose and the instruments had simply slipped around to the other side of my wrist. In my state of confusion, I did not notice this." He was very relieved and very thankful to have survived to tell the tale.

I was very grateful to regain possession of my 'twins', aware of the irony of the cylinders, which presumably had been used by professional divers on many visits to the Lusitania, revisiting the wreck again on the back of a very confused and frightened amateur. Don's foolishly brave lone dive was discussed at committee afterwards and it was with great regret that he was invited to look for another club if he wished to continue diving. Don parted amicably from us, he graduated some time afterwards and the last we heard of him was that he was practising medicine in Australia.

*     *     *     *     *     *     *     *

The Club was based at the Curragh Camp and our Dublin members drove down every Monday night, for the swim and for 'refreshments' at the Officers Mess in Ceannt Barracks and later at the 'Winning Post' in Newbridge. Unfortunately, external pressures, in the shape of the disturbances in Northern Ireland, forced a major change in our routine. Because of increased security at the Camp, it became difficult for our members to travel within the Camp to and from the swimming pool. We tried to organise special passes, but eventually and with great regret, we decided to leave the Curragh Camp and to look for a new base in the Dublin area. This was a great setback, and over the next few years, the Club moved about between locations in the Dublin area. We used swimming pools in Crumlin, Castleknock, and Terenure, none of which were really suitable for our purposes. Fortunately however, a new swimming pool, for which I had helped to raise funds, was opened at Glenalbyn around 1968 and we settled in there with relief. It was the biggest pool in Dublin and, while being a little too shallow for the purposes of training new divers, it was in all other respects ideal for our purposes. But we still needed our own premises.

As it turned out, we were in for another stroke of good luck. I received a phone call from Micky Lynch, a member of the Committee. "Mick", he said, "Dun Laoghaire Corporation owns an old building at Sandycove. It used to be a swimming baths, the old Victoria Baths, built in 1907, but it is in such a state of decay that they are planning to knock it down. The Corporation engineer, Bill Reidy, said that it would be a shame to destroy it. He feels that it should first be offered to a water-based sports club of some kind, and then if nobody wants it, it could be knocked down. He is a friend of mine and has given us first refusal". I was only vaguely aware of the building, and knew little of its condition but even though I did not know about its condition, I immediately said "We will take it". I did not even wait to consult the rest of the committee just in case some other group got in before us. The Corporation accepted our willingness to become tenants but said that we would have to share the building with a troop of adventure scouts.

Working to improve the dressing rooms at Sandycove, Sarah Lyle, Alan O'Dowd, Peter Davitt, Joe Delaney and Peadar Farrell

We had no problem with this. In fact it suited both the scouts and ourselves to be sharing the building, from a security point of view, as the more people using the building the better. About five weeks later, we found ourselves tunnelling our way through the inner brick walls and clearing up inside and outside the building. It was a huge task and it meant that diving had to take a back seat. The Scouts occupied a separate portion of the building with their own entrance. Builder Mick Duffy, a member of the Club, did a marvellous job in building internal walls and doors and in bricking up all the unwanted window and door openings. The building was rescued and it is now giving enjoyment to large numbers of people of all ages who have a love of the sea. It was very fortunate for the club that, having been displaced from the Curragh, we ended up using the best pool in Dublin, and having the best and biggest clubhouse right at the water's edge.

Thirty years later we are still there, sharing the building with the Sandycove Sea Scouts. The present day Club facilities comprise a large lecture room, changing rooms, toilets, hot showers, and a kitchen. There is also ample space for the large electric compressor and two inflatables. Unfortunately, the tide comes up to the front of the building, indeed, at times, it can even come in under the doors. This ensures that the building is always fairly damp. A high spring tide would not normally cause a problem

John Hailes lecturing at the Clubhouse, Sandycove, Co. Dublin.

in the Clubhouse, but when it is accompanied by a North Westerly gale, the waves will mount the front wall and pour in under both sea-doors.

It was the custom for many years to hold the Christmas dinners in the Clubhouse. One particular December, the committee forgot to check the tide tables for the night of the dinner. The wind was strong and from the Northwest and the worst happened on this occasion. The floor was inundated to a depth of about two inches. But, in the best spirit of diving, the diners did not falter. Led by the Committee, everybody simply took off their shoes and socks and carried on celebrating Christmas.

\* \* \* \* \* \* \* \*

Today, most diving is done from boats, usually from the rigid inflatable boats, (RIBs). A RIB combines the attributes of an inflatable with those of a rigid hulled boat. RIBs are both fast and rugged, and are used for diving at locations further out from shore. Before these boats became popular, we used smaller inflatables, which were very suitable for close-to-shore diving but not at all suitable for long journeys out to sea.

In the days before either type of boat became widely available to divers, it was common to hire a trawler for the far-out diving locations. Up to twenty or more divers and even 'camp-followers' could be carried. Trawlers were popular but they placed some additional demands on the divers. Apart from surviving seasickness, the divers had to be prepared to jump into the sea from a heaving, rolling deck. Timing was crucial in such circumstances! If you launched on an up-roll, you might get hurled into a low orbit about the earth. If you launched on a down-roll, you might find yourself dangerously close to the flank of the rolling trawler.

On completion of the dive, the diver was faced with a difficult climb on board; an old tyre hanging over the side was the usually means of boarding. For anyone who was fit, young, and active, it was not a big problem, but for many it was a daunting challenge. However, once diving was over and the trawler was moving again with a regular motion, happiness would break out and bottles would be opened.

On one occasion many years ago, the Curragh Sub Aqua Club was returning to Slade Harbour from a day's diving on the south side of the Great Saltee Island. Most divers were still in their diving suits, and some had opened bottles of beer. Micky Lynch was standing at the stern with some others, when an unexpected lurch of the trawler tipped him into the sea. There were some unkind people afterwards who suggested that Seamus O'Reilly from Belfast might have been responsible. There were frantic shouts of "man overboard", and some were putting on masks and snorkels in preparation to go to his rescue. The shouting quickly changed to laughter, however, as Micky surfaced in the wake of the trawler, giving the 'OK' signal. He was facing the receding trawler with his arm held straight up in the air in the approved manner. But we all could see that he was also clutching his bottle of beer upright with his thumb securely over the open neck!

Diving is most definitely not a spectator sport, but in the early Sixties, there was great interest in diving and it was common for clubs to be invited to give a demonstration at a Gala or a Regatta. Once the divers had gone under water, there was no more to be seen and the whole thing proved to be a bit of an anticlimax. So, when the organisers of the Dun Laoghaire Festival invited the Curragh Sub Aqua Club to give a diving display, the Club came up with a novel plan.

The display took place in the water in Scotsman's Bay close to the East Pier, where the huge crowd would have a good view. The plan was that Johnny King would drive the inflatable at speed parallel to the pier and towards the shore. Four divers, two pairs at a time, would drop into the water and submerge. They would locate a large canvas bag that had been laid on the bottom earlier, inflate it and raise it to the surface. Club member Des Hearns was on the pier to broadcast a commentary the display.

As the boat raced along parallel to the pier, the first pair of divers tipped backwards into the water without problems. But trouble arrived as the second pair of divers left the boat. As he was rolling backwards out of the boat, one of the divers kicked Johnny King so hard that he also fell into the water. Johnny held on to the throttle, but the engine was now at maximum revs and the boat started to spin around at high speed with its bow high in the air, as he could not twist the throttle to reduce speed without letting go. This was a most dangerous situation, but Johnny was a strong and determined man and he managed to haul himself back on board and regain control once more. After it was all over, when thanking the Curragh club for the interesting demonstration, Des Hearns said that as a result of popular acclaim he had one more request, "Would Johnny King please repeat his demonstration of boat handling skills"!

# CHAPTER 4
# THE EVOLUTION OF SPORTS DIVING

While there can be many arguments as to where the sport of modern diving originated, the Mediterranean in general, and the South of France in particular, could certainly lay claim to having been the cradle of the new sport. Guy Gilpatric, an American writer living at Cap d'Antibes, was an early spearfisherman from 1920, who developed his own hand spear and goggles and published a book called the 'Compleat Goggler' in 1938. A French Navy officer, Comdr. de Corlieu invented flippers, (fins), as far back as 1920, even taking out a patent for same in 1937. He had probably studied the design drawings of Leonardo da Vinci, who had made drawings for an underwater swimmer, showing not just fins, but also webbed gloves. Even earlier, Paul Bert, French physiologist, 1833-1886, conducted pioneering studies on the toxic effects of oxygen, as well as studies on blood gases. These studies were of great value to modern aviation as well as to diving. His work on air and compression formed the basis for the first useable diving tables compiled by Haldane much later on in England.

A Russian, Alec Kramarenko, living in the South of France, designed and used the first spring-propelled spear gun in 1937. He invented a new diving mask in 1932, and patented it in 1937. He realised that the problems with vision underwater was caused by having separate glass eye-pieces (goggles were usually worn by divers at that time), which could move into different attitudes relative to each other and to the diver's eyes. As the diver descended, the rising pressure caused the eye-pieces to be driven into his eye sockets, causing discomfort or damage. So Kramarenko mounted a single flat glass plate on a frame that maintained it at the same angle to the eyes, thus overcoming the vision problems of previous models. As it also covered the diver's nose, so the diver could pinch his nose to equalise his ears by blowing air into the mask to prevent it being squashed onto his face as he descended. Georges Beuchat invented a rubber-powered spear gun in 1934, while Maxine Forjot, in 1937, invented a new design of mask and snorkel, as well as a new type of rubber-powered spear gun.

Commander Jacques-Yves Cousteau, of the French Navy, spent as many as eight years spearfishing and snorkel diving before WW2, having become totally enthralled with the underwater world. He had tried the demand valve invented and used by Comdr Le Prieur, another French Navy officer but found it unsatisfactory. Later, in occupied France, he went to a gas company engineer called Emil Gagnan to seek help with the development of a better breathing valve. He wanted a valve that would be an improvement on any of the existing models, all of which had flaws of one sort or another.

Because Emile Gagnan was accustomed to dealing with valves that reduced gas pressure, he was the right man for the job. At the time that Cousteau approached him, he was working on a valve that was designed to feed gas automatically to car engines. As in Ireland during the war, an entire mini-industry had arisen in France devoted to the substitution of gas for scarce and rationed petrol for motor engines. After one or two attempts, Emile Gagnan produced a simple and effective valve that supplied compressed air to a diver at a pressure slightly above that of the surrounding water. It was described as an open-circuit valve whereby the used air was expelled directly into the water when the diver exhaled. Two corrugated hoses ran from the demand valve to the mouthpiece, the right-hand hose being the intake hose and the left-hand hose being the exhaust hose. However, the design initially had one flaw. When the diver was in any attitude other than the horizontal, the twin-hose demand valve would not perform properly. Cousteau quickly realised that the air exhaust needed to be as close as possible to the intake so as not to affect the flow of the air. After this simple alteration was made, the valve worked to his entire satisfaction. He then arranged a harness for the air cylinder so that the entire assembly could be carried on the diver's back. It was designed so that the demand valve would be in a position level with the top of the lungs and between the shoulder blades - the optimum position for the valve.

Despite many improvements since 1942, the basic concept of this wonderfully simple device has been used to supply air to divers ever since. It was the one device above all others that launched the modern sport of diving, a sport which has spread across the world in a remarkably short time. Cousteau had found himself at the focus for all of the advances in diving that had previously taken place before this breakthrough in war-time France, and he was in the perfect position to take advantage of his good fortune.

The armed forces of all the major nations produced many versions of underwater breathing equipment, of which the most important was called a 're-breather' set, which uses oxygen rather than air. The diver's expired air was not released into the water; it was circulated within the equipment and purified by passing it through filters and fresh oxygen, to be inhaled once more. The re-breather sets gave divers a much longer underwater endurance than if they were using compressed air. The principal advantage of the set was that it did not create any telltale bubbles that might alert the enemy sentries, and for that reason it was the preferred equipment for military use. A major drawback of the set was that the diver was limited to a maximum depth of about 10 metres, because of the toxicity of oxygen at greater depths.

Re-breathers were regarded as dangerous and unsuitable for amateur divers. The Curragh club placed a warning in its first Logbook stating that members must have the permission of the Committee before attempting to dive with a re-breather set. Modern versions of these re-breathers have been gaining in popularity, but opinion is divided on the wisdom of amateur divers using this equipment and there have been some fatalities.

The 'Frogmen', 'Swimmers', or 'Charioteers', as they were variously called during WW 2, took enormous risks in carrying out quite elaborate exploits. These divers were following in the traditions of the warriors of ancient times who swam under water to cut the anchor ropes of the besieging fleets. The extraordinary courage shown by the individuals involved was not confined to any particular nation. In WW2 this element of underwater warfare was probably initiated by the Italians, lead by a team in which Prince J. Valerio Borghese played a prominent role. One of his team was a young Lieutenant called Luigi Ferraro, who became the President of the Sporting Commission of Confederation Mondiales des Activities Subaquatiques (CMAS) many years later.

There can be little doubt that World War Two provided a huge impetus to the development of all aspects of diving, be it in underwater medicine, technology, photography, exploration or navigation. After the war ended, the large numbers of ex-service divers, seeking gainful employment, quickly moved to take advantage of their training and experience. They turned to the sea and set about realising the potential of the skills they had acquired during hostilities.

*    *    *    *    *    *    *    *

Irish scientists and engineers have also played a part in the development of modern diving. While he certainly could not have foreseen the development of sports diving, physicist the Rt. Hon. Robert Boyle, (1627-1691) of Lismore, Co. Cork, developed his 'Boyle's Law', which states that where the temperature is constant, the pressure and volume of a gas are inversely proportional. Knowledge of 'Boyle's Law' is a basic requirement for all divers today, amateur or professional.

Sir Francis Beaufort (1774-1857) of Navan Co. Meath, was the chief Hydrographer to the British Navy from 1829 to 1855, retiring with the rank of Admiral. He developed the Beaufort Scale of Wind Force for the estimation of the strength of wind over water and produced a tabulated system of weather registration. Today, because of the huge increase in offshore diving, divers must know all about the sea and understand the weather, particularly the winds.

John Philip Holland (1840-1914) a teacher from Liscannor, Co. Clare, was not a diver but his career after had he moved to the United States deserved to be mentioned in any account dealing with underwater exploration. Holland designed one of the earliest viable submarines in 1878 that he called the Fenian Ram. A later version, called Holland, was successfully demonstrated in the Potomac in 1898. His submarine incorporated many of the design features that are found in the modern submarine. It had the classic pear-shaped hull, a petrol engine for use on the surface and an electric engine for use underwater. It had ballast tanks, hydroplanes, torpedo tubes and a retractable periscope. The periscope was made by in Dublin by a company in Rathmines, Thomas and Howard Grubb. This company was more famous for making large telescopes for observatories all over the world, as well as optical instruments for military use.

A later version, Holland 6, became the first submarine to be commissioned in the US Navy in 11 April 1900, while a number of the same design were later purchased for the British Navy. His Holland Torpedo Boat Company was later absorbed into Electric Boat, the company that today builds nuclear submarines, but in 1904 he was eased out of the company. It is only in relatively recent times that he is being acknowledged as the inventor of the modern submarine. The US government's first commissioning of Holland's Underwater Torpedo Boat No. 6 was commemorated in Ireland and in the United States during 2000. His earlier submarine, the Fenian Ram, has been raised and can be seen today at the Naval and Space Museum in New York. A number of very fine models of his submarine can be seen in the Museum of the Maritime Institute of Ireland in Dun Laoghaire, Co Dublin.

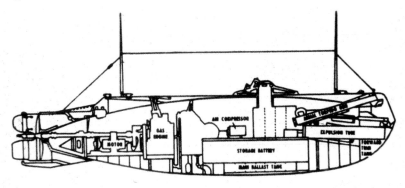

**Official U.S. Navy Photo**
**Plan of the 54 ft. HOLLAND, 1st U.S. Navy sub.**

Plan of the Holland Submarine

Thomas Steele, 'Honest Tom'(1788-1848) from Ennis, Co. Clare, was an engineer, inventor and politician. Although a Protestant, he was a devoted follower of Daniel O'Connell. In 1825 he designed and patented a new form of diving bell. For centuries, the only way to achieve useful heavy work underwater was by means of a diving bell, and even that only in shallow water. The original diving bell was so named because it was shaped rather like a large church bell. It was heavily weighted to prevent it from tipping over as it was lowered into position. On the way down it had trapped enough air inside to enable one or two divers to do limited work on the seabed directly under the bell. It was exceedingly difficult and dangerous work and it was very limited in effectiveness. Later models were vastly improved by having air pumped down from the surface. Steel's diving bell included two chambers, one dry and one wet. While there were other 'bells' with two chambers by this time, his was regarded as a major advance in design over the others.

He designed and patented a new system for underwater illumination in the same year. A diving enthusiast, he worked with Charles Deane, who at that time was one of the foremost commercial divers in England. They dived on the 'Intrinsic' at Kilkee in 1836 and on the 'Mary Rose' in England in 1840. In 1828, Tom Steele advised on the general

Steele's Rock, Ennis, Co.Clare.

improvement of the navigation of the Shannon between Limerick and the Atlantic. There is a monument to him on the river Fergus in Ennis.

Augustus Siebe, a German artillery officer and inventor, moved to London where, in 1821, he founded a company to manufacture diving equipment. He was responsible, with the two Deane brothers, for many of the crucial advances in design during the 19th century, especially in the design of the traditional closed 'hard-hat' diving suit. He took on a partner one William Gorman, who married Siebe's daughter. The name of the company was changed to Siebe-Gorman, by which it is known today. William Gorman's father was from Limerick.

Robert Davis (1870-1965) was a renowned designer, inventor and engineer. His book, 'Deep Diving and Submarine Operations', is still, to this day, a classic account of diving and the development of new equipment. His mother was from Dublin.

Jacques-Yves Cousteau had an Irish connexion, a fact of which he was very conscious, as he confessed to Des Branigan in London in 1962. His great-grandfather was an O'Moore and his great-grandmother was an O'Shea.

*　　*　　*　　*　　*　　*　　*　　*

After WW2, with the introduction of Cousteau's demand valve, there was an explosive growth in the number of new clubs and diving centres. In France the most famous was Club Alpin Sous-Marin, formed at Cannes in 1946 by Henri Broussard, whose membership list was a whose-who of diving. It included Comdr. Le Prieur, Jacques-Yves Cousteau and Lord Louis Mountbatten.

The proliferation in the number of clubs was such that at an early stage, the need for national organisations to control and co-ordinate their activities and interests was perceived. Many of the European countries had established their own national bodies by the late 1940s and the early 1950s. The logical next step was to establish an international organisation. This would bind all the national organisations together in common purpose, and it would give them a forum to create proper diving standards in training and in examinations. It would also provide a forum for the resolution of disputes and for representation to governments in matters of importance to the sport.

Confederation Mondiale des Activites Subaquatiques (CMAS) the World Underwater Federation, - was formed at Monaco in January 1959. The national diving organisations of the following countries were the founder members:

West Germany, Belgium, Brazil, Spain, The United States, France, Great Britain, Greece, Holland, Italy, Malta, Monaco, Switzerland, Portugal, and Yugoslavia.

Jacques Cousteau became the first President of CMAS, and Oscar Gugen, who was one of the founders of the British Sub Aqua Club (BSAC) became Vice-President as well as President of the Technical Committee. The new Federation was composed of an Executive Committee and initially two subsidiary committees, or commissions, which dealt with sport and technical diving matters. The Sports Commission dealt with matters of diving sport of all types, but mainly spearfishing and breath-held deep diving attempts, as they were particularly popular at that time. The Technical Committee was the most important Commission in that it was charged with responsibility for the setting up of standards in the training programmes, diver grades and examinations. This was a huge task, as they were starting almost from scratch, having only the practices of the various navies and their own national experiences to go on.

Despite having administrative troubles, CMAS continues to expand and prosper. Initially it was based in Paris, where it was heavily subsidised by the French government, but the headquarters was moved to Rome in 1993. Today, it can claim to represent as many as eighty national diving organisations, representing some 20,000,000 divers.

In 1995, a new diving organisation was established in Europe. It was called 'Confederation de la Communauté Européen des Activités Subaquatiques' (CCEAS) - The European Underwater Federation (EUF). It was often alleged that CMAS was biased in favour of European member states, so the foundation of the new body was intended to change this perception by shifting some of the emphasis away from the European countries. The founder member countries were: FDR, Belgium, Denmark, Spain, Great Britain, Greece, Netherlands, **IRELAND**, Italy, Luxemburg and Portugal.

# CHAPTER 5
# THE EVOLUTION OF SPORTS DIVING IN IRELAND

Despite much debate and enquiry at the time, it has not been possible to establish with certainty who might have been the first amateur sports diver in Ireland, but we do know that Dr Boyd undertook his first dive at Portaferry in 1945. He was using a type of oxygen re-breather set which he had put together himself from ex-War Department surplus equipment. Later on that year, he dived at St Tropez and at Nice, and in 1947, having met Cousteau's underwater cameraman-to-be, Jean Oniac, Dr Boyd made his first dive using one of the new Cousteau aqualungs, breathing compressed air. This obviously made a big impression on him because, once back home in Belfast, he bought his own diving suit and aqualung.

Another early diver in Ireland may have been a retired Colonel P. Kaulbeck who had lived in Ardnagashel House, Bantry, County Cork in the early 1950s. The first diving facility to be provided in Ireland was called Courtmacsherry Diving Services, run by Paddy Allan and his wife Joan. They lived in Bandon but operated out of Courtmacsherry Harbour, County Cork. Paddy brought visiting divers out in his boat and he also owned one of the few compressors in Ireland would fill air for passing divers.

His compressor was sited in a shed in the back garden and one day when he was filling a cylinder, he became distracted by something in the house. The unattended compressor continued to fill the cylinder beyond its safe working pressure until it failed explosively. The explosion damaged the shed and sprayed fragments of steel around the garden. Fortunately, nobody was injured, but it was a great lesson for those of us who frequently undertook the duties of filling cylinders for our clubs. All modern air compressors are fitted with safety blow-off valves, which are designed to prevent such overfilling accidents. The valves are set to the safe working pressure of the average diving cylinder and when that pressure is reached the compressor will vent the excess air, making a loud whistling sound to attract the urgent attention of the operator.

Organised sports diving began in Ireland in February 1955, when a meeting was held at the house of Dr Douglas Boyd in Belfast to establish a branch of the British Sub Aqua Club. Dr Boyd, a Manchester-born radiologist who had been working in

Belfast, was elected as the first Chairman, a post that he retained for many years. Following the formation of CFT in 1963, he was appointed as the first Honorary Medical Adviser.

\* \* \* \* \* \* \* \*

In January 1956, the Irish Sub Aqua Club (ISAC) was founded in Dublin, followed by the Curragh Sub Aqua Club on the 15th of May 1958. ISAC had expected to follow the example of BSAC with affiliated branches around Ireland, and indeed branches of ISAC were established in Killaloe and in Cork, but neither lasted for long. The Killaloe Branch became the Limerick Sub Aqua Club in April 1965. There are certainly many benefits to be associated with a unitary organisation; it would permit of easier control, direction and greater efficiency. A single very large club would carry considerable weight when speaking to government on behalf of the many branches and the thousands of members across the country. However, here in Ireland, the representatives of the early clubs preferred to retain their autonomy, they felt strongly that it was essential to retain control over their own affairs in their own localities. It was preferable to be known as the Mullingar Sub Aqua Club rather than the Mullingar branch of a national club. It was correctly assumed that local interest and support for fund-raising and recruiting would be much better as a result.

In 1960, four members of the Irish Sub Aqua Club decided to open a diving equipment shop in Dublin. Hugh Quigley, Brian Pim, Brendan Redmond and Hugh Crawford formed a company called DISCO (Diver Supply Company), opening for business in Hatch Street, in Dublin. This was the first shop for selling diving equipment in Ireland at the time. They initially concentrated on stocking equipment made by US Divers and invited over the Vice-President, whose name happened to be Carroll from Dublin! The company traded successfully for a number of years, moving from Hatch Street to Drumcondra, and then in 1965 to Dun Laoghaire Shopping Centre, even though by then diving equipment formed only a small part of the business.

\* \* \* \* \* \* \* \*

By the early 1960s, the sport of diving in Ireland was growing very rapidly and, as divers from the clubs met and discussed aspects of the sport, concern was expressed about the need for standard techniques in training. The only instruction manual available was that of the British Sub Aqua Club, and individuals or committees were interpreting the manual as they thought fit. Danger could arise when members from different clubs dived together, using different procedures and different hand-signals. The opportunities for misunderstandings were evident. I give the following humorous story as an example.

Val Kennedy, then a member of the Curragh club, dived with Mick O'Driscoll and Palmer Lyons of the Cork Sub Aqua Club on the wreck of the City of Chicago off the Old Head of Kinsale in 1963. Before the dive, Val asked the others, "What hand signals are you using"? "Oh, the BSAC signals." said Mick. This answer satisfied Val as the Curragh also used the BSAC signals. Some time into the dive, Palmer went up to Val, nodded, bent backwards and tapped his buttocks. Val had never seen such a signal before, and became even more confused when Palmer then repeated the signal to Mick. In response, Mick somersaulted twice with his head tucked between his legs and shook his head at Palmer. Val assumed that this was a reply to Palmer, but had to wait until they were back in Paddy Allan's boat before he got an explanation. "Oh", said Palmer, " I touched my bottom to tell you that we had arrived over the stern of the wreck." "Was that it," said Mick, "I thought you were telling me that I had torn the a—- out of my diving suit!"

The concerned divers amongst us felt that the lack of common training and knowledge could not be allowed to continue. We wanted to protect not just the individuals but the good name of diving itself. A few disastrous incidents at this early stage could give diving a reputation from which it might never recover. The earliest recorded reference to a 'federation' of clubs was when the Chairman of the Irish Sub Aqua Club, Anthony Bishop, made the proposal at a committee meeting of his club in 1959, and it was decided that he would contact myself and Dr Boyd of Belfast about the matter. However, nothing came of that proposal and the subject did not 'surface' again until Derek Nelson from Belfast made the suggestion in 1962 to the approval of all the active divers of the time. A number of formal meetings to discuss the project were then organised to which each of the five existing clubs was asked to send two representatives.

The first of these meetings were organised by Shane O'Connor and myself and it was held at the house of Jenny Simcox in Naas, Co. Kildare on the 24th of November 1962, followed by another short meeting on the following day at 6.30pm. This latter took place in the Gymnasium after a sub-aqua gala at the Curragh Pool. Jenny happened to be the Secretary of the Curragh club at the time, so she acted as secretary for both meetings. The divers knew each other quite well, which was a great help, so it took only two more meetings, one organised by the Garda club in January and one by the Irish Sub Aqua Club on 23rd March 1963, before the final details were thrashed out. The entire process had taken only about 18 months to complete. On Sunday 29th of September 1963, four clubs were represented at the inaugural meeting of Comhairle Fó-Thuinn (CFT), the Irish Underwater Council, held at the Officers Mess, Ceannt Barracks, Curragh Camp. They were the Irish Sub Aqua Club, The Curragh Sub Aqua Club, Limerick Sub Aqua Club and the Garda Sub Aqua Club. Representatives of the Belfast Branch British Sub Aqua Club and the new Galway University Sub Aqua Club were present at the meeting as observers only. However, both of these clubs became members of CFT in January 1964.

The first officers of CFT were elected as follows:-

President:  Captain Shane O'Connor, Curragh Sub Aqua Club

Secretary:  Tom Shakespeare, Irish Sub Aqua Club

Treasurer:  Sgt. Niall Bracken, Garda Sub Aqua Club

Press Officer: Hugh Quigley, Irish Sub Aqua Club.

Some time before the inaugural meeting, the Irish Sub Aqua Club had applied for affiliation to BSAC. However, they changed their minds and applied to CMAS for affiliation instead. Following on the formation of the new national organisation, and in the spirit of the recent events, ISAC allowed their international application to lapse in favour of CFT. Shortly after the first meeting in the Curragh, the new CFT applied to CMAS and was accepted as a member affiliated to the Technical and Competition Commissions of the international body in early 1964.

A word of explanation is needed here about the divers of the Belfast Branch BSAC. In January 1964, the committee of the Belfast Branch sought the permission of their Head Office in London to become members of the new Irish organisation. Approval was granted promptly and with the very best wishes of the Executive of BSAC. An EGM was then held in Belfast and those present overwhelmingly approved of membership of CFT. Because of our close friendship and common interests, the first constitution of CFT had been drawn up in such a way as to allow them to participate. From the outset, the Belfast divers were absolutely committed to CFT, and they contributed hugely and effectively to its establishment and its success.

So, only eight years after organised sports diving had first arrived in Ireland, a national body called 'Comhairle Fo-Thuinn - The Irish Underwater Council' - was established. The Irish title means literally, 'The Council under the Waves', and it was the late Kevin Danaher of the Folklore Commission who advised me on the title. We spent a lot of

Left: A proposed logo for CFT, designed by Shane O'Connor but never used.
Right: The CFT car decal as used for some years from 1968

time and energy looking for a suitable figure or legend on which to base our logo. We examined the Celtic legends, and found only one sea god, Mannanán Mac Lir, (Mannanán, son of Lir). Mannanán was regarded as the Overlord of the Tuatha de Danaan, the Lords of Light and Life, whose main rivals were the Fomorians, the Lords of Darkness and Death. In old Gaelic 'fomor' or 'Fo Mor' meant 'under the sea'. The Celts associated the sea with vastness, darkness and danger, the lair of monsters. This may well explain why so many latter-day Irish appear to have such little regard for the sea and matters maritime. We decided against using Mannanán as his portrayal in old Irish books too closely resembled Neptune as used by BSAC in their logo.

So Shane O'Connor designed the first logo in the appearance of a trident, making skilful use of the capital letters 'I.U.C.', (Irish Underwater Council). The trident was a reflection of the great interest in spearfishing at that time. When a new and more 'international' logo was required, I spent many hours doodling and eventually devised the present logo, which was also to be used on the medallions for award to competitors at galas or other national competitions. It still incorporates a trident but the trident is now imposed on a large shamrock, with stylised waves beneath. Shane O'Connor completed the detailed drawings with his own inimitable precision.

A number of important principles were accepted at an early stage in the discussions. The delegates felt that they wished to retain their independence and that CFT should not interfere in the internal affairs of any affiliate club, except in matters of safety. The diving standards in training and testing, as agreed by the delegates to CFT, would become the acceptable minimum standard consistent with safety for all the member clubs to follow. Internally, Clubs were permitted to impose even higher standards on their own members if they so wished, providing that these conformed with safe practices as laid down by the new body. A number of decisions, which were to have far-reaching effects on the future success of the new body, were made in relation to the examiners and the way in which diving tests were conducted. All CFT examinations and testing for 3rd Class divers, (now CMAS Diver Two Star), and higher were to be conducted by examiners from an outside club. This was regarded as a very important measure as it reduced the chances of favouritism and ensured that candidates had to be well prepared for their tests.

Initially CFT had used the same diver grades as the BSAC, but after some time it was felt that the holders of a 3rd or 2nd Class grade might well develop feelings of inferiority after some time. To the uninitiated, a first class diver would be a highly respected diver whereas a second-class, or worse a third class diver might well be a very dubious diver indeed, partly trained, not to be trusted! So, in 1970, the titles of Trainee Diver and Club Diver were adopted, as proposed by Brian Cusack, the National Diving Officer, at a Delegate meeting in the Crofton Hotel, Dublin. Another early stipulation was that the principal tests had to be conducted in open water, be it sea or lake, rather than in a swimming pool. This meant that the abilities of each diver were assessed in the medium in which he was going to continue to practice his sport. The examinations for higher-level grades that followed some years later continued under the same general principals, with examining juries appointed for the purpose. As a result of these early basic provisions, Irish divers are among the world's best-trained divers and conform to a very high standard.

One of the early challenges presented to CFT was the announcement that the Minister for Agriculture and Fisheries proposed to introduce a ban on the taking of shellfish by divers. Over the preceding twelve months a certain amount of tension had arisen, particularly in the southwest of the country, where local fishermen were complaining that divers were stripping the coastal areas of shellfish. Certainly divers were catching shellfish, mainly crawfish, scallops and later, sea urchins, and they were selling them on to agents for export to France. There were no regulations or restrictions on the activities of divers in the matter of taking shellfish, as was the case also in Great Britain. Fishermen were seeing small groups of amateur divers taking holidays in their areas and making good profits into the bargain. They said that divers had no right to take anything from the sea; they argued that this was the sole privilege of those who made a full-time living from fishing. A new fisherman's organisation was formed in the southwest, and they started to lobby their politicians for the introduction of controls on divers.

The matter was brought to a head by the arrival of a group of divers from the South of England. They had been working in a crowded 'industry' over there and had decided that the catches could be much better in Ireland. This was highly ironic, because about that same time, a British MP, Mr John Knott, was complaining bitterly about 'the deplorable activities of Irish divers' catching crayfish off the Cornish coast! The Irish diving community was very small, we had a good idea of what was going on and we were satisfied that we posed no threat whatsoever to the shellfish stocks in South-West Ireland or any where else.

There was considerable anger amongst divers over the possibility of being forbidden to perform an activity that was, for the majority of us, comparable to picking blackberries from a roadside hedge. CFT, of which I was Secretary at that time, held a number of special meetings where delegates from the clubs debated over how best to respond to the Minister's proposal. It was decided to send a delegation to the Minister in order to present our side of the argument, and on 13th June 1966, Tom Shakespeare and myself were ushered into a meeting room in the Department of Agriculture and Fisheries in Dublin. Mr Haughey received us courteously and listened to our arguments. Our strategy was that instead of rejecting his proposal completely, we would seek to present a counter-proposal to amend it. We proposed that the example of other countries should be followed instead. We informed him that in the US, Canada, Australia and a number of other countries, the 'bag' system was in use for a long time.

According to the 'bag' system, a catch of one, or a specified small number, of shellfish per diver per day was permitted by law. Apparently, such restrictions worked very well in those locations, where the climate and conditions permitted a far greater level of diving activity than would be the case in Ireland. We felt that this system had a number of benefits. It would allow the diver to bring home a lobster for his dinner without having to break the law. It would provide a legitimate bonus to the quality and satisfaction of his dive and he would be less likely to take a chance and break the law by exceeding the specified bag. Above all, it would prevent the movement into Irish waters of commercial divers from the South of England or anywhere else, while still enabling the fishing community to retain their perceived 'rights' to the produce of the sea.

We informed the Minister that if he went ahead with his proposed Byelaw, there was every possibility that it could result in unpleasant confrontations between divers, fishermen and the Gardai. There had already been some nasty incidences where trawler men drove their boats at divers who were in the water, and shots were fired on at least one occasion. We felt that fishermen might go running to the Gardai every time they saw divers come out of the sea, demanding to have their bags and boats searched for illegal shellfish. The potential for conflict was very obvious to us at the time.

Mr Haughey was not inclined to agree with us that it was necessary to take a lobster simply to enjoy the dive. He claimed to have tried out diving for himself and felt that there was sufficient enjoyment to be had without taking a lobster. He thanked us for our trouble, wished us well and said that he would consider our proposals. We left the Ministry feeling happy that we had taken a reasonable stand and had presented a reasonable alternative. The very next morning, 14th June 1966, we read in the national papers the Official Notice by the Department of Agriculture and Fisheries proclaiming the introduction of a new regulation entitled 'The Skin-diving for Shell Fish Bye Law, No. 533, 1966'. The Bye Law made it illegal for an individual to take any shellfish - unspecified - while using diving apparatus.

It also informed all parties that they had 28 days notice in which to lodge an appeal against the Bye Law, if they so wished. Unfortunately, CFT was a new and very small organisation, without adequate funds, and we felt that we were not in a position to mount a challenge to the Bye Law in the High Court. In Britain, the State has resisted, to this day, all such calls by fishermen's groups for a ban on shellfishing activities by divers. We now have the ridiculous situation where it is legal to take shellfish in Northern Ireland, but not on our own coasts. It was obvious to us that the Official Notice had been prepared for publication at the time the Minister was actually talking to us and that he was merely going through the motions of consulting the 'interested parties', should he be asked a question in the Dail. Equally, it was obvious that our arguments and point of view had been found not worthy of further consideration.

Irish divers were then, and are still to this day, very much in favour of conservation in our seas, but we also feel very strongly that the wrong method of control has been chosen. It is still not too late to adjust this Byelaw in the interests of fairness and rationality. Perhaps there is a politician somewhere willing to give this his consideration.

In dealing with state organisations in the early years, CFT suffered from a problem that has persisted to this day. Just as in other outdoor sports, there are many 'rogue' divers who are not affiliated to CFT or any of its clubs. Some may have been affiliated divers at some stage but who, for reasons of their own, decided to operate without any regard for the ethics or indeed the rules of good diving. Their activities such as poaching lobsters or removing valuables from the sea bottom, getting into difficulty at sea, or even in a few cases losing their lives, reflect badly on the good name of CFT and its members. It is very difficult for CFT to counteract such bad publicity.

\* \* \* \* \* \* \* \*

As the new sport of diving gained in popularity, it became necessary to protect the members of CFT against claims for 3rd party liability in the case of accidents or injuries. Initially, the State did not provide any support to help cover the cost of running an increasingly more complex organisation. So, despite the protests of some members, an initial capitation fee of 10p was charged to cover insurance and administration costs. Today that fee is £48. With the intention of bringing divers closer together under CFT, it was decided to organise an annual national diving rally. The first of these was held at Whit Weekend in Slade, Co. Wexford in June 1965, where 96 divers, mostly accommodated under canvas, experienced a happy get-together in excellent weather.

Initially, CFT boasted of excellent communication with all its divers because of the small numbers involved and because two Delegate meetings per year were held in addition to the AGM. The Delegate meetings were especially valuable as divers from the clubs could participate directly and effectively in the affairs of the Council. But as the organisation grew, divers began to feel more remote from the decision making process. To overcome this, the Secretary or the Diving Officer issued information bulletins from time to time, but these did not solve the problem. Many of the clubs produced their own club news sheets or magazines. In the Curragh, Shane O'Connor and I produced 'Diving News', a quarterly stencilled magazine with a printed coloured cover that ran for four years from Summer 1963. The magazine of Belfast Branch BSAC, also a stencilled production, was a major factor in that club winning the Siebe-Heinke trophy for the best-administered Branch in the BSAC in 1964.

In 1967 the first of a short series of CFT Yearbooks were published giving a summary of the events of the previous period, as well as statistics, results of competitions and other information relevant to divers. With the intention of making it a commercial venture, Donal Douglas of the Irish Sub Aqua Club published 'Dive 67', a magazine that sadly lasted for only about twelve months. Barry Kinsella of the Trident Sub Aqua Club then stepped in to produce a very good magazine called 'Diving Ireland', which ran from November 1977 to June 1980. However, neither of the magazines fulfilled the needs of

CFT as they were not official organs of the Council, even though Barry had begun to print a centre-fold section in 'Diving Ireland' giving current CFT information.

Hugh Hennessy, then a member of BSAC in Belfast, who produced the first Yearbook in 1967, volunteered in 1973 to publish an A5-sized magazine to be called 'Subsea'. Subsea was an instant success, and is sent to each diver on the National Register of Divers. It has gone through a number of changes of content and size over the years as it developed. Today it is an excellent quarterly journal, circulated to all the registered members of CFT and to a wide number of national federations around the world. Produced by volunteer editors and helpers, Subsea has maintained very high standards in content and presentation. But the burden on these volunteers is getting greater as life in Ireland becomes more complicated and more frenetic. I feel that some time in the future, the production may well have to be 'farmed out' to a professional company. I believe also that editorial policy should be more independent and more critical of the official CFT Executive line in order to widen the magazine's attraction. However, its place in Irish diving is assured and it has fulfilled the need for regular communication with the members of CFT.

In the early years of diving, few enough women were involved as it was regarded as a man's sport, requiring strength and endurance. It was in an era also when money was scarce and diving equipment was expensive and difficult to acquire. There were many notable exceptions of course, particularly in the Belfast club where Margot Sydney-Smith, Hilda Maguire, Maureen McGladdery and Isobel Dobbyn were amongst the most active women members. However, following on the change in circumstances and the rise in the standards of living in Ireland, many women today are active and dedicated divers, contributing very effectively to diving at all levels. I believe that women divers are every bit as good as men, in many ways they are better because they are less likely to take foolish risks. Irene Harrison, daughter of a retired Army officer, was the first woman to serve as National Diving Officer to CFT from 1994 to 1997. She also served as Chairman of the Curragh Sub Aqua Club in 1998 during which same year Sue Cobbyn was the Diving Officer. In any diving club, the posts of Chairman and Diving Officer are the most important and the most senior posts. Mary McKenzie served as Diving Officer to the Curragh club in 1997 while Deirdre Davitt held the post of Chairman in 1999. Many of the RDOs have been women who have been very successful in their appointments. At present, 'Subsea' is produced by Editor Polly Dolan and a team where all bar one are women. The current Vice-President of CFT, Roisin Maguire, may well be in line to become the first-ever woman President in 2002.

I served as Secretary to CFT from 1964 until 1973, (as well as Treasurer for one year in 1965), during which time I was also acting as Registrar, issuing diving certificates. But the rapid growth in the number of clubs meant that the workload became too much for any one person to handle, so a Diving Sub-Committee was formed on the 3rd of December 1967. Tom Shakespeare was appointed Chairman and Paddy Chritchley, Michael Clarke, Shane Gray and Val Kennedy were members. This Sub-Committee was expanded and given wider powers and a larger number of members in 1970.

At the Hook, Jun 1995, CSAC members Dr Mary Taafe and Captain Paula O'Riordan preparing to dive.

At the same Meeting in December 1967, a Competitions Sub-Committee was established with Joe Murray, of the Navan club as Chairman and Ted Spendlove, ISAC, and Bernie Brennan, CSAC, as Members. At my suggestion, the first Executive was formed on the 25th of January 1970 with the intention of further spreading the workload. Ted Spendlove of ISAC, who succeeded me as Secretary in 1974, further proposed that in order to bring CFT into line with CMAS, committees should be established to cater for medical, scientific, technical and sporting activities. These proposals were adopted at the AGM of 1974, but the term 'commission' was to be used for each and not 'committee'. Another development in the organisation of the Technical Commission was introduced as the number of clubs continued to rise rapidly. With the intention of lessening the burden on the National Diving Officer, the island was divided into regions and each region was allocated a Regional Diving Officer who functioned both as the representatives of the NDO and as assistant. Currently there are nine regions, one, the Northern Region, includes the CFT clubs in Northern Ireland.

\*   \*   \*   \*   \*   \*   \*   \*

As the new CFT was developing not all went smoothly. The unified all-island body suffered an unfortunate blow in 1972. The problem arose when the British Government decided to make changes in the manner in which it allocated funds to sporting bodies in the UK and Northern Ireland. In order to take advantage of the substantial funds that would become available, the divers within Northern Ireland felt that a federation of diving clubs was the best option for them. This seemed a reasonable path to follow, and as CFT had already been able to cope with clubs having dual membership, it needed only another tweak of the constitution to cope with the new problem.

Unfortunately, it generated a considerable amount of heated debate amongst the representatives of the clubs from the North. Some divers were most unhappy at the possibility that the Northern Ireland Federation (NIFED) might seriously weaken CFT, while others maintained that they could retain the close link with CFT but still gain financially from the British Government's attractive financial offerings. It was a traumatic episode for CFT, aggravated by the particularly difficult security situation in Northern Ireland. A protracted and strained debate arose within CFT where the matter of the Northern Ireland Federation, (NIFED) as it was called initially, was argued at great length over a number of months. While all divers in the Republic wanted the northern clubs to benefit from the potential riches that would flow, few wanted it to be the cause of a split between friends. The problem was aggravated to some degree by the fact that the State here did not support CFT financially at that time.

On a personal basis, it was particularly difficult for me also, because I was President of CFT for part of that year during which the protracted and sometimes acrimonious debates took place. Worse, I was on close and friendly terms with both sides in the debate. The debate was undoubtedly aggravated by the political and security events occurring in the North. A Northern Federation of Sub Aqua Clubs (NIFSAC) was formed in 1973 and the close, friendly and valuable relationship between divers on both sides of the Border changed. The BSAC branches withdrew from CFT, although a smaller number of northern non-BSAC clubs have continued with their affiliation. The hope is that it will be possible in the future to mend the fences and to restore the links between all the clubs. Whatever solution or formula is found, the result can only be of great benefit to diving on this Island.

\* \* \* \* \* \* \* \*

Past Presidents of CFT pictured at the 21st anniversary.
Back row L-R: Billy Nott 1984-88, Ronnie Hurley 1968, John Hailes 1977-78, Ted Spendlove 1975-76, John O'Connor 1992-94, Mick Moriarty 1973-74, Gerry Stokes 1978-81, Bart McMullin 1983-84, Paul Ryan 1991-92.
Front row L-R: Jim Whelan 1969-70, Hugh Quigley1966-67, Shane O'Connor 1963, Hugh Hennessy 1964-65, Brian McGuinness 1981-83, Pat Bergin 1988-90.

While the many national federations were developing and prospering through their membership of CMAS, a new diving organisation was formed in the United States that was to have a major impact on the world diving scene. In 1967, John Cronin and Ralph Erickson founded the Professional Association of Diving Instructors, known all over the world today as PADI. A story is related that the two men, one Irish-American and one Swedish-American, were having great difficulty in deciding on a name for the new body. So they decided to have a drinking competition to see which of them would make the final decision. John Cronin, bearing a good Cork name, won the competition, so naturally the title PADI was adopted!

PADI has expanded enormously since 1967. It is represented in 180 countries around the globe, and over 8 million certificates have been issued, 750,000 alone in 1998. The PADI school system provides a one-stop shop for anyone who wishes to become a diver, providing qualified instructors, first-class training, (in most cases), facilities and the best of equipment for rent or sale. PADI has over 90,000 professional members around the world, mainly Instructors, Assistant Instructors and Dive Masters. A number of important ancillary services are provided to members such as the PADI Retail Association, which covers all aspects of diving equipment and the industry. The PADI Travel Network helps members to improve their skills through experiencing diving in the world's best locations, in co-ordination with another branch of the organisation, the PADI International Resort Association. PADI arrived in Ireland on the 17th of March 1989 with the establishment of its first Dive School and Equipment shop at Oceantech Adventures, Dun Laoghaire, Co. Dublin run by Willy Siddal. Within a short ten years, PADI is represented in many locations across Ireland.

The arrival of PADI on the world stage was not exactly greeted with open arms by the established clubs and federations, as it was seen as a direct threat to their continued existence. The long serving sports divers and organisers, whose loyalty, energy and dedication had been completely bound up with their federations, felt that they would shortly be out of business. All the years of debate and hard work might be lost to the brash and cash-rich interloper. There was much uninformed opinion and even hostility towards the PADI concept, as it was seen as an organisation designed simply to make money for the organisers in the US. It has to be accepted that in the fast-moving, ever-shrinking world of today, the PADI system does offer a very appealing training package of short courses, slick presentation and professional standards. The impatient and affluent young people, who might have joined their local clubs in the past, would rather get their certification to dive as quickly as possible, and they do not mind paying considerably more to achieve this.

CFT is understandably concerned that a situation might arise where the 'club concept' may become redundant. If a person can get a certificate to dive in a week or even less, why should he bother with a club, where he might have to wait three to six months to reach much the same end result, i.e. a certificate of suitability to dive safely. In diving, just as in other sports, there are always some individuals who are not interested in the 'club scene'. They are selfish 'loners' and they join for the sole purpose of learning how to dive, disappearing as soon as they have acquired their certificates of qualification. Such individuals are of no benefit to clubs anyway, so it is better if such people were to go to PADI instead. The CFT clubs prefer to get members for the long haul - divers who will give something back to their chosen clubs.

A well-organised diving club with a bright, intelligent and active committee can provide for its members an atmosphere and a feeling of belonging that PADI can never hope to equal. Such clubs should have nothing to fear from PADI. In fact they will reap the benefits because the better PADI divers will naturally gravitate to these clubs. This process is already underway and many Irish clubs have benefited by acquiring eager and active PADI-trained divers. Unfortunately, there are a small number of clubs in Ireland that could be described as 'sluggish', operating something of a closed shop, limiting or refusing membership to newcomers. They seem to hang together simply because of the insurance, certification and appearance of credibility that membership of CFT provides. This type of club does nothing for the image of diving in Ireland or anywhere else, and they may well find that they have more to fear from the presence of PADI than do the healthy active clubs.

Within CFT there have been many proposals to try to counter the arrival of PADI schools in order to protect the Council and its systems. None of these are practical or even desirable. What CFT has to do is to look carefully at its own system, and to make improvements where possible, particularly in the manner in which the Council is administered. CFT should welcome the challenge posed by PADI and if the right attitude is adopted, the Council could actually benefit from the competition. I believe that we can co-exist. The pool of diver potential in Ireland is small and if both organisations are sensible, it is surely possible for both to prosper.

Well before the arrival of PADI, the first Irish diving school was established by Shane Gray and Bernie Brennan at Dalkey, Co Dublin in 1974. The company was called Scubadivers Association and they aimed their courses at those people who were in a hurry and who did not mind paying the extra in order to go diving without the bother of being a member of a club. It was a great success but the numbers were such that it was found necessary to establish a club called Dalkey Scubadivers in order to cater for the large 'surplus' of trained divers. This club, affiliated to CFT, was a great success, even though they suffered the loss of their base at Dalkey on two separate occasions through development of the waterside properties. Dalkey Scubadivers Association has changed too, and its descendant, Scubadive West can now be found in Renvyle, Co. Galway, run by Shane and his family.

\*  \*  \*  \*  \*  \*  \*  \*

Many years ago, in an effort to boost the attendance at the annual general meetings, CFT decided to improve on the AGM format and to make it more attractive to divers by arranging for concurrent lectures, films and a display of diving equipment. The first of these new-style weekends was held at the Prince of Wales Hotel, Athlone, Co. Wesstmeath in January 1971 and the principal speakers were Des Branigan, of Marine Research, Dublin and David Bellamy. Marine Sales, of Dalkey, Co. Dublin set up the first-ever public display of diving equipment, manned by Aidan Kelly and Willie Sidall. The success of the new format was such that a much more ambitious AGM was held at the Prince of Wales Hotel in Athlone in January 1973, organised by Roger Fitzgerald. Films on the wreck of the Gerona and the recovery of the Wasa

At the Prince of Wales Hotal. Athlone in 1971. The first exhibition of diving equipment at a CFT AGM weekend, by Marine Sales, Dalkey. On left is Aidan Kelly and on the right his co-director, Willie Siddall.

were shown, together with lectures on underwater research by Nigel Mathers, Galway, underwater photography by Dermot Fitzgerald, Limerick, and the Association for Adventure Sports (AFAS) by Pat Colleran, CSAC.

The CFT AGM weekends, operating under the title 'Underwater Ireland', have expanded wonderfully since those days. A large trade exhibition of diving equipment, boats and related equipment forms a very important part of the weekend. Some travel companies who specialise in diving holidays are also represented. The weekends provide an opportunity for all divers to meet and to renew old friendships, to look at the latest in equipment, to enjoy the films and lectures, and to plan new ventures. The CFT weekends have attracted many of the world's most important divers and underwater filmmakers, such as Hans and Lotte Hass, Ron and Val Taylor, Ralph White, Robert Ballard and many others. Some of the most challenging and beautiful underwater films have been shown which attract large audiences, many of them from the non-diving community.

Irish divers have been dedicated supporters of CMAS ever since CFT first became an affiliate, and CFT officers have contributed effectively to its aims and activities over the years. In particular, the Irish delegation of Paul Ryan, Gerry Stokes, Rory Golden and Pat Bergin can claim to have played a major role in saving CMAS from its own possible demise at a critical meeting in Nagoya, Japan in 1989. As a result of that meeting, CMAS was strengthened, reorganised, and eventually, in 1993, its headquarters was moved from Paris to Rome. Paul Ryan of Galway University and the Galway Sub Aqua Club was elected President of the Scientific Commission, which automatically made him a Vice-President of CMAS as well. He held the post for three eventful years from 1989, and his Secretary for that period was Irene Harrison of the Curragh Sub Aqua Club.

The Technical Commission of CFT has produced a two-part personal diving logbook, the novel and practical format of which was so good that it was copied by many other national diving organisations. The first part is the diver's personal Logbook, or 'passport', which is accepted all over the world. It contains the photograph and all the details of the holder's training, grades, experience, and current medical condition from the time he started his diving career. Part Two of the logbook is purely for the purpose of recording the owner's dives, allowing for a wide range of details such as depth, dive duration, temperature, clarity of the water, the buddy diver, marine life seen, decompression stops, as well as personal comments on the dive. Snorkelling was gaining rapidly in popularity with the juniors so Ronnie Fitzgibbon produced the first Snorkel Diving Manual and Logbook in 1988. A new and modernised Logbook was introduced in 2000.

Having designed and produced an excellent two-part logbook, the Technical Commission of CFT then recognised that there was a need to produce its own training manual. The diving conditions on Irish coasts are fairly demanding, and very different to diving in warm clear waters like the Caribbean. It was intended that the Manual should reflect the diving practices and ethos that had been developed through experience over the years. After a lot of hard work by many divers, the Club Diver (CMAS 2 Star grade) Training Manual was published. It has been protected by copyright and at the CMAS General Assembly in Egypt in 1991 the CFT training format was adopted as the world standard for all federations to follow. It has been sold to a number of national diving bodies across the world, or reproduced by them.

Initially, divers here had difficulties in arranging their annual registrations with CMAS. The process was very cumbersome and slow. The fee in dollars and the details for each individual had to be sent to CMAS in Paris, and frequently there was a considerable delay before the card was returned to the diver. CFT devised a new and much more efficient system whereby the cards were printed in Ireland with the CMAS logo on one side and the CFT logo on the other. When an application for registration was received, the name and grade was typed in at CFT and sent back to the individual while a copy of the details and the appropriate fees were sent on to CMAS. The CFT delegates proposed this new system of registration to CMAS and it was eagerly accepted and has been applied to all countries ever since. Another card, this time an MNBA loyalty card, displaying the CFT Logo, was put into service in 1996. Two videos promoting sports diving in Ireland have been produced, one by Ronnie Fitzgibbon in Tralee in 1985, and another by Peter O'Doherty, CSAC, in 1993.

The CFT building at 78a Patrick Street, Dun Laoghaire.

CFT has continued to grow and to prosper. It now has the affiliation of 83 clubs and can boast of an annual registration of about 2,700 divers. It took a very long time, but the state eventually recognised CFT and its contribution to the community at large and to youth in particular, and now provides a small but variable annual subvention to assist in its administration. For many years, CFT was administered from the homes of the various early officers, until the strain of the rapidly growing organisation became too much for any individual. In 1971, Secretarial Services, Ltd, Baggot Street, (later at Upper O'Connell Street) was given the contract to provide all necessary secretarial support. In a major new initiative in 1993, CFT decided to go it alone and a Portacabin was purchased, fitted out as an office, and placed in the grounds of the National Maritime Museum in Dun Laoghaire. Mrs. Enda Roche became the first full-time employee as the office manager, and, although not a diver herself, she has brought about a dramatic improvement in the administration of the Council. In 1994, CFT moved again and purchased a two story building in Dun Laoghaire, which provides accommodation for an Executive Board Room, a public office, a number of storage and stock rooms and the Diving Archives. In January 1993, CFT became a Limited Liability Company.

So from humble beginnings in 1963, CFT has become a large, complex, and effective organisation that can be said to reflect very closely the needs and wishes of its diver members. An amateur sporting organisation run by its members, CFT is a tribute to all those who have voluntarily given of their time and energies over the years to make it the successful organisation that it is today. The sport of diving is regarded as being one of the best-regulated sports in Ireland and CFT is widely respected in the wider international diving community.

# CHAPTER 6

# OUR UNDERWATER HERITAGE

In Lough Lene, near Mullingar, a logboat recovered by members of the Mullingar Sub Aqua Club 1968. From the left: B. Healy, National Museum, Des Coleman and Bob Acton, MSAC. Photo; Sean Magee.

As the sport of diving developed in Ireland, a number of divers made accidental discoveries of artefacts in lakes and rivers, mainly in the midlands of Ireland. The Athlone, Mullingar and Cavan clubs, in the early years in particular, located and reported on some fine examples of 'dugout' canoes, or 'logboats' as diver Nessa O'Connor of the National Museum called them. In 1991, a bronze axe and a bronze spear were found in the Shannon at Athlone by Harry Smith and a very fine book shrine, the Kinale Shrine, dating from the 8th Century, was found in a lake in Longford by members of the Cavan club. These were all handed over to the National Museum. In view of the history of the Viking raids on the centres of learning and wealth, especially along our rivers, there is every possibility that the lakes and rivers of Ireland may still conceal some very important and valuable artefacts. It was the practice of the time, apparently, to throw the valuables into the water, to be recovered after the raiders had left.

As a result of these and other previous discoveries, the Irish Underwater Archaeology Team (IUART), a sub-division of CFT, was established in 1990. CFT representatives and representatives of the National Museum, the Maritime Institute of Ireland, and the various institutions responsible for the archaeological

heritage on the island of Ireland met and agreed to establish the new organisation. The objectives of IUART were to foster working relationships between professional archaeologists and the sports diving community and to increase awareness of the need to protect and document our underwater heritage. Many successful projects have been completed by IUART since 1990, including surveys of the river Boyne, investigations of ship remains at Portaferry, Newcastle, the Aud in Cork, a monastic harbour in Strangford Lough, and a bridge remains at Clonmacnoise. More recently, a survey of a prehistoric petrified forest was conducted at Bray, Co.Wicklow, and a study of the landing stages in Dalkey Sound is ongoing. IUART has also organised many conferences and studies with other interested organisations across the island of Ireland.

It was originally intended that IUART would supply the statutory bodies with specially trained volunteer divers to work as assistants on archaeological projects. However, with the establishment of diving elements within government departments in the Republic and Northern Ireland, and with the arrival of a commercial archaeological underwater sector, the work of IUART was radically curtailed in the years between 1995 and 1997. In particular, under the new Health and Safety Act, a diver engaged in commercial or government archaeological work has to be in possession of a current Certificate No.4. This certificate is acquired by undergoing an expensive six-week full-time training course with FÁS. This effectively sidelined the amateur divers of IUART or at best reduced their role to a peripheral one.

Because of the new constraints imposed on the activities of IUART, an assessment was made of their situation and eventually a meeting was called to propose a new organisation and constitution. This meeting took place in conjunction with the Annual General

Meeting of CFT in March 2000 at Limerick. It was decided that IUART would cease to exist and be replaced by a new organisation to be called The Irish Maritime Archaeological Society (IMAS). The objectives were to remain as before, to study and foster an interest in Irish maritime and archaeological matters amongst its members. Training courses have already commenced under the auspices and technical standards of the Nautical Archaeological Society in London, a body of worldwide standing and reputation.

A National Maritime Sites and Monuments Record, (SMR), was established in 1997 by the Department of Arts, Culture and the Gaeltacht with the following principal aims:-

• To document and map all know archaeological sites in Irish waters.
• To create a large archive of data relating to maritime sites.
• To create a computerised database of all known sites.
• To carry out a programme of fieldwork on a number of maritime sites.
• To publish county inventories of known maritime sites.

In recent times, the Applied Geophysics Unit of University College, Galway, under Dr Colin Browne and Mr Kevin Barton, has developed new techniques and introduced electronic equipment that will have a major impact on future underwater archaeological operations. The Unit has already worked on a number of projects using a combination of a side-scan sonar, a ground penetrating radar, a remotely operated vehicle (ROV), Differential Global Positioning System, and a high-resolution proton magnetometer. Projects executed include the remains of a wooden bridge at Clonmacnoise on the Shannon, previously investigated by the amateur divers of IUART, and the 'Surveillante', a French frigate from 1798 lying at 34 metres in Bantry Bay, discovered some years ago by Tony Balfe.

In the past, many of the principal underwater finds have been made by amateurs in our inland rivers and lakes. It is fully accepted that the manner of the recovery and the treatment of the finds have not been in accordance with the proper preservation standards necessary to protect them from long-term damage. There has been under-standable tension between the amateur and professional diver archaeologists since underwater archaeology became popular in Ireland.

Certainly, there are rogue divers operating outside of the clubs of CFT whose motives are purely mercenary. An active member of the Curragh club was ejected from the club in the 1960s after it was discovered that he had been using explosives on a wreck off the East coast. Unfortunately the activities of these rogue divers, many of whom had never been members of clubs, tarnish the good names and best intentions of the disciplined divers of CFT.

In general, divers have always felt very strongly about the need to protect wrecks and important underwater sites and are fully supportive of the new legislation designed to preserve the underwater heritage. There is little doubt that there exists a wealth of discoveries yet to be made in the lakes and rivers of Ireland, and it is essential that the search for and recovery of such treasures are conducted in a disciplined manner for the benefit of all who live on this island.

Events and experiences over the years have clearly indicated that there are occasions on which the professionals can benefit from the assistance of trained and dedicated amateurs, many of whom are eminently qualified for these tasks. Because of their enthusiasm and dedication, the members of IMAS should be regarded as a reservoir of experienced manpower, willing and able to work side by side with the professionals, and under their direction. They can, and should be, encouraged to provide a 'reserve force' to be employed where the manpower requirements are beyond the limited resources of the professionals.

\* \* \* \* \* \* \* \*

Under the National Monument (Amendment) Act 1995, all archaeological sites over 100 years old in Irish waters are automatically protected. No interference of any sort is permitted and a licence is required to dive on any of these sites. The punishments for contravening these laws are severe, and include possible confiscation of all diving equipment, even boats and vehicles. Anybody who finds a site on the seabed must report it to the National Museum and to the Gardaí immediately. The first underwater excavation licence ever granted to amateur divers was granted to members of the Athlone club in 1989. The Project Manager was Donal Boland and the Office of Public Works (OPW) supplied an archaeologist and a surveyor under the direction of Ned Kelly of the National Museum. Two sites on the River Suck were excavated with some urgency as major drainage works were imminent. The site at Correen Ford in particular, yielded many items of a military nature, as it was associated with the Battle of Aughrim of 1691.

Under the Merchant Shipping Act – 1993, all divers are required to report any objects that they find to the nearest Receiver of Wrecks, who can be the local customs officer, Harbour Master or even a member of the Gárda Síochána. The question of salvage and the ownership of wrecks is still a potentially problematic area for individuals, despite recent court decisions, and divers have to be very wary. The penalties are as stringent as those already outlined in the National Monument (Amendment) Act, 1995.

\* \* \* \* \* \* \* \*

The story of the Spanish Armada and the 23 or so wrecks that are believed to have been lost along the north and west coasts of Ireland has always fascinated Irish divers. The weather in the summer and autumn of 1588 was such that it accounted for more loss of life and ships than did the running battles with the English and the Dutch in the Channel. It is believed that as many as 5,000 soldiers and sailors may have been lost at sea and in the ships that were wrecked on our shores. Despite the common belief, not all were Spanish nationals. The ship that was stripped, abandoned and set on fire off Scattery Island in the Shannon estuary, was the Ragusan (modern-day Dubrovnik) argosy called the 'Presveta Anuncijata', or in Spanish, 'Santisimo Anunciada'. The records show that the ships of the Armada were manned by Portuguese, Italians, (from Venice), Germans, Dutch, Ragusans, (from Dubrovnik), as well as many prisoners and slaves/servants from North Africa. There were even a small number of English mercenaries and about forty Irish on the rolls.

The Portuguese galleon 'São Marcos', with a Spanish captain, was wrecked on the coast near Quilty in Co. Clare, where only four of the four hundred Portuguese on board survived. The four survivors, along with about sixty other survivors of the carrack 'San Esteban' a Basque vessel, lost at the north end of Doonbeg Bay, were later hanged at Cnoc na Crocaire (Hill of the Hanging). Their remains were cast into a common grave at Tuama na Spáinneach, known today as Spanish Point. In view of the nationality of the majority of sailors from these two vessels who lost their lives, it probably should have been called Portuguese Point. A plaque to commemorate the tragedy can be seen on the pier wall at Seafield, near Quilty.

There are many excellent accounts of the Armada wrecks available but I intend only to deal with those wrecks that came to the attention of Irish divers in recent years. The 'Santa Marie de la Rosa' was a ship of the Guipuzocoa (Basque) squadron, of 945 tons, armed with 26 guns. It had a crew of 64 sailors, while 233 soldiers were carried as passengers. The captain was listed as Martin de Villafranca from San Sebastian. The pilot was Giovanni de Manona, an Italian, who was fated to become the only survivor of the sinking, which occurred soon after it arrived in the Sound at the Blasket Islands in mid-September 1588.

Two other Spanish ships were already there at anchor, the 'San Juan Bautista' and the 'San Juan de Portugal', of which only the 'San Juan Bautista' managed to get home safely to Spain. An eyewitness, Marcos de Armaburu, on the 'Bautista', described the arrival of the 'Santa Maria de La Rosa' and its sudden and dramatic loss in the channel. As many as four hundred men may have been lost in the sudden sinking, caused when the ship dragged its anchors and struck a 'rock in mid-channel'. Two Irishmen were among those lost, John Rice and Francis Roche. The Captain of Infantry on board was called Matuta, and in Dublin in 1969, Sydney Wignall showed me a pewter dinner plate with that name crudely inscribed on the underside. A number of cannon balls, and other items recovered from the Santa Maria are now to be seen in the Ulster Museum in Belfast.

Sydney Wignall, from Old Colwyn, Wales, an amateur diver with a special interest in ancient shipwrecks, started to do research on the Armada wrecks on the Irish coast in 1961. He quickly identified the 'Santa Maria de la Rosa' as the best 'target', given the amount of information available on its sinking. He was assisted in this research by Des Branigan of Marine Research in Dublin. Des had carried out his own diving search in the Blasket Sound in 1963 prior to joining forces with Sydney Wignall. Colin Martin, marine archaeologist, provided valuable and active direction to the expedition. After a lot of very hard work in difficult diving waters, the wreck of the 'Santa Marie Santa de la Rosa' was located in the Blasket Sound in June 1968.

Earlier Sydney Wignall had applied for a salvage licence from the Department of Industry and Power in Dublin, and after some delay, he was told to get in touch with the Spanish Government which had been adjudged to be the legal owners of the wreck. The Spanish government then granted him a licence to all Spanish wrecks on the coast of Kerry from 1967 to 1974. The licence was subject to the payment of a deposit of £1,000 and his agreement on some other conditions. He was permitted to become the rightful owner of any items of historical interest, such as guns, cannon balls, that he might recover.

About that same time, the decision of the Irish and Spanish governments proved to be of interest in another jurisdiction. Robert Stenuit, a Belgian diver, had located the wreck of the 'Gerona' in Antrim in 1967. As in the case of the 'Santa Maria', the 'Gerona' was fairly well documented and this caught the eye of Robert Stenuit who had been carrying out research on the Armada wrecks in Scotland and Ireland. He read various accounts of three ships that had ended up in Killybegs Bay. They were all in a very poor condition. One sank on arrival, a second was driven ashore where it was stripped and abandoned and later it provided some of the materials for the repair of the 'Gerona', the remaining vessel.

The galleas 'Gerona' was made seaworthy with the help of locals and the decision was to return home via the north of Scotland. Around the same time, the 'Duquesa Santa Ana' was driven ashore in Loughros Bay in Donegal. The surviving members of the crew, including a number of Spanish noblemen, made their way overland to Killybegs. There they were taken on board the galleas and the over-loaded and over-crowded 'Gerona' set out for home. But luck was against the Spanish as the Gerona was wrecked on the Antrim coast soon afterwards and all were lost.

Diving in accordance with the official English and Spanish accounts of the wreck, Stenuit and his team were not having any luck. Local people told him that he had been diving in the wrong place, as tradition in the locality had placed the wreck further to the East off Dunluce Castle, home of Sorley Boy McDonnell. On examining the Ordnance Survey map, Stenuit saw that a rock a short distance out from the shore there was called 'Corrig na Spáinneach', the Rock of the Spaniard. This in itself is not a certain indicator that a Spanish wreck may lie there. A ship might have struck there and a misfortunate crewman may have been seen hanging on to the rock, but the vessel itself could well have travelled quite a distance before it foundered. The coastline of Ireland is dotted with quite a few 'Corrig na Spáinnaigh'. But on this occasion, the tradition proved to be startlingly accurate.

In 1967, on the first dive on the new location, one of his divers came up with a gold necklace. Robert Stenuit had discovered what turned out to be the biggest find of coins, jewels and gold ornaments to be recovered in Irish waters up to that time. The treasure trove was purchased by the British government and it is on exhibition in the Ulster Museum in Belfast ever since. Stenuit, claiming precedent from the decision of the Spanish Government to Sydney Wignall in court in Dublin, went to the High Court in Belfast in 1968 to get an order restraining divers from the Belfast Branch of the British Sub Aqua Club from diving on, or interfering with, the wreck.

Another vessel of great importance to Irish divers was the 'La Trinidad Valencera', badly batterd and in urgent need of water and food which struggled into Kinnagoe Bay, Glenagivney, Co. Donegal in October 1588. The third largest vessel in the Armada, it was a Venetian ship of the Levant squadron, weighing 1,100 tons, with 42 guns. It had a crew of 79 and carried 281 soldiers. The ship was abandoned and all on board were safely brought to shore. The ship sank in the Bay shortly afterwards. In 1971 the City of Derry Sub Aqua Club started to search in a disciplined manner for the wreck of the 'Valencera', and eventually their efforts were rewarded. They found and raised six fine cannon, two of which carried the coat of arms of Phillip of Spain, his name 'Phillipus Rex' and the date of the casting, 1556. They also recovered a considerable variety of artefacts, such as cannon and musket balls.

There are some interesting points to be made about the above story. Firstly, the entire project was conducted and brought to a successful conclusion by amateur sports divers. These divers displayed a remarkable dedication and discipline in their approach to what turned out to be a long campaign that has yet to be finalised. They were fortunate to have had the close guidance and assistance of marine archaeologist Colin Martin amongst others.

Secondly, the legal aspects were significant. When Eamon Molloy, Paddy O'Doherty, Fr.Mick Keaveney and others approached the National Museum in Dublin in 1972, they were told that the Museum was not interested, as the Armada wreck was not of Irish historical value! Fortunately, they persisted and after a considerable passage of time, the nineteenth century laws governing wrecks in the Republic were modernised, as described earlier in this chapter.

Thirdly, a novel three-way 'deal' was made between the Irish Government, the City of Derry Sub Aqua Club and the Ulster Museum. The then Taoiseach Charles Haughey, agreed that the artefacts would be made available for display in a special Museum in Derry. The proposed museum would have the necessary facilities to continue the process of conservation for any additional artefacts recovered in this or other wrecks. Unfortunately, the Museum has yet to be built and in the meantime, the artefacts remain at the Ulster Museum pending a decision. The BBC 'Chronicle' team made an excellent film of the process that was since broadcast in many countries around the world. If it is lack of finance that has delayed the project, perhaps the Fund for Ireland could find the one or two millions required.

There are clear records and eyewitness accounts available depicting the destruction of three ships of the Armada on Streedagh Strand, which is north of Sligo. Because of this and because of the publicity relating to the discoveries mentioned above, it was only a matter of time before these wrecks would be investigated. A team of British divers came to Ireland in the early 1990s and, working under very difficult conditions in the waves of the beach, they made some wonderful discoveries. However, the State stepped in and a prolonged dispute arose over the ownership of the artefacts, which ended eventually in the High Court where Mr Justice Barr made a landmark judgement. He adjudged that the State was the rightful owners of the artefacts but that the diving group who made the discoveries were entitled to adequate compensation for their efforts. There is an excellent BBC 'Chronicle' film of some of the activities and discoveries of the team.

In 1968, Sydney Wignall wrote about the relatively new science of marine archaeology. He said 'The mere thought of what an Armada wreck could contain in bronze guns, astrolabes, jewelled crucifixes, or muskets, would make the average Mediterranean wreck seem as dull and uninteresting as a nineteenth century coal barge'. He also said that 'In the diving world of today a great deal of young and very enthusiastic talent is wasted due to the lack of direction. There appears to little sense or purpose in being a diver if one restricts one's activities to weekend trips to the seaside and to pointless dives into the same familiar waters year after year'.

\*　　\*　　\*　　\*　　\*　　\*　　\*　　\*

While the Gerona yielded up the biggest haul of treasure ever found in Irish waters, it pales into insignificance beside the cargo of gold ingots recovered from the SS Laurentic, a liner of the White Star Line, which had been converted into an armoured cruiser. In 1917 it was carrying part of the gold bullion of the Bank of England, valued at £5 million, to Canada for safekeeping when it struck a mine off Lough Swilly, Co. Donegal. It sank in a depth of 38 metres with the loss of about 200 lives. Lying on its port side on a sandy bottom, with its position well buoyed, it was assumed that it would be a simple enough task to recover the bullion. But the very strong tides, the frequency of severe Atlantic gales, and the rapid disintegration of the vessel meant that the entire operation took no less than seven years to complete. All but three ingots have been recovered in a diving operation that is vividly described by diver Desmond Young in his book 'The Man in the Helmet'. The wreck was subsequently purchased by the Cossum brothers of Derry, and rumour has it that they have been searching for the remaining ingots ever since.

In 1979, a group of about eighteen divers of the Army Sub Aqua Group went out in a hired trawler to dive on the 'Laurentic'. The skipper had brought divers to the location many times before and knew what to do. Having lined up with his markers on the distant headlands, he dropped his anchor and used the strong current to drag along until the anchor snagged on the wreck. Captain Harry Smith and myself were the second pair of divers to enter the water, after a tricky jump from the heavily rolling trawler. It was a hard swim to the anchor line because of the strong current, but after that it was an easy task to drop to the bottom. I was not prepared for the surprise that greeted us when we reached the bottom at 37 metres in poor visibility. The anchor had fouled on a large gun, probably a deck gun of about 4inch calibre, which was sitting upright on the sand.

For an artillery man this was a great start to the dive. I was carrying my Nikonos 2 underwater camera with electronic flash, so the first thing that I did was to gesture to Harry to sit on the barrel of the gun while I took a picture. This he did promptly, straddling the barrel and moving forward at my signal so that he would be closer to the camera. As he moved up along the barrel, I noticed that a large conger had put his head out of the muzzle to see what was going on. I was now presented with a very difficult ethical dilemma. Would I warn Harry that his manhood might be threatened if he continued to advance towards the muzzle, or should I set aside my scruples and try and get a very dramatic photograph! I compromised and took the picture before Harry reached the danger zone. The conger disappeared, shocked by the flash. To my regret the photograph turned out to be very poor as the water was too dark and the flashgun was too weak. Harry never knew until after the dive just how close he was to disaster.

We continued on the dive, reaching the wreck itself, which was only about 20 metres away. It looked like a huge scrap yard of rusting metal with occasional larger mounds of junk. It was not very interesting, and the 11 minutes available to us went too quickly and we had to head back for the surface. At the surface, it was a hard swim again against the current to reach the line trailing from the stern of the trawler. Harry kept falling behind me and I had to signal to him several times to catch up. It was only when we reached the deck of the trawler that Harry noticed that one of his fins was almost severed just forward of where his toes lay. It must have been cut on a piece of sharp metal when we were moving across the wreck on the bottom. This explained why he could not keep up with me on the surface, he was working on half-power.

A very sad aspect of our expedition to the 'Laurentic' occurred only a short time after we had regained the deck of the trawler. Two of our divers got into difficulties on the bottom and were forced to make an emergency ascent from 37 metres. One of the divers collapsed immediately into unconsciousness on reaching the surface, while the other seemed to be unaffected. An Army doctor, who was in attendance on the trawler, possessing the standard oxygen and resuscitation medical equipment, began the struggle to save him. An Air Corps helicopter from Finner Camp was called and both divers and the doctor were taken by helicopter to Craigavon for treatment in the Recompression Chamber. Tragically, one diver died about twelve hours later while the other made a full recovery.

I have always maintained that divers, particularly inexperienced divers, are taking risks when they dive on wrecks, especially those wrecks that lie in deep water, in bad visibility, or in strong tidal waters. This is only a personal opinion, not shared by all, but I have met divers over the years who seem to live only for a visit to the next heap of scrap. I firmly believe that divers can become distracted by the search for souvenirs and they are likely to forget where they are and the constraints of their dive.

A diver is trained to notify his buddy and to start for the surface when he reaches a particular pressure in his cylinder, usually 50 Bars. If he is distracted by trying to get a souvenir and has remained too long at depth, he may find that he does not have enough air to do the compulsory safety stops during the ascent, a very dangerous situation indeed. In the era of the wrist–held diving computer, the diver is given all the information he needs to complete his dive in safety, so such events should never occur. However, human nature being what it is, incidents and tragic accidents can and do occur. It should also be borne in mind on this type of dive that some wrecks are often associated with considerable loss of life and divers should have due regard for this and accord the wrecks the respect that they deserve. Bearing all these matters in mind, a visit to a wreck in relatively shallow clear waters, especially a recent wreck, is an extremely satisfying experience.

# CHAPTER 7

# SNORKEL DIVING

The word 'snorkel' is a German one, coming from the word to snore. In the later stages of WW2, the German U-Boat engineers developed a means of refreshing their air supplies and re-charging their batteries without having to bring their submarines to the surface. They would float a wide-bore tube up to the surface through which the submarine could 'breathe' while holding out of sight at a shallow depth. After the war, somebody somewhere used the word 'snorkel' to describe the simple breathing tube that he was using. He was probably practising what we divers now call 'snorkelling' or 'snorkel diving'.

The snorkel has nothing to do with enabling the diver to remain under water for a long period. It merely allows him to continue observing the underwater scene without having to lift his head to breathe. It has been frequently suggested that if this snorkel is so effective, why not use a longer one. Why not even dispense with an aqualung altogether, for the shallows at least. This might seem like a great idea but sadly even the strongest diver could not physically draw down air to his lungs if he is more than about one metre below the surface. The water exerts too much pressure on the diver's chest, and he would become exhausted very quickly.

Such is the importance of snorkelling to the development of diving skills that CFT has included a section on snorkelling in the training programmes, tests and examinations for each diver grade. In addition, CFT requires all divers to start each diving season by doing three snorkel dives of 30 minutes duration that are designed to improve the 'water-fitness' of divers before they resume aqua-lung diving. One member of the Executive of CFT, the National Snorkelling Officer (NSO), has responsibility for snorkel diving for all ages. As NSO, Ronnie Fitzgibbon of Tralee Sub Aqua Club produced the first Snorkelling Manual and Logbook in 1975 while a new Snorkel Diver Logbook was produced by Polly Dolan in 1999, incorporating all the latest advances in snorkel diving techniques and practices.

One of my most memorable snorkelling experiences came about unexpectedly at a very early stage in my diving career. In the summer of 1959, Jim Motherway and I went to Slade, Co. Wexford for a weekend of diving. We arrived too late to go diving, but the weather was exceptionally calm and warm. 'Come on, Jim', I said, 'let's go for a night snorkel instead'. This was something that neither of us had done before, so it said much for his enthusiasm that Jim agreed without hesitation, even though neither of us owned diving suits at this time. We went along the rocky shore to Carrigahoy, enjoying the balmy, evening and admiring the full moon, which was high in a cloudless sky. Conditions were excellent, the air was still, and the water was lapping gently against the rocks. It was getting dark as we got into the water but we knew the layout of the rocks and the underwater terrain very well so we had no worries. From the surface, the water was dark as I peered down, but I found that when I dived to the bottom, I could see around me very well. That was my first surprise.

My second surprise came when I looked over to watch Jim arriving at the bottom near me. He was trailing a plume of glowing bubbles behind him, each scuttling madly towards the surface. I looked at a large bubble. It was a perfect but miniature full moon! I watched in fascination as it wobbled its way upwards. Looking behind me, I could see that I too was leaving behind me a trail of tiny 'full moons'. I looked closely and I could see where there were hundreds of them trapped on the hairs of my arm. Every so often, a bubble would escape and struggle away towards the surface. The calmness, clarity and relative darkness of the water allowed the moonlight to be reflected beautifully in every bubble.

The third surprise was the phosphorescence, or more correctly the bioluminescence. Every movement of hand or leg generated a shower of tiny 'sparks'. The disturbance made by my movements caused the myriad tiny organisms suspended in the water to glow briefly. I had read stories about the tropics where the passage of the boat through the water left a glowing wake. I had never expected to see anything like it in our waters, yet I now know that it is a common natural phenomenon and can be seen at night underwater, even in the much-maligned Irish Sea. (Night dives on aqualung are a required practice for all trainees, where there is a special emphasis on safety and support. Those making their first dives are usually overwhelmed by the experience and are quite surprised to see the luminescence).

It was the same Jim Motherway who introduced us to the joys of snorkelling into the series of blowholes that can be found on the western side of the Hook peninsula not very far from the Lighthouse. The rock formation in the area is very brittle and layered and the ceaseless pounding of the storms creates fractures where the sea tunnels inwards. The waves eventually break upwards to give the blowholes so beloved of all shore watchers when the seas are rough. There was a small network of tunnels under the rock leading to three blowholes about 20 metres inland, and they can only be approached in calm conditions.

Jim was an excellent snorkel diver and on one fine day he decided to explore one of the underwater passageways. Moving very cautiously, he inched his way in, noticing that the walls and floor of the tunnels were completely devoid of seaweed. He only continued when he was satisfied that he had enough air to return to the sea and to the surface. After a short distance he could see light ahead of him and when he moved forward, he found that he could surface in a small pool in the rocks. He shouted out and his friends arrived, astonished to see him in the water of the pool about 3 metres below them. Taking a deep breath, he dived again to make his way back to the sea by the opening through which he entered. As he went, he noticed that there were other branches to the tunnel, leading to other blowholes and also back to the sea. So he developed a new game where he teased his friends by submerging in the sea and appearing in one blowhole and then another. The children in particular enjoyed rushing from one place to another, trying to anticipate him. The blowholes gave us great fun in the snorkelling days, but they are extremely dangerous in any but the very calmest conditions.

Snorkelling is a very suitable activity for young people and many of the Irish clubs provide a junior section, where children between the ages of six and sixteen are given the opportunity to enjoy the sea at an early stage in their lives. Some of the groups have very apt titles. In the Irish Sub Aqua Club the juniors are known as 'Sea Urchins' and in the Curragh club they are called 'Tadpoles'. Diving suits are now freely available in very small and small sizes, and although the wearers grow rapidly, there is a ready market for trading between the sizes. Apart from training in snorkel techniques in the pool and in the sea, junior divers also receive training in safety, First Aid, CPR, and related subjects. There are four grades: Junior, Senior, Leader and Instructor. There is an annual National Junior Sub Aqua Gala, which includes fin-swimming races, on the same lines as for the Senior events, and the competition between clubs and individuals can be intense. This Gala is held at a different venue each year.

CFT introduced a 'National Snorkelling Day' in 1985. This event is usually on St Patrick's Day or the Sunday closest, and clubs all over the country are encouraged to hold a public snorkel swim in their own localities, sponsored if possible. In Dublin, this takes the form of the 'Round Dalkey Island' Race, probably the biggest of the events held on National Snorkelling day. This public display has a number of purposes: it publicises the club and diving, it encourages recruiting, it furthers fitness amongst divers, and it raises money for the Royal National Lifeboat Institution (RNLI). The RNLI is a popular and worthy cause and after a few years, the funds raised enabled CFT to hand over a fully equipped inshore lifeboat to the RNLI on the 5th November 1993. Called

CSAC Junior snorkellers                                    Photo by Peadar Farrell
Standing: Robert Harris, Gerry Van Ommen Kloeke, Ciaran Meghen,Noel Whelan, Fergus Wheatley, Fintan Van Ommen Kloeke, Tara Morris, Adrian Kavanagh, Micheal McMullin.
Sitting: Marianne McMullin, Natasha Renwick, Laura Nolan, Adele Buckley, Maeve Brannigan.

'The Irish Diver', the lifeboat is based at Dun Laoghaire, where it still contributes to safety for all those who enjoy the waters of Dublin Bay. Some time previously an incident occurred with the predecessor to 'Irish Diver' in which a small group from the Curragh Sub Aqua Club led by Fred Esby went to the rescue of the Inshore Lifeboat. The Lifeboat had gotten into difficulties in rough weather and was drifting towards the rocks south of Bulloch Harbour. Fred, who was a Lifeboat supporter, heard their radio distress call and he and some others put to sea in a Club inflatable from Sandycove and brought them safely into Dun Laoghaire. The Club received a very gracious letter of thanks from RNLI afterwards for this gesture. Since the presentation of the 'Irish Diver' to the RNLI at Dun Laoghaire, a need arose to renovate the Recompression Chamber located at University Hospital Galway, and since then, the monies raised as a result of National Snorkelling Day have been devoted to this equally worthy cause.

Spearfishing was a great way to get fit for the water, but it is no longer practised. To some extent, this loss has been replaced by other sports such as fin-swimming competitions, underwater hockey, and more recently underwater rugby. These are minority sports and are confined to a fairly small number of totally dedicated divers. In the very early days of diving, some clubs became involved in a number of experimental schemes at Carlingford Lough and other locations to see if divers could get rid of starfish in oyster beds. Des Branigan of Marine Resources also did a detailed study of the problem at Clarinbridge in 1969 for Bord Iascaigh Mara. In all cases, the results indicated that while divers could be of some help in the war against starfish, it was slow and tedious, and it proved to be wildly unpopular with the participating divers themselves.

It was probably as a result of these starfish culling activities that the 'starmop' competition received its name. The Starmop competition, also known as the 'Davy Jones' competition, represented an attempt to involve more divers in a fairly non-competitive snorkelling activity. Hundreds of small objects, such as metal bottle tops or similar objects were scattered over the sea bottom within the competition zone. The bottom would be sandy and relatively free of seaweed, and the water would be between two and five metres deep. Then within a specified time limit, the diver who came in with the greatest number of recovered items would be the winner of the competition. It is a very suitable exercise requiring little training, equipment or preparation. It can involve any number of divers, and it is particularly suitable for the junior divers.

Not long after CFT was established a new organisation was formed in which CFT was involved. Called the Association for Adventure Sports (AFAS), it was established in 1969 by a group of mountaineers led by Paddy O'Leary, Joss Lynam and Noel Masterson. Others in the group were Ernie Lawrence and Bill Hallowes, representing canoeing, Donal Gilhuys and Brian Farrell representing caving, and Mike Lunt representing orienteering. From their own observations, Paddy O'Leary and Joss Lynam had come to realise that there was a need to co-ordinate the activities and endeavours of the participants in what they termed the 'outdoor pursuit' sports. These they identified as canoeing, orienteering, mountain walking, mountaineering, caving and diving. At that time, some of the sports represented by AFAS did not even have a national organisation of their own, nor did many of them have a set of training and examination standards. This was a very undesirable state of affairs, most especially for the leaders and organisers of those sports. They could be exposed to embarrassing questions or even to litigation in the event of an accident. Therefore, the advent of AFAS was very important for the protection of the leaders and organisers of these adventure sports.

AFAS diving was confined to snorkelling only, as snorkelling was expected to appeal more readily to the younger people than scuba diving, it would also be cheaper, and the training for snorkelling would be easier. Because CFT was seen as an established and effective organisation, AFAS learned many lessons from the manner in which it was organised and administered. CFT was invited to participate by providing instructors in snorkelling to the scouting and other youth organisations as requested. Because of the association of CFT with AFAS, the new post of National Snorkelling Officer (NSO) was instituted, and given a seat on the CFT Executive Committee.

The duties of the NSO were to promote snorkelling within CFT, and to act as the liaison officer to AFAS. John Hailes of the Curragh club was the first to hold that appointment. John and myself attended many of the early AFAS meetings, and we provided AFAS with its first constitution, which initially was merely a re-worked version of the constitution of CFT. Later, John and I spent many enjoyable weekends in schools and colleges across the country teaching snorkelling to students. However, of all the activities covered by AFAS, snorkelling was possibly the least successful. There were many problems of which the biggest were the shortage of swimming pools in those years while there were great difficulties in providing an adequate supply of small-sized diving suits. In the cold Atlantic, an ill-fitting diving suit was nearly as bad as no suit at all. Most of the initial training had to take place in the scarce swimming pools of the time, while the open-sea part of the training was very dependent on the weather and the state of the sea. The support from state funds was less than adequate, especially as it had to be shared among so many sports. Fortunately, many of these problems do not arise today, due to increased affluence, the prevalence of swimming pools and the availability of diving suits for children.

A National AFAS Centre was established at 'Tighlin' in the Wicklow Mountains in 1971, in a former 'An Óige' hostel. Run by Paddy O'Leary, it provided a badly-needed base for AFAS, at which most of the training for AFAS activities could be carried out. Other centres were to have been established as well, but the financial support did not materialise. Since then, a little of the slack has been taken up by the Vocational Education Committees in some of the counties, especially on the West coast, where adventure training centres are established during the summer months. In August 1972, the first issue of a magazine called 'Irish Adventure Sports' was produced, featuring articles relevant to all the sports represented by AFAS.

\* \* \* \* \* \* \* \*

Ursula O'Leary instructing AFAS pupils at the swimming pool in Lahinch,Co.Clare, 1970.

The following story serves to illustrate the value of snorkelling in warm, clear waters, in a situation where there is no opportunity to go aqualung diving. In October 1964, I found myself in Cyprus as part of the United Nations Force in Cyprus (UNFYCIP). The Battalion was stationed initially at Famagusta and I found many opportunities to snorkel at the nearby beach. The following story is taken from the magazine of the Curragh Sub Aqua Club issued in Spring 1965.

'At the northern end of the beach I noticed a line of rocks stretching out from the shore not too far from the onshore ruins of Salamis, an ancient Roman settlement. History had it that the port of Salamis was founded sometime after the Trojan War by Teucer, son of the King of the Greek island of Salamis. It was fought over on many occasions, but in 306-301 BC, a long siege of the city ended when Ptolemy and his fleet were defeated by the Roman General Demetrius in a sea battle somewhere offshore. Cicero was the Proconsul of Salamis in 51 BC and Salamis was the home of St Barnabas when St Paul visited there in 45AD on one of his missionary journeys. Following earthquakes and tidal waves, the port was abandoned in favour of the new port of Famagusta.

The tremendous history of the place was present in my mind as I snorkelled happily around the rocks of the reef. The first time I slipped into the water close to the line of rocks, I realised for the first time that the rocks were really the remains of the breakwater or pier of the ancient port of Salamis. Almost immediately, I spotted a slab of masonry that turned out to be a large copingstone. It was about five feet long and three feet wide, and was in an excellent condition. This find really aroused my expectations and I moved eagerly along the line of the broken pier wall, alas, never seeing anything as well preserved as that first stone. However, there were thousands of pieces of shattered stones in a tumbled mass stretching away from me, many of them bearing the marks and straight edges of the stonemasons of old. As well there were enormous quantities of broken pottery scattered everywhere on the sand, many of them being the necks and handles of amphora, in which wine and oils were carried by sea in ancient times.

I explored the deeper northern face of the pier where the depth dropped more rapidly to the sandy bottom. Here the rocks were much larger, but it was obvious that the sea had scoured the area clean of any artefacts, or had buried them beneath the sand. So I returned to continue my exploration of the inner side of the pier. It was on my fifth visit to the site that I discovered the anchorage. It lay some distance out from the pier, and there was an obvious channel of water, approximately 25 feet deep, running parallel to the pier. Down below me I could see that the seabed was littered with the largest fragments of jars and amphora that I had seen to date. I dived repeatedly to inspect them at closer quarters. The neck and two handles of many of the pieces were intact and in very good condition. I also saw many fragments of vases of a slate-blue colour with small close-set grooves running around the sides.

I came to the conclusion that these pieces of pottery were exposed from time to time by the action of the waves, after which they were slowly ground down by succeeding storms. How I longed for x-ray eyes so that I could see even one foot below the sand and silt. Goodness knows what wonderful artefacts lay just under the surface. I speculated as I finned along, how the sailors, the merchants or the slaves simply pitched any broken vessels over the side of their ships or into the water from the pier wall. When I was on the bottom, I could picture in my mind's eye the ropes, the anchors and the undersides of these pitifully small wooden vessels and their human cargoes. I could imagine St Paul arriving in his ship, creating a flurry of excitement when he stepped on to the pier. I also pictured the Roman galleys arriving back after defeating Ptolemy's fleet, thus securing Salamis for the Romans. These thoughts and many more filled my mind as I drifted along, hoping every moment to make a dramatic discovery. I knew that I was not the first diver to inspect this site, but it had become a place of special significance for me. I planned to come back as soon as possible with an aqualung to take a closer look. Alas, that was not to be, as our Battalion was transferred suddenly to the other side of the Island, thus precluding the possibility of visiting once again my own ancient harbour of Salamis. It was a month or two later that I discovered that the

Cypriot authorities were very protective of their archaeological sites over and under the water, and the penalties for examining this site as I had done, could have earned me severe penalties.'

\*    \*    \*    \*    \*    \*    \*    \*

Snorkelling is a safe and gentle activity, it requires the minimum in equipment and training and, while a diving suit is needed for our cold northern seas, a T-shirt is enough in the tropical waters. It is an excellent way of passing time, watching the colourful fish in the shallow waters instead of baking for hours on the sand. So satisfying is it, especially in the tropics, that I believe it could well be practised by all ages. Like swimming, it is quite suitable for those suffering from certain back, knee and leg problems, as they will find welcome relief from gravity. In 1961, I met and dived with an English diver who had suffered severely in a motorcycle accident. One leg was deformed and shorter than the other, but he was otherwise an excellent diver. Unfortunately, when snorkelling on the surface he was always pleading with his companions to wait for him as he could not keep up with us.

In the past in Ireland, many young people left school without ever learning how to swim, while today, thanks to the widespread presence of swimming pools, most young people are competent swimmers. I now believe that it is desirable and feasible that every swimmer should also learn how to snorkel. The swimming pools of Ireland are crowded each morning by the retired citizens, who are getting great exercise in a gentle and relaxing way. For those who may have become tired of swimming and who want something new, I believe that they should be introduced to snorkelling. The training is simple, the equipment is cheap, and I believe that the elderly could derive many hours of beneficial exercise, not just in Irish waters, but also on their holidays, in the warm blue waters of the Mediterranean or the Caribbean.

# CHAPTER 8

# SPEARFISHING

Scuba diving is a relaxing, non-competitive sport, and this in itself is a major part of its attraction for many people. It requires of its practitioners simply average basic fitness, careful training and due regard for the hazards involved. It is very much for the average Joe and Josephine. Spearfishing, however, was not for sissies! It involved a process whereby a diver holds his breath, dives down and attempts to shoot a fish using a hand-held harpoon or a speargun. It required excessive zeal, low cunning, high ideals, great deviousness, individual fitness, team spirit, careful preparation, extraordinary disregard for creature comforts, and, quite often, for one's own personal safety as well. The sport was a lonely one, even during a team event. Hours could go by during a competition without seeing another diver, and of course, all the action took place far from the gaze of others. It was a deadly, silent action, fought below the surface between the diver, the fish and the laws of nature, with the balance very much against the diver.

There are no laws against spearfishing in Ireland, apart from the obvious prohibitions against fishing in private fisheries on rivers or canals, or in estuaries where salmon fishing rights are established. There are no restrictions on the kinds of fish that can be speared either, except under the limits as mentioned. In many warm-water countries, particularly along the Mediterranean, spearfishing divers made a handsome living by selling their catches to the local hotels. Initially, there were no laws against the practice, but in most countries today, a diver must possess a licence to fish commercially or even to simply own a speargun. Many of these 'commercial' divers were so good at shooting fish that they became automatic choices for inclusion on their national teams. This made it very difficult for the amateurs like ourselves to make an impact when it came to competing at international level.

Unfortunately, leisure divers also went spearfishing, but using their aqualungs, which made it much too easy for the diver and very unfair on the poor fish. In the warm waters countries, again it was a lucrative occupation, as the fish were bigger, more flavoursome, more popular, and were present in greater numbers. In particular, the divers were going after the grouper, (merou), a fish related to our own wrasse, but much larger. These unfortunate fish have a major weakness, which was exploited by unscrupulous divers. They make their homes in a particular group of rocks and when frightened they would retreat to their homes rather than flee. The hunters would spear them at close quarters and spend as much time as was required in bringing the fish to the surface. The practice of using an aqualung while shooting fish had a disastrous impact on the numbers of fish in the shallower waters, along the Mediterranean coasts in particular. Spearing fish while using an aqualung never became a regular habit in Ireland. It was regarded as being unethical and in any case most divers here were just not interested in the practice.

In the Ireland of the 1960s, spearfishing developed for a more prosaic reason. When a group of divers went to the coast for a weekend's diving, the number of potential aqualung dives was limited, because once the cylinders were emptied, there was no way of re-filling them again, as air compressors did not exist outside of Dublin or Belfast. Unless a gullible volunteer, usually a new member with a large, fast car and little sense, could be persuaded to take all the cylinders back to Dublin or Belfast to be re-filled, the only solution was to go snorkelling. Better still, if you owned or could borrow a speargun, you went spearfishing. For many divers in those early years, snorkelling was only the first step to spearfishing. Equipped with a speargun, a diver was provided with an additional motivation for extending his time in the water. In contrast with aqualung diving, the time spent in the water was only limited by fitness or the ability of the individual to withstand the cold.

While there were many spearguns on the market at that time, Beuchat in France, produced probably the widest variety of guns to cater for all tastes. The spear was propelled by two, or four, lengths of surgical rubber. The ends of the rubbers were attached at the head of the gun, while the other ends were attached to heavy wire wishbones. To load, the diver slid the spear into the gun until it engaged in the sear of the trigger, then he placed the butt of the gun in his groin, reached up and grabbed the wishbone of the rubbers. He then stretched the rubbers back until he could get the wire wishbone to engage in the groove cut into the spear. Where the gun had a double set of rubbers, he then pulled back on the second wishbone and engaged it in the same way in a second slot in the spear. The gun was then loaded, the diver released the safety catch and proceeded on the hunt.

Pressing the trigger released the spear which was then propelled very rapidly towards the target fish. To prevent the loss of the spear, it was secured by a length of light line to the head of the gun. In this manner, if the hunter missed, he was able to recover the spear and start again. The spear was tipped by a removable head on which was fixed one or even two swinging barbs. When the spear struck the fish and passed through its body, the barbs would open and prevent the fish from getting off the spear. There was a crude aiming device on the hollow barrel of the gun, but in practice, the hunter aimed more by instinct than by sighting along the barrel. The Beuchat models had a number of important features. They were slightly buoyant - they would float for a while if they were released. Also, they were remarkably silent when fired, by comparison with other guns, especially the compressed air guns. Even so, if a diver happened to be underwater at that moment, it was possible to hear the 'twang' when a near-by diver fired his spear. Silence of operation was a very important feature, because the fish were very sensitive to any sudden sound or motion, and reacted accordingly. Most fish were so swift to react that it was the norm to aim slightly ahead of the fish's head - even for a more or less stationary fish - to allow for that instinctive jump forward as the spear was released.

The fisherman carried a second belt in addition to his weight belt. It was usually made of rubber, and was designed to carry the diver's catch. We called it a fish belt or a 'keeper' belt. It would clearly be a huge waste of time to have to come back to shore each time a fish was caught, as it could often mean a round trip of many hundreds of metres. So it was necessary to bring the catch along while the diver continued hunting. The keeper belt had a short length of line attached to it, at the other end of which was a metal rod through the centre of which the line was threaded. When the diver shot a fish, he pulled the struggling fish back to him, and took hold of the spear, releasing the gun. While he was doing this he also had to rise to the surface to get a breath of air. Next, he would thread the short metal rod of the keeper belt through the gills of the fish, so that the fish could not get away. Then he unscrewed the spearhead, removed the spear shaft from the fish, and released the fish. Finally, he replaced the spearhead on the spear before re-loading and continuing on the hunt. This was a slow process but it was not a waste of time as it gave the diver time to recover his breath before resuming the hunt.

If the diver was having a good day, the number of fish on his fish belt would eventually start to pose problems for him. Apart from the sheer bulk of his catch, which created a resistance to his forward movement, the diver would also begin to get heavier. Usually, all divers deliberately carried a little extra lead on their belts, as it helped them in getting down to where they might find fish. But with the additional and increasing weight of his catch, the diver would find that he had to work harder simply to get back to the surface for a breath of air. This condition only started to take effect towards the end of a four or six hour competition at the very time when the diver's energies were on the wane.

Most of the prominent Irish spearfishermen were capable of diving down to 25 metres at least and staying down for as long as one minute or more. They could keep at this for hours without a break. However, although impressive, their abilities still fell some way short of the abilities of the professional divers of the warm waters of the world. During

The author spearfishing at Sandycove, 1966.    Photo: Tony Balfe

the brief time available to him under the water, each diver had to hunt, shoot, and bring up his catch. He had to search under rocks, move along the bottom, or, more usually, hang onto a rock at a likely spot and wait for a curious fish to come within range. If the sea conditions were marginal, as they often were, the extra weight caused by his catch would begin to pose a progressive threat to his safety. I well remember, at a competition at Kilkee, seeing Billy Nott coming ashore with a fine catch. He said that although he was seeing plenty of fish, he had to give up as he was finding it more and more difficult to regain the surface after each dive!

When a diver left the surface and plunged down, clearing his ears as he went, the water pressure squeezed his thoracic cavity to as much as one third of its normal size, depending on the depth reached. This normally did not create discomfort for the diver or have any lasting affect on his condition, as the ribs, being quite elastic, would return to normal on regaining the surface. As he was carrying in his lungs only what air he could inhale at the surface, he was not in any danger from the bends or from narcosis. However, he was very much in danger from shallow-water blackout, a condition that could strike without warning, rendering the diver unconscious.

If a diver over-stayed his time underwater, holding his breath against the frantic urgings of his body, he would reduce the pressure of oxygen in his blood below that which was sufficient to maintain consciousness. Unconsciousness could then come upon him without any warning. If he had reached the surface when he lost consciousness, he might well recover after a few minutes. If he had been on the bottom, or had been rising when he lost consciousness, he might not survive. Now, it might seem to the casual reader that no diver would be so foolish as to allow himself to get into that situation. But when there is a good fish to be had, and a competition to be won, most divers would take the risk and push themselves well beyond their limits. In all the years of spearfishing in Ireland, there was only one fatality, at Killybegs, Co. Donegal, and one case of unconsciousness, in Bantry Bay, Co. Cork. In this latter case, another diver happened to be passing by and went to the assistance of the unconscious diver.

Another dubious practice in spearfishing was to hyperventilate before diving. The purpose of hyperventilating was to prolong one's time under the water. A diver would spend up to five minutes on the surface before descending, breathing forcibly in an attempt to build up the level of oxygen in his blood stream. He knew when to stop, because he would start to get quite dizzy. This 'overload' of oxygen would then enable him to stay a little longer under the water. It was, and is, a very dangerous practice, as it made the onset of shallow-water blackout more likely. But while all divers were aware of it, and even preached against it, we all practised it. Later on when we were in Italy at the World Championships in 1969, I had the opportunity one day to watch the eventual individual winner, Massimo Scarpatti, in action. He would spend up to 15 minutes hyperventilating before he submerged, and he could then stay down for as long as two minutes at a time, often at a depth of 30 metres or more. As a matter of interest, he was also the individual winner when the European Spearfishing Championships were held in Ireland in 1974.

In the Ireland of the early 1960s before CFT was established, it became the norm for each club to organise a spearfishing competition and to invite divers from all the other clubs to take part. The competitions were generally very well supported and divers came to know each other well, a factor that was very important later on when coming together in the formation of a national organisation. Spearfishing was becoming so popular and so competitive that divers were actually required to go into the sea for training in preparation for forthcoming competitions. This was both expensive and time-consuming and the divers who lived near the sea possessed a distinct advantage over those who lived inland. At this time I was stationed in Magee Barracks, Kildare and the sea was some distance away, so I decided that I would attempt to improve my skills without having to travel to the sea. I built an underwater firing range in the Curragh Pool in order to keep my shooting eye in tune.

Out of a sheet of tin, I cut a fish shape, about 25cm long. Next I cut about 30cm from my old homemade wooden handspear and mounted the fish shape at the top, weighing it all down with a 2kg lead weight attached at the other end to keep it upright. Finally I attached a length of light line to the weight. Next, I placed the target on the bottom at the deep end of the pool and got a volunteer to do safety cover from the security of the side of the pool and to hold the line for me. The pool had to be cleared, just in case of accidents. I then unscrewed the spear head from the spear, as yet another safety precaution, and I was ready to go. I had laid down a number of rules to make it more difficult for myself. The target was near the other end of the pool, about 25 metres away. I would submerge at the shallow end and make two complete right-angle turns from one side to the other as I approached the target. Finally, I would not permit myself to fire at the target until I was passing across, rather than heading straight at it, and my volunteer would pull the target along the bottom of the pool just when he thought I was about to fire! It worked, after a fashion.

I was unhappy that the ballistics of the spear would be different because the spear point had been removed, but it was the best I could do and it saved me having to go to the sea more often. It was very unpopular with the other users of the pool, naturally, so after a while I discarded what may well have been the only indoor spearfishing range in the world. It may be just coincidence, but in France in recent years a new and novel competition has arisen called 'Tir sur Cible', literally, target shooting. The competition is held in a swimming pool and the divers, using their spear guns, shoot at a target very like the target butt used in archery. It is a very popular competition, so much so that it rates a separate organising and controlling committee at national level in Fédération Française d'Etudes et de Sports Sous-Marin (FFESSM).

* * * * * * * *

In Ireland, as many as five or six spearfishing competitions were held every year, North and South, so it was only a matter of time before a national or open competition was organised. Up to then the most popular locations for spearfishing were at Kilkee, Co Clare; Bulloch Harbour, Dalkey; Co Dublin, Slade, Co. Wexford and Killybegs, Co Donegal. The committee of the Irish Sub Aqua Club, based in Dublin, were the ones to recognise the need for a national competition that would not just involve our own divers, but would bring in 'spearos' from abroad as well.

In 1959, Des Lavelle and Dermot Ring established an excellent dive centre at Valentia Island, which they called Sub Aqua Services. It was aimed at attracting both Irish and foreign divers, and it was a great success. Both Des and Dermot had been employees of the Western Union International, Inc., up to the time when it closed down in the mid-1960s, so they had been forced to turn to other means of making a living. They also opened a very nice hostel, the 'Dive Inn', to accommodate divers, located only a short distance up the hill from the pier at Knightstown. They provided a compressor and rented out diving equipment and boats as required. It was a very successful venture for Des, but Dermot did not stay on, eventually moving off to London. Des was a stalwart supporter of diving and he contributed much to the early days of spearfishing and to the formation of CFT. All the clubs in Ireland, and many from Britain, made great use of Valentia for diving, as there was a wide variety of excellent dive sites. Because of the topography, only the very worst of weather would prevent divers from getting into the sea.

So, in 1963, the Irish Sub Aqua Club organised the first Irish Open Championships at Valentia Island and invited divers from Britain as well as from home to participate. ISAC provided a marvellous solid silver trophy, called the Glaucus Trophy, for the winner, with a bronze Glaucus for the runner-up, as well as many sponsored prizes to tempt the divers. The Trophy was named after a fisherman called Glaucus from Anthedon, a small Greek town widely known for the devotion of the entire population to fishing. Glaucus found an apparently dead fish on the beach one day and he returned it to the sea in the hope that it might revive. It transpired that the Gods were watching and because of this act of generosity to the 'dead' fish he was allowed to become an immortal and to live in the sea.

At that time in Britain, there were many diving clubs, mostly in the south of England, whose members specialised in spearfishing only. They lived for spearfishing and like Fintan Mullowney, regarded those who went under water with cylinders of air on their backs as wimps. I had been preoccupied with the duties of National Secretary to CFT at that time and had paid very little attention to the new competition. It was only at the urgings of my wife Anne, that somewhat reluctantly, I entered for the competition, and to my great surprise and delight, I became the first winner of this beautiful trophy. This happy event became the principle motivation for my involvement in the sport for the next seventeen years. I was runner-up in 1964 and won again in 1966.

The Irish Open turned out to be a very popular event and for as long as it lasted, it regularly attracted entries from Britain, Sweden, Belgium, Jersey, as well as from most of the clubs in Ireland. Attracting as many as 80 divers, the competition began as a one-day event, lasting for four hours, where the competitors worked from shore, without benefit of a supporting boat. However, after the second year, it became a two-day event, the first day of four hours and the second day (Sunday) of six hours duration. On the Sundays, a boat and boatman was provided for each team of four. The boatman himself was not normally a diver, but he stood to gain a boatman's prize if his team did well, so he had an interest in the welfare of his team. The competition zone was usually very generous, as the entire inner side of the Island was safe, and little affected by the weather.

The author with the Glaucus Trophy for the Irish Open Spearfishing Championship of Ireland, Aug 1966. Photo, M.Fleming, Kildare

The teams and individuals were free to select their own fishing areas within the designated Competition Zone, which was usually a very large area between the island and the mainland. The competition started at the pier-head in Knightstown to the sound of a shotgun blast, fired by Des Lavelle, who was a superb master of ceremonies and the chief organiser. Divers were free to enter the water at whatever point they fancied, usually trying to get an area to themselves, so that the fish would not be disturbed by the presence of other divers. Competitors had to be back at the pier-head and checked in before the time was up, otherwise they would have points deducted or they could even be disqualified. Des was correctly quite strict in this matter, and the fact that he was holding a shotgun in his hand while making decisions and issuing orders meant that there was rarely any confrontation!

Each diver was given a numbered wire loop on which to place his catch for handing in at the end of the day. Most divers carried more than one speargun, often of different powers, as well as a range of spare spear shafts, spear heads, rubbers, and wishbones, and the loop for his fish catch. It would be impractical to carry such items with them in the water, so they were 'stashed' on land until they were needed. When a boat was in use, the additional equipment was much closer to hand. 'Spearos' rarely wore gloves or boots, as they did not require them. If they wore gloves it would be of the heavy garden or industrial variety to facilitate the handling of fish, some of which were equipped with very sharp spines. Apart from a diving watch, no other instruments were carried. Spearfishing was so strenuous that cold was never a problem either, the diver was, if anything, liable to overheating because of his exertions. Thirst and dehydration could cause problems however, but they did not pose a serious problem in Irish conditions. On at least one occasion, I remember turning my face up to the heavy rain for a drink!

The Saturday competition was effectively an individual event, as each diver in a team would select his own area depending on his knowledge or assessment of the zone, and he would usually work away there for the day. At the end, each diver's catch was weighed in and recorded for the individual event, but the points were also combined with those of his team-mates, to give the team result. Points were awarded on the basis of one point per gram, the minimum weight of fish to be accepted for weighing was 500 grams, (later 1kg), and any fish below that weight were discarded. There was always great excitement at the weigh-in, watching the opposition, and trying to assess one's chances for the second day. The results of the four members of the team were simply totalled in order to nominate the winning team. As well as the trophies for the winner and runner-up, separate prizes were awarded also for the greatest number of fish, the heaviest fish, or the most unusual fish, all of which added to the interest. The merest novice might have speared something unusual like a trigger fish, or perhaps he may have shot the heaviest fish, and this would put him among the prize-winners, even though he may not have shot anything else of value.

When the Irish Open competition was extended to include Sundays, things were much more interesting. It was here that the team effort and the careful planning and preparation really counted. The tactics employed by a team were very important. A diver would have decided on a plan prior to entering the water. He knew where he would go first and how much time he would give to an area before moving on, but mostly he worked on instinct, experience, or knowledge of the area. Generally, more and bigger fish were to be found in the deeper water, close to reefs, where there was tidal movement or broken water, and where the bottom conditions provided food and cover for the fish. In particular, more fish were to be seen when the tide was coming in than when going out. When a boat was not available to him, a competitor was very much on his own. Once he had entered the water, he did not have a team manager or a coach close by to advise him. He had to make his own decisions, based on the success or lack of same, on his experience as to when and where he should move, or how well he felt physically.

However, when a team boat was provided, it was a different matter. In this case the diver had a means of getting and giving advice or information. This provided an enormous advantage not just to the individual but to the entire team, and the information passed between divers could make the difference between winning and not winning. This is why in spearfishing competitions, the home competitors had a great advantage over all others. Not alone did they know the area as a result of previous competitions there in which they had competed, but they would also know the types of fish to be encountered and, more importantly, their habits.

When competitions started first in 1958, there were no restrictions on the species, quantity or weight of fish permitted; it was a free-for-all. However, after a number of competitions had been held, it became obvious that control was needed. The easiest fish to hit were the flat fish, once you learned to spot them. They relied on their remarkable skills of camouflage, but once a diver knew what to look for, it was 'caput' for the poor fish. Skate and rays also fell into this category, and were even easier to hit because of their size. The most frequently seen fish in Irish waters though, are the many types of wrasse, often called 'connor fish' locally. They were easy targets because they are large, slow and very curious fish. They like to frequent a group of rocks that provides both shelter and a variety of entry and exit points. When a wrasse dived into cover, all you had to do was to hang around for a while. He would inevitably come back out, via a different route, to have another look. In fact, when I suspected that some wrasse lived in a particular location, I would dive down, and zoom along the kelp near the bottom. On surfacing, I would turn around and prepare to go down again immediately, as one or more wrasse would have come out to see what was going on.

One of the pleasant side effects of being a dedicated spearfisherman was just how much more one learned about the sea and the fish that lived there. The anti-aircraft gunners or the fighter pilots of World War 2 were trained to identify an aircraft just by seeing the merest hint of a portion of a shape. So also, the experienced spearfisherman became expert at recognising a fish by catching just a glimpse of a fin, a tail or even a silhouette. This was important information because one could decide if the fish was worth chasing or not. Also, depending on the fish, you could predict what it was most likely to do next, and you prepared accordingly.

On 2nd August 1964, the Curragh team was lying poorly enough in the tables after the Saturday weigh-in, so we were very anxious to do well on Sunday. Our allocated boatman was Dominic Bourke, a school teacher from Valentia Island, working in Dublin. He had been home on holiday, and was 'shanghaied' into service by Des Lavelle to be our boatmen for the day. He knew the waters of the Sound very well, having grown up on the Island, and he said in his Kerry brogue, "I know a spot that at certain stages of the tide, there are often skate to be caught". So, after the competition had started, we told him to bring us there immediately. I can still recall very clearly what ensued. The seabed in the area where we stopped was crowded with skate, all easily spotted, even though the visibility was poor. They were lying in about 5 metres of water on a muddy /sandy bottom, with scattered patches of long seaweed.

Poor Dominic now put in one of the hardest episodes of his fishing life. We had arranged beforehand that each diver had a designated part of the boat for his own fish loops, spare guns, spare parts bag etc. When any diver shot a fish, he would simply hand up both gun and fish to Dominic. Dominic then handed out the relevant spare gun, with which the diver went off to get another fish, loading the gun as he went. (One of the most important safety rules in spearfishing, was that the guns must only be loaded in the water, because of the dangers of accidental discharge). Meanwhile, back in the boat, Dominic had to take the fish off the spear, put the fish on the appropriate numbered wire loop for the diver concerned, screw back the head on the spear, and prepare to take in the next gun and fish. He was kept very busy trying to keep up with the demands of four very happy 'spearos'. At times we were actually queuing up for his services. It was sheer murder, but we were all laughing our heads off at our good luck in finding such a concentration of fish in the one spot. Anyway, at the end of the day, between the large numbers of skate, plus some good fishing in other locations, we had a huge total catch, our biggest ever.

As we approached the pier at Knightstown to check in, I found that I could not lift my particular wire loop, it was so heavy with fish that the wire was cutting into my un-gloved hands, softened by nearly six hours of immersion. Bernie Brennan, John Hailes, and Tommy Coyle had the same problem, so I suggested that we should use an oar to carry all four fish loops from the boat to the check-in. This we did and it created a sensation when the four of us staggered up to the weigh-in with our combined catch. It created a photo opportunity that was used by a local hotel, the Towers Hotel in Glenbeigh for some years afterwards to demonstrate just how good the fishing was at Valentia Island. Another photo of this event, showing myself, Tommy Coyle and Bernie Brennan, appeared in the July 1993 issue of 'Diver' magazine, the magazine of the British Sub Aqua Club, in an article celebrating 50 years of British diving! 'Diver' had previously taken over another British magazine, 'Underwater World', for which I had been the Irish correspondent for about 18 months, and the photo supplied by me to UW, presumably came from the old files of that magazine. We won the team event that year with ease, Bernie Brennan becoming the Irish

CSAC with their winning catch at Valentia Island, August 1964.
From the left: John Hailes, the author, Bernie Brennan and Tommy Coyle.

Open Champion with a catch of 114lbs, while I was runner-up with a catch of 89lbs. Dominic Bourke won the boatman's prize.

One of the outcomes of this and other competitions was that with the obvious rise in spearfishing standards in Ireland there was equally a need to introduce new conservation measures to protect certain types of fish. So the minimum weight for any one fish was raised to one kilo, and all flat-fish and other bottom-living fish and conger eels were banned, as they were considered much too easy to shoot. All divers were in full agreement with these measures and, unknown to any of us at that time, by upping the standards, we were actually helping to prepare Irish divers for the international competitions that lay ahead. We believed then that Ireland was the first country in CMAS to introduce restrictions on the weights and species of fish permitted in competitions. This process of restriction on what could be taken was revised upwards in 1969, 1971 and again 1974. CMAS officials praised the Irish approach and indicated that similar measures would be introduced in future international competitions.

In 1968, the weather had been excellent for weeks leading up to the August weekend, when the Irish Open Competition was due to be held. The members of the Curragh team were discussing tactics for the following two days in a quiet corner of the bar in the Hotel at Knightstown, making sure that we were not being overheard. I made a proposal. I said, "Bernie, for several years now we have been doing all our spearfishing in the inner parts of the harbour, and while the fishing has been good, we are in need of some new grounds. And in any case, other divers are watching where we go and are inclined to follow". "I have been thinking the same thing," said Bernie, "the weather has been better than usual, so conditions for bigger catches should be ideal". I proposed that we say nothing to anyone, but when we get the starter gun tomorrow, instead of getting in at the nearest entry within the inner harbour, as all competitors would normally do, we should run all the way to the sea near the Lighthouse. I said "this will cost us a lot in time and energy but it should be well worth it in terms of catch". Bernie saw the value of this idea immediately, while John Hailes and Padraig McSweeney agreed, perhaps more reluctantly.

It was not a very long route in mileage terms, about a mile, but it meant running up hill first and then down hill into Glanleam, followed by a long fin swim to the open sea. Each of us was dressed in a wetsuit, wearing a diving watch and approximately four kilos of lead on a weight belt, and carrying snorkel, fins, mask, two spear guns, spare spear shafts, and spare spear points. We wore diving boots but did not use gloves, and we all wore a special fish belt to retain our catches while in the water. We also had to carry the numbered loop for our catch, which was to be handed in at the end of the competition.

We were taking quite a risk, because we had never fished on the outside of the island before, and it was quite possible that there would not be many fish in those areas that were accessible to us. As well, there was the problem of losing so much time in getting to and from the chosen site, time in which we could have been fishing in the inner harbour as in other years. If one or other of us did not leave enough time to get back to the pier at Knightstown, we risked a large penalty or even disqualification. So it was an indicator of our fitness and confidence, as well as our appreciation of the fishing grounds around Valentia Island itself that we were prepared to make such a bold move.

We were not to know it at the time but the Mullingar club, members of which had never participated in a spearfishing competition up to this, had decided to enter a team for the very first time in the Irish Open at Valentia. It was not to be an auspicious debut for them however, because in deciding tactics for the competition, they had selected the Curragh team, with its proven track record in this competition, as the ones to imitate. They figured that if they watched us closely, and did what we were doing, it would save them much time and effort. If they went where we went, they felt that they could hardly go wrong. I regret very much that I was not in a position to have seen the faces of Des Coleman and his team as they saw their "mentors" disappearing up the hill at Knightstown, away from the water. I could imagine their feelings of dismay, if not panic. They had come to Valentia expecting to get straight into the water to chase fish, but were completely unprepared for a cross-country race as well!

The return route to the check-in became a 'marathon'. We had very little time to the finishing gun, and we ran as hard as we could, across and up through Glanleam, over the top of the hill and down into Knightstown. It was a warm day and as I ran, I started discarding some of my burden, the speargun here, the weight belt there, throwing them into the undergrowth of the hedges, to be retrieved later on. Eventually, I was carrying only my fish catch as I reached the check-in, where I saw that Bernie had gone even further, even taking off the top of his diving suit. Fortunately the rules at the time did not cover this type of behaviour, so we survived. The gamble paid off handsomely for us and by the end of the second day, we had won the team event once more, even though Colin House of Weymouth Association won the Individual prize.

$$* \quad * \quad * \quad * \quad * \quad * \quad * \quad *$$

The Belfast Branch of the British Sub Aqua Club ran an annual competition in Northern Ireland that was very popular with all divers. It was also notorious however for the small numbers of fish that were taken by divers during the competitions. It was called the Noslen Kered competition after Derek Nelson (spelt backwards), one of the prominent members of the club, who had donated the trophy before emigrating to Sydney. Now, I had always preached to spearfishing novices that a diver must be on the alert from the moment he entered the water to the very moment he left the water, he should never waste a moment, never relax or give up hunting. I had an early experience of this myself at Kilkee when I had decided that I had enough and was heading for the shore. Just as I was about to stand up, in quite shallow water, I saw and shot a fine mullet, which made a big difference to my score.

Employing that principal at Ardglass, Co. Down on 11th of September, 1966, I won the annual Noslen Kered competition. I had spent almost four hours in the water without even seeing a fish, but I persisted. Just when I had decided that it was time to get out, I saw a smallish wrasse and bagged him. He weighed in at just over one kilo. I had barely enough time to get back to the check-in, to discover that I was the last diver out of the water. All the other divers had given up earlier, discouraged by the complete lack of fish. I could not believe my luck when I was told that I had caught the only fish of the day! I had swept the boards, ending up with the Trophy for the largest catch, the prize for the heaviest fish, the most unusual fish, and even the team prize! This was a perfect example of why one should never give up. Tom Shakespeare from the Irish Sub Aqua Club had won the same competition in a similar manner with just one fish in 1961.

* * * * * * * *

There are countless tales of spearfishing escapades and each diver has his own to tell. Ronnie Hurley from the Limerick Sub Aqua Club was competing in a competition when he encountered a most unusual emergency. He had shot a fairly large dogfish, put it on his fish belt in the normal way and continued on his hunt. Now dogfish, when attacked, will often coil up into a tight ball and stop struggling, but after some time the fish will revive again, as did Ronnie's. The angry dogfish did what all dogfish had to do, he bit the nearest object to him, Ronnie's bottom! Despite all his efforts, Ronnie could not shake off the grip of the fish (he could not see it properly as it was behind him) so he had no option but to make his way ashore to seek help. Ronnie was not hurt because he had two layers of neoprene protecting him, but he had to put up with a lot of ribbing from his friends for a long time afterwards.

One I like to tell happened to me when the Irish Sub Aqua Club held their annual club competition at Wicklow Harbour in 1970. Up to this time I had never shot a conger eel, partly because they had a fearsome reputation (undeserved) and partly because they were rarely seen in open water during the daylight hours. However, after about two hours in the water, I was getting desperate, I had only three small fish, and one of those was likely to be rejected at the weigh in.

On one particular dive I found a small underwater reef, which had a vertical face. It was eight metres down and about three hundred metres from the shore. To my surprise, when I looked more closely, I saw no less than three conger eels living in the holes in the rock-face. One of them was fairly big and he looked out aggressively at me. I went back up to the surface to think about what I was going to do. Was it wise, was it safe, could I get this guy back to shore? Congers had a bad reputation for being powerful and aggressive and I had never shot one before. Did I really need to go for one of these? Would I be better increasing my efforts to find the more usual fish before it was too late?

Eventually, the shortage of time and my willingness to 'have a go' decided for me. So I went down and went almost nose to nose with the conger and planned what I had to do. He glowered back at me, sending out vibes - "leave me alone"! I had heard from others that when one shot a conger, it was necessary to hit it behind the head, and that the spear must penetrate the fish's body and protrude out the other side. The diver then had to grasp the spear on both sides of the conger's head, effectively retaining control of his struggles and hoping to avoid being bitten. So I took a deep breath, dived down, went right up to the fish and put the point of the spear close to his head and fired. The conger, on being struck, retreated back into the rocks as far as he could, the spear having penetrated his body just behind his head as planned.

I had no time to lose. I found that tugging on the line had no effect, I could not pull him out as he had jammed himself into the rock. So I put one foot, and fin, each side of the hole, took hold of the spear with both hands and yanked with all my strength. It worked, and then I realised that I had a problem, as an astronaut might say. I tumbled backwards away from the reef, and suddenly the sea seemed to be full of conger eels. Fortunately, I had my hands on the spear or he would have broken away from me and might even have managed to bite me. He twisted and writhed and at one stage his body was wrapped around one of my legs. He knocked my snorkel violently against my mouth and as I discovered afterwards, he broke a front tooth and loosened another.

The snorkel I was using was made of metal and it had a rubber mouthpiece. When the conger's body struck my face, the metal was driven through the mouthpiece and did the damage. I had dropped my gun in order to hang on with both hands to the spear and the line had become entangled around one of my legs while the barrel of the gun was catching in the seaweed on the bottom. The body of a conger is all muscle, and just then, it seemed to me to have been made of steel. With great difficulty, I was able to get my legs clear of the line and managed to get to the surface for a badly needed breath. In order to keep the conger under control, I was compelled to hold its head uncomfortably close to my face. I could even see down his throat! Having reached the surface, I headed for the shore, gasping for breath and eventually got there in a tangle of line, fish and gun.

As I was lifting the conger out of the water, I changed my grip and he nearly succeeded in clamping his jaws over my left wrist. He did manage to tear my diving glove and to break the strap of my watch, which fortunately fell into my glove rather than down into the water, where it might have been hard to find. After a break, and with the confidence of that success behind me, I went back for one of the other smaller congers, and landed him also. The first conger weighed in at 23 pounds and when I held him up he was nearly as long as myself. However, it was at some cost. I had to go to the dentist to get a crown, eventually another, and I am now sporting a denture, all as a result of my determination to win a competition!

The rewards of spearfishing were few, but for me at least, the thrills and challenges over the years in which I was actively involved were a source of great personal satisfaction, while the de-briefings in the pub afterwards in the company of like-minded enthusiasts were magical! In particular, I was fortunate to have participated in a number of World, European and other competitions during that period mainly as Team Captain, something of which I am very proud.

You may notice that I have written this chapter in the past tense. I do so because this branch of diving has all but disappeared in Ireland. Certainly competitions, at either club or national level, are no longer held, and perhaps that is a good thing too, in view of the need to protect the undersea environment.

# CHAPTER 9

# INTERNATIONAL SPEARFISHING COMPETITIONS

In the spring of 1967, I opened a letter from CMAS in Paris announcing that Cuba was hosting the 9th World Spearfishing Championships in September and that Ireland was invited to send a team. This letter was very different to anything that we had received up to now from CMAS. I was the Secretary of CFT at that time, and messages about international events such as underwater photography or fin-swimming, came to us from time to time without arousing any great reaction. CFT was a very new organisation, it was only four years old, and it was still trying to find its feet. There were four officers: President, Secretary, Treasurer and Press Officer. We had very limited funds, and at that time the State did not provide any assistance.

If CFT had decided to start sending spearfishing teams abroad to compete in competitions in other countries, it would have been as part of a planned and deliberate programme of selection, preparation, and training. This would have been followed by a careful introduction into less important events, so that the teams could gain experience in a controlled way. What happened in 1967 went against all common sense. An Irish spearfishing team had never competed outside Ireland before this, the opportunity had never arisen, and now suddenly we were presented, at short notice, with the need to send a team to the World Championships. We were starting at the wrong end!

The letter from CMAS was most unusual because it stated that the Cuban Government would pay all the costs for an Irish team of three, plus a Team Captain, for three weeks. We would be flown to Havana from Prague, and returned via Prague on a date to be notified later. The unexpected invitation from the Cuban federation hit the diving community in Ireland like a tidal wave. Our community was small, and the number of spearfishermen was even smaller, although they were a very closely-knit group, who competed regularly against each other at competitions around the island. The discussions began at club and CFT level and it became clear that this offer could become the first serious test for the new organisation. Should we respond to this request and if so, how? Even as far back as 1967, there was a strong anti-spearfishing faction within CFT, but to be fair to the individuals concerned, even they were in favour of acceding to this most unexpected and generous invitation.

The problem was, in the absence of any experience in this matter, how were we to go about selecting a team? After much debate and consultation with other sporting organisations, we decided first to tell CMAS that we would participate, and then worry about where to begin afterwards. Eventually, it was decided to hold special competitions on the four Sundays in May, to be organised by the Galway University Sub Aqua Club. As a matter of Club policy, the members of GUSAC did not approve of spearfishing, and as a result did not have any individual member who might have hoped to travel to Cuba. So they agreed to become the organisers for the four days. They would select the locations and provide the officials, guides, safety, medical support, and so on, for each day.

The locations they chose were top secret, as it could be of great advantage to any individual to know of the competition zone in advance. Only when all the competitors had assembled for the briefings at Eyre Square in the centre of Galway early on each of the four   Sunday mornings, did they tell us where we were going. In case we did not know how to get there the club provided divers on motor-cycles to guide us to the sites. The interest in these trial competitions was immense, as could be expected because of the quite exceptional prize for the winners. At the end of May, the combined results were announced. Four divers were nominated to travel to Cuba: myself and Bernie Brennan, from the Curragh Sub Aqua Club, and Fintan Mullowney and Joe Roddy from the Limerick Sub Aqua Club. I was nominated as Team Captain.

Then followed three intensely busy months for me. Not alone was I the Secretary of CFT, with all the duties of that post, but I was also preoccupied with moving my wife, Anne, and son John, from Kilcullen to a new house in Dublin. I had to find sponsors for the team uniforms and decide on blazer and crest design. Souvenirs of Ireland, swimwear, what diving and spearfishing equipment and spares to carry, how to organise the publicity, were all discussed at length. I asked for and received medical advice and a medical kit for the team from the Army Medical Corps. Fintan and I were called to Defence Forces Headquarters (DFHQ) to be briefed on the hazards of going to a communist state. We were reminded that we represented the Defence Forces and that we had to be vigilant against the dangers of being compromised or subverted in any way. Even though we were representing our country, we were still required to take 22 days annual leave, as at that time, the Department of Defence would not allow us to take special leave. We had anticipated this however and had wisely saved our annual leave against such an eventuality.

Because CFT had not been in a position to send teams abroad before this, a whole range of decisions had to be made very rapidly. While CFT had an official flag, logo and tie, it did not have a blazer or a pocket crest, or indeed a 'uniform' to be worn by our representatives

At Golum Head, Connemara May 1967. Team trials for the World Championships in Cuba.
From the right: Joe Roddy, Pat McSweeney, the author, Fintan Mullowney, Donal Douglas, Shane Gray, Cyril Foster, John Hailes. At rear; Dr Jim Doyle, Peter O'Beirne and Peadar Canavan.    Photo, J.Hailes

when abroad. We decided to copy more or less what all other Irish teams had worn before us, namely, grey slacks, white shirts and dark green blazers. The crest on the blazer pocket was the crest of the four provinces, with 'Irish Spearfishing Team' in silver thread beneath. With the intervention of Ronnie Hurley, a good friend and a member of the Limerick Sub Aqua Club, the Limerick Clothing Company provided us with grey slacks and blazers. Dick Pender, of Manor Street in Dublin made us the crests to be worn on the pockets of the blazers, and a sports shop in Stillorgan, Co. Dublin, provided us with beach wear. We had to buy or borrow additional spear guns, spare parts, and other items of new or additional diving equipment as required. Ronnie Hurley was a great help to us here also, as he owned an agency that supplied much of the equipment that we needed and he gave us very special terms. We decided to take a risk and not bring our diving suits, as we expected the water to be warmer than anything that we had experienced up to this time in spearfishing.

CMAS had told us that we must go to Prague to be picked up with all the other Northern, Eastern and Central European teams. The southern European teams were to travel from Madrid. However, I discovered that Cuban Airlines aircraft were required to stop at Shannon airport to refuel on all its westward flights. It seemed to me that it was wasteful to have to travel to Prague first in order to return through Ireland a few hours later, so I was able to get them to agree that the Irish team could be picked up at Shannon. It was a hectic time but eventually we found ourselves at Shannon, watching the Cubana aircraft taxiing in. To our surprise, the British team turned up at Shannon as well, having made the same arrangements as ourselves, and it was fortunate that we knew some of them already from the Valentia competition days. The aircraft was full of teams from central and Eastern Europe, none of whom we had met before.

We flew to Havana via Gander in a Britannia turboprop, arriving to a great welcome at the airport. We were waved through Customs, given drinks, introduced to our guide-cum-translator, Orestes Bla, and then to our driver. At an early stage we christened our driver 'Fangio' and he was delighted to be compared with the World Racing champion. Both Cubans were to be with us for the entire period in Cuba. We were driven to our hotel in Havana in a large American 'gas-guzzler' which, although elderly, was in great condition, probably because it received tender loving care from 'Fangio' whenever the circumstances allowed. Later on that evening, all the teams were brought to the best nightclub in Havana, the 'Cabaret Tropicana', for a wonderful night's entertainment.

The following morning we drove to Varadero, a tourist city to the East of Havana where we were ensconced in a modern hotel just off the main beach. We spent the next two weeks at the hotel, where each of the 28 teams had a chalet to itself in the grounds. We dined at the hotel, and attended the cabaret each night. The teams were provided with small fishing boats driven by inboard petrol engines to use as we wished in the beautiful waters off the beach. Every day we spent up to six hours in the water, trying to come to terms with differences between spearfishing there and at home. The water was so clear and warm that our performances began to improve rapidly. While we were out training, a 'canteen' boat would come around every so often to shower us with chilled watermelon, fruit drinks and fresh water. Further out near the horizon, a naval patrol vessel moved up and down. There had been threats by the Cuban exiles in Miami to disrupt the Championships in some way, in an attempt to embarrass Castro and his Government. Fortunately, the threats were never translated into action.

Many notable incidents occurred in Varadero during our time in the sea, but one in particular remains very vividly in my mind. We were all fairly near each other, happily fishing away in an attractive area, enjoying the clear and warm water, when I heard Joe Roddy calling to Fintan. "Fintan, I've shot a fish but I can't get him out of a hole in the rocks, and I had to leave my gun below. Can I have a loan of your gun"? I moved over to

The Irish Spearfishing team at Varadero, Cuba, Aug 1967. From left; Bernie Brennan, the author, Fintan Mullowney and Joe Roddy.   Photo; Cuban Organisers.

watch. Fintan gave him his gun and Joe dived down. After what seemed like an age he reappeared with two guns and one medium-sized grouper. He had dived to 80 feet, approximately 24 metres, shot the fish again, and brought the fish and guns back to the surface. This was without a doubt the best dive yet by any of us on the team. Joe was a wonderful diver with natural talents; he had not put in the same amount of preparation as had any of us back in Ireland prior to departure, and yet he was able to outperform us with ease. Not surprisingly though, over the two weeks of practice, we had all upped our performances considerably.

On another occasion, we were preparing to finish up for the day, when both Fintan and I saw a shark on the bottom. Because my gun was loaded and his was not, I won the race to shoot the shark and bring him to the boat. Fintan was miffed but delighted for me at the same time. Mind you it was a fairly small nurse shark, which is about as inoffensive as one can get. I remained secretly chuffed about it and ribbed the others that the team captain could get a shark and the others could not! It weighed about eighteen kilos. It was the only shark that any of us shot during the entire three weeks, even though Bernie and I teamed up to have a 'go' at another that he had spotted. As we got nearer, it became obvious that it was a lot bigger than we had realised. So we gave it a miss, strictly in the interest of conserving our guns and scarce spare parts. At least that was the excuse we gave to the others!

Each evening when we came back to the beach, we would line up our catches on the sand for photographs, after which we would invite the onlookers to take what they wanted. The fish were always taken away in seconds. The spearing of sharks, barracudas and all types of flat fish were banned during the competition, and the minimum weight of fish for weigh-in purposes was set at 2 kilos. The Cubans had warned us, not about sharks, but about barracudas; we were advised to treat them with great caution. There had been five incidents of attacks on swimmers by barracudas during 1967, and certainly every time we went into the water, we found that at least one barracuda was tagging along behind. It was a little bit unsettling, but we eventually forgot about them.

On Saturday 02 September 1967, we left Varadero for the official opening ceremony that was held in the Baseball Stadium in Havana the following morning. It remains in my memory as a very special moment when I led our little team out into the stadium to the sound of our national anthem. The next morning we were taken to the airport and flown down to the Isles of Pines. The plane used was a twin-engined Soviet model, and on our flight, the pilot had to make two attempts to put down on the unsurfaced runway at a tiny island. We had to walk for some distance from the airstrip, carrying all our gear and sweating profusely in the evening humidity. Eventually we rounded a corner and a wonderful and colourful sight met our eyes.

We were looking at a small fishing harbour full of trawlers. All twenty-eight fishing boats were of the same design and appeared to be very new. They were decorated with bunting and the national flags of the participating teams. We were able to locate our trawler easily by spotting the tricolour and we gratefully climbed aboard. Each team had been allocated a fishing boat, which was to be its home for the next five days. In addition to the normal crew of four, one the cook, on board also were a Cuban Army doctor and three Cuban military divers, complete with Soviet-made aqualungs. They remained with us for the next few days. It was a wonderful moment of excitement and a spectacular sight as the twenty- eight gaily decorated trawlers set out in convoy for the competition zone. We slept on deck under the stars while the fleet travelled all night to the fishing zone at an uninhabited island, Cayo Avolos.

The Opening Ceremony at the Baseball Stadium, Havana, Aug 1967.  Photo; Cuban Organisers.

The island had been prepared for our arrival and a complete tented village had been constructed on shore for any teams that might wish to be based onshore. We preferred to live aboard, an experience that we all enjoyed. Our meals were prepared for us each day and we had a swim in the clear warm waters every morning before breakfast. The next day was devoted to a reconnaissance of the fishing zone. The zone was huge, measuring about 10 by four kilometres, one half of which was to be used on each of the two days of the competition. However, we just weren't given enough time to do a proper inspection of either zone. This proved to have been a major drawback for teams like ours, lacking in the experience of previous competitions under such conditions. The competition itself took place over the following two days, six hours each day.

As with all the other teams, we were allocated four small boats. One was a motorboat similar to those that we had used at Varadero, intended for use by the team captains. The other three were rowing boats, one for each competitor, manned by a Cuban army diver from our trawler. In the rowing boat, the diver carried his spare guns, spears and also his fish as they were caught. The organisers considered it to be too dangerous to permit the divers to carry the catches on their belts as was the custom at home in Ireland.

The Cuban organisers had emphasised before the competition that all countries affiliated to CMAS had been invited, and we were given to understand that the US team was expected. But they failed to show up at the last moment and surprisingly, so did the Soviet team. The Cubans won handsomely, with a magnificent catch, mostly of big grouper. This was not an unusual result, as out of the seven world championships held up to then, the home team won on no less than four occasions. The prize for the biggest individual fish was won by a Swiss. He had spent all six hours of the second day in trying to bring up a magnificent black bass, which weighed almost 160 kilos. We remembered the warning we had received previously about barracudas, when, during the second day of the competition, Fintan shot a fine blue parrot fish. The large barracuda that had been tailing him all day flashed in over his shoulder and bit the fish in two. When Fintan was handing in his catch at the end of the day, much was made by the Cubans of the half-eaten fish.

We were very definitely out of our league amongst the big boys of spearfishing, but out of 28 teams we managed to be 18th after the first day, slipping to 20th on the final day. We felt very satisfied with our placing at our very first international appearance. Jean Tapu, from Tahiti, won the individual event for France while Cuba won the team prize. It was a tremendous learning experience, and it made us more determined than ever to try harder for the next event.

As well as my duties as Team Captain, I was also occupied with taking movie film of our diving activities. I had brought along my Eumig Automatic standard 8mm camera, complete with its aluminium underwater housing. In such conditions as we were experiencing, it was a joy to be able to record some at least of our activities. But after I had the films processed at home, I discovered to my horror that a few   rolls had 'melted' in the heat and were useless. This had probably happened on the trawler coming back to the mainland after the Championships. For whatever reason, on our return to the mainland, the Yugoslav team and one other were put aboard our trawler, so we had a very cramped and extremely hot 30hr journey back to the Cuban mainland at Batabano. Fortunately more than enough of the film survived to convey the flavour of our experiences in Cuba.

In view of the warnings from DFHQ before we left Ireland, I remember being vaguely disappointed each night when I found out that 'Olga from the Volga' was not waiting for me in my bedroom. No attempt was made to compromise any of us! The Cubans were preoccupied with more important matters, as Che Guevara was killed just two days before we left Havana for Ireland. As a result, Fidel Castro, himself a keen spearfisherman, who had been billed to present the prizes, did not show up.

\*     \*     \*     \*     \*     \*     \*     \*

Once the international boundary had been crossed, the invitations to spearfishing competitions started to turn up frequently, and CFT readily responded to each opportunity, having had a taste for the heady challenges that they provided. The next one to 'surface' was the 8th World Championships at Sicily in August 1969 - they normally, occurred at two-year intervals. On this occasion we were better prepared and felt more confident. The competition was based on Vulcano Island, the most southerly of the Aeolian Islands, which lie to the north of Sicily. We were sponsored by USI Travel in Dublin. They provided our return airfares to Milan, and also our return train fares from Milan to Messina. The team consisted of myself, as Team Captain, Bernie Brennan and Shane Gray of the Curragh Sub Aqua Club and Fintan Mullowney of the Limerick club. Ronnie Hurley, from Limerick, who was President of CFT at that time, came along as our official representative at meetings and receptions.

The waters around the Aeolian Islands were surprisingly cold, especially after Cuba, where the water had averaged about 75 degrees Fahrenheit. By good fortune we had brought the tops of our suits with us and they were of great benefit. Conor Doyle and his wife June had come along to have a holiday and together with Ronnie, they formed our 'supporters club'. Conor had hired a small inflatable that he put at our disposal for some of the practice days. This was fortunate as all teams were required to provide for their own needs and we discovered that boats for hire proved to be quite expensive. While we did all our practising around Vulcano Island, the competition zones were at Filicudi Island on the first day and at Salina Island on the second day. 30 countries sent teams, and while Ireland ended in 21st position, we did not feel too bad about this as the British and the South African teams were at 19th and 20th positions respectively. Italy won the team prize and Massimo Scarpatti won the individual prize. The fish were quite scarce and again, the unfortunate grouper formed the bulk of the catch, especially for the divers from the Mediterranean countries. Although I was fully occupied throughout the fortnight as the team captain, I managed to find time for filming also, both under and over the water, in an attempt to record the event.

*　　*　　*　　*　　*　　*　　*　　*

Over the next few years, Irish divers took part in a number of other competitions. Tom Stopford and myself competed at the Jersey Open Championships on 28th of May 1970, without having any luck. The competition was won by Ted Grimshawe, from Jersey. Ted, along with his three team mates, had once spent a cramped overnight in my house in Dublin, on their way to Valentia Island to compete in the Irish Open. Tom Stopford, Billy Nott and myself competed at the North European Championships at Plymouth in September 1970 but we were only in the also-rans. Eight nations competed. During that competition, about my only claim to fame was that I was interviewed for local radio. A boat pulled up beside me as I was fishing and I was asked

The French and Irish Teams with the Mayor of Plymouth after the Opening Ceremony to the North European Championships, September 1970.   Photo: Western Morning News, Plymouth.

would I mind being interviewed. As I was having very little success with shooting fish, I said yes, and to my astonishment the interviewer jumped into the water beside me to do the interview. On the following two days we competed in the British Open Championships at Looe and at Pembrey, again without making much impact either on the scoreboard or on the fish population! It was all great fun though.

In 1971, an Irish team consisting of Shane Gray, Billy Nott and Tom Stopford, all from the Curragh club, and Manuel di Lucia, from the Limerick club, travelled to Iquique, Chile, to take part in the 9th World Spearfishing Championships. Ted Spendlove accompanied them as Team Manager and CFT representative. Twenty five national teams competed and the Irish team ended up in 15th place, after competing in very difficult conditions in quite cold water. Raul Choque of Chile was the individual winner and Chile also won the Team event. But while the Irish team did not make waves

The Irish team at the World Spearfishing Championships, Iquiqe, Chile, 1971.
From the left: Shane Gray, Ted Spendlove, Team Manager, Manuel di Lucia, the CMAS Secretary,
Billy Nott, Tom Stopford.

in the water, they were easily the winners at public relations. The Irish team generally, but Manuel di Lucia in particular, had become known to everyone, not just to the competitors and officials but also to the local inhabitants. He became the recipient of a fine special award for the 'Personality of the Competition', the first time that such an award was made at any spearfishing competition.

In 1972, the North European Spearfishing Championships were held at the Isle of Man from the 12th to the 18th of September. The Irish team consisted of team captain, Fintan Mullowney, Manuel di Lucia, both from the Limerick club; Bernie Brennan, Vernon O'Byrne, and Roger Fitzgerald, from the Curragh club; and Jim Fox from the Belfast Branch, BSAC. The Irish team ended in 11th place out of fourteen teams, but Fintan Mullowney was at a very creditable 15th in the individual placings. In 1973, the North European Spearfishing Championships were held at Malta. The Irish team, consisting of Billy Nott, Curragh; Fintan Mullowney, Limerick; and Jim Fox, Belfast BSAC, came 4th out of the six teams that competed. Billy Nott was placed 6th out of 18 individual competitors.

In hindsight, it is likely that the interest in spearfishing amongst Irish divers reached its high point in 1974. I had been one of those who proposed that CFT should hold a major spearfishing competition in Ireland. The idea was accepted with enthusiasm, not realising just how much work was ahead of us. Having suggested the idea, I was promptly sent off for duty with the United Nations in Israel for the next 18 months, so I missed out on the fun and the hard work. No international diving event of any sort had ever been held in Ireland, so it was felt that the time was right to show ourselves to the general European diving community. Because of the strength of spearfishing at the time, it was the logical competition to host.

It was decided that Kilkee offered all the facilities that would be required and the year was to be 1974. An application was sent to CMAS for permission to organise the 6th European Spearfishing Championships. Ted Spendlove, Secretary of CFT, and myself were sent to Cadaques, Spain by Bord Failte in 1973 to be observers at the 10th World Spearfishing Championships. Ireland was not in a position to enter a team in this event. We were to report back on the manner in which it was organised and the lessons to be learned. After a bit of 'too-ing and fro-ing', and after an inspection of facilities by Raimundo Sague, a member of the Sports Commission of CMAS, CFT was given permission to host the Championships.

Kilkee had been selected as the location because the fishing was very good, and the fishing zones were very accessible and close to shore. We asked for and received the enthusiastic support of Bord Failte and the Shannon Free Airport Development Company (SFADCO). The teams were flown in and out of Shannon, and we had the support of hotels and car hire firms in the area. Seventeen teams took part in the competition, and are shown as follows, in the order of their final placing at the end of the second day:-

Great Britain, (Team Winners), Italy, France, Jersey, Portugal, Bulgaria, Belgium, *Ireland,* Spain, Monaco, Yugoslavia, Guernsey, Finland, and the Faroe Islands. Massimo Scarpati of Italy was the individual champion, with Jose Amengual of Spain and David Heaphy of Great Britain second and third respectively. Best Irish competitor was Ray Dunne, of the Irish Sub Aqua Club, who finished in 10th place out of 52 competitors, an excellent result.

Before the competition there had been many protests at the decision of Competition Director, Shane O'Connor, and his officials to allow the taking only of free-swimming fish with a minimum weight of 1kg. Shane also ruled out the taking of wrasse, probably one of the most common fish in the sea. Wrasse were ruled out because of the fact that they were sedentary fish, easily shot, and also because of the huge numbers of wrasse that had been taken during the North European Championships at the Isle of Man in 1972. The decision on the species of fish and the minimum weight of fish to be permitted for the competition is always a contentious issue between the team captains and organisers before a competition. The teams made their plans on the assumption that certain fish would be permitted, and they resented any deviation from their expectations.

To the surprise and delight of Shane and his officials, the two CMAS officials present, Prof. Luigi Ferraro, President of the Sports Commission, and Monsieur Perraud, Secretary of CMAS, both supported him fully. As an aside, Luigi Ferraro, from Tripoli, had been a 'frogman' during WW2 for which he had received a gold medal for bravery from the Italian Government. After the war, he worked for the Italian diving equipment company, Technisub, ending up as Chairman. He remained as President of the Sports Commission of CMAS for many years, and was to be seen at nearly all the international competitions.

In the end, despite the restrictions about which they had protested, the competitors were very pleased with the numbers and size of fish that they found in the waters at Kilkee, and the catches reflected that. A total of 1,950.4 kg of fish were weighed in, representing 1,210 fish. The competition was judged to have been one of the best ever, and many of the visiting divers were astounded that it was run in its entirety by volunteer workers, most of whom had taken annual leave for the week. Looking back over a span of 26 years, it is perhaps ironic that the decline of organised spearfishing in Ireland should have commenced when the standards and the interest in spearfishing had never been higher.

# CHAPTER 10

# SEALIONS

By 1972 spearfishing in Ireland had become so popular and so developed that divers felt that there was a need to regularise the circumstances under which competitions were being organised. The prize for being a high achiever at spearing fish had become extremely attractive, namely, membership of a team that would travel to an international competition in some exotic part of the world. Up to this, clubs or even individuals within a club could make the decisions as to when, where and how a competition was to be organised. The more active spearfishermen amongst us felt that there was a real and urgent need to formulate standards of training, equipment and to control the manner in which competitions were being run. This would provide for better assessments of individuals while the selection of teams for international competitions would be fairer and more transparent. The proposed organisation was to be in effect another offshoot of CFT, reporting to it and being subject to its rulings and precepts.

On the First of October 1972, a group of actively involved spearfishermen came together at a meeting at the Victoria Hotel in Kilkee, County Clare, to establish a new regulatory body to be called 'Sealions'. Amongst those present were:- Fintan Mullowney, John Murphy, Jack Meade, Billy Nott, Vernon O'Byrne, Roger Fitzgerald, Manuel di Lucia and Jim Fox. Billy Nott was elected as Secretary/Treasurer, in addition to being the Liaison Officer reporting to the Executive of CFT. Fintan Mullowney was elected to the post of National Coach and Vernon O'Byrne was elected as a member of the committee. The National Competitions Officer of CFT was to become the Chairman of 'Sealions', who would in turn report to the Executive of CFT.

The aims of Sealions were to raise the standard of spearfishing in Ireland, to encourage young divers to take up the sport, to prepare for international competition by organising both winter and summer training camps, and to administer the sport of spearfishng on behalf of CFT. Membership was open to all divers from CFT clubs. They competed for their own clubs in the normal way, but would also be considered as eligible for a place on the national team for future international competitions. Sealions was a very good idea and had great potential, but fairly quickly it ran into difficulties. The weakness in the new organisation quickly became evident. Because the majority of Irish divers were by then not particularly interested in spearfishing or were simply not competitively minded, it fell to the spearfishermen themselves to organise and run their own competitions around the country. This created many difficulties, particularly as the original enthusiasts were not being replaced by up-and-coming young spearfishermen. Inevitably personality clashes also detracted from the best intentions of the founders.

About the only notable training event held by Sealions was a weekend session at the Two-mile Inn in Limerick organised by Fintan Mullowney. Fintan, who was always a superbly fit man, believed that all others could be like him, and he intended to prove it. All the active hopefuls in spearfishing turned up, if for no other reason than to improve their chances of being selected for the next international competition. The weekend turned out to be a harrowing series of very   demanding pool exercises, three times a day, starting before breakfast, with lectures for relaxation in between! The exercises became progressively more difficult. The divers on the first session had to fin for forty lengths of the pool without resting, alternatively one length over and one length under the water. This was easy enough but by the following morning, the requirement had risen to finning 40 lengths, without pause, in alternate sets of three lengths over and three lengths under the water. This final exercise was to prove virtually impossible for anyone but Fintan himself.

It was an exhausted group of divers who crawled away from Limerick, muttering about medals for endurance, or T-shirts proclaiming 'I Survived Two-Mile Inn'. The training weekend was not repeated. Sealions had arrived on the scene about ten years too late to be effective, as spearfishing was already losing its appeal for many divers, both at home and abroad. Sealions disappeared quietly by 1975, with the National Competitions Officer, a member of the Executive of CFT, taking on all responsibility for future events.

For me, spearfishing was far and away more exciting, challenging and rewarding than any other aspect of diving. I look back on those times with great affection for the many friends I made and for the places to which spearfishing has taken me. In those early years, I probably spent many more hours chasing fish than in aqualung diving, but like all things in this world, it had to end. Spearfishing is very much a sport for the young person from about 15 onwards and like all sports, it required training and practice. Divers had to retain their skills and this meant spending hours in the sea killing fish when your friends were having fun on a diving boat or in the pub! Like everything in life, attitudes and interests change.

I remember clearly the incident after which I started to turn away from spearing fish. I had been practising in the sea for some hours near the Hook Lighthouse in Wexford, and maybe I was tired, or cold, but I was certainly bored. The sea was lumpy and grey and I felt that I would have been better employed ashore. I had seen and shot a reasonably sized pollack and was starting to put him on my fish belt when I accidentally knocked out one of his eyes. The eye floated up towards me, glaring accusingly. I was suddenly horrified at what I had done. It struck me very forcibly that I was inflicting great pain and death on this poor unfortunate fish, against which I had no grudge or gripe whatsoever.

I felt a wave of revulsion pass over me, because I was killing this fish, not in order to win a competition, although that in itself should not be sufficient justification. No, I was killing this fish just to keep my hand in, just so that I could be better able to kill yet more fish at another time. I needed to retain my ability to win, to retain my reputation. I was on an ego trip, it was for my own pride that I was doing this. I had no right to do this to another creature and I felt very badly about it for quite a while. Although I did not give up there and then, I gradually started to ease out of spearfishing for good. In all walks of life, a greater awareness of the environment and the need for conservation has gradually gained acceptance, and diving has reflected this welcome trend. Organised spearfishing is no longer practised in Ireland, although it continues at international level.

# CHAPTER 11

# OTHER DIVING COMPETITIONS

Club Chairman Shane O'Connor presenting the Moriarty Trophy to his wife Betty for winning the 100m Fin Swimming Championship of Ireland at the Curragh pool, Nov 1960. Also in the photo from left: Margot Sydney-Smith and Cora Brennan. Photo: E. O'Connor.

As I have already explained, spearfishing was easily the biggest and most popular of the competitive offshoots of diving, but as diving became established in Ireland, some individuals who disagreed with spearfishing expressed a desire to demonstrate their abilities and to compare their performances against others in a different manner. As a result, a number of other sports appeared, of which fin-swimming was easily the most successful. Fin-swimming was similar to conventional or 'steam' swimming except that the swimmers wore fins, mask and snorkel. The competitions are organised in the manner of swimming galas, incorporating varying distances and categories, as well as squad races and novelty events.

The Curragh Sub Aqua Club organised the very first Inter-Club Gala to be held in Ireland at the Curragh Pool in 1959. As well as fin-swimming races at 100, 200 and 1,500 metres, for both men and women, there were novelty events also. One was a tug-o-war event with teams of four divers, which was very popular with the spectators, but proved to be extremely demanding on the participants. Another event, adapted from army swimming galas, was where competitors, wearing mask, fins and snorkel, were invited, in one dive, to pick up as many as possible of about thirty numbered flat metal discs which had been scattered about on the bottom of the pool. It was a breath-holding exercise that tested the endurance of the individual. The discs were large, about four inches across and although easily seen, they were difficult to pick up. One diver from Connemara lost consciousness while underwater - he had obviously exceeded his ability to hold his breath. He was picked up immediately by the stand-by rescue divers and taken to hospital as a precaution but he suffered no after effects. It was a sharp lesson for us in the dangers of 'underwater blackout', and this event was not repeated.

The sub aqua galas, as they were titled, have become very popular. Some clubs, like Aquatec in Dublin, specialise in certain events such as the sprint and squad events with great success. There is a national senior gala, which is held annually at different venues across the country. Among the many trophies awarded for the different events, the premier trophy is called the Harp Lager Trophy. It is awarded to the club that had gained the most points from successes at the gala. This fine trophy was presented to CFT by Harp Lager, Belfast, as a result of the representations of the divers of BSAC,.

Not all fin-swimming is conducted indoors, however. Each year there is an Irish Championship race over 1,500 metres in Lough Owel, Co Westmeath. Competitors are allowed to use the free style stroke, and to adapt their masks and snorkels as they wish. There is a strong international aspect to fin-swimming too. Over the years, groups of Irish divers have competed at fin-swimming events in the British and European Championships, where they have done very well. Certain countries of Eastern Europe, where conditions were not conducive to good diving or to the development of spearfishing, particularly some of the land-locked ones, took to fin-swimming with great enthusiasm. They rapidly became dominant, not having the distraction of open-sea diving to divert their energies. A new invention called the monofin appeared on the scene in the 1980s. It is a large single fin that looks like the fluke of a whale. The diver's feet are inserted into double shoe-type fittings and forward propulsion is achieved using the dolphin kick. The result was most impressive and all serious competition swimmers now use the monofin. During the race, the modern competitor spends more time under the water than over, where he can move more rapidly. The arrival of the monofin ensured that the standards rose rapidly everywhere.

CSAC aqualung relay team in action. Brian McGreevey, Peadar Farrell and nearest camera, Dougie Browne.
Photo: P.Farrell

Joe Delaney and Sue Cobban, after their drag race event.

Tony Boyle, ISAC, winner of the BSAC 100m and 200m mens Fin Swimming Championships at Blackpool, Oct 1985.    Photo. Subsea.

The Irish Fin Swimming team training for the World Championships held at Rome in Sep 1990. LtoR, rear: Roisin Maguire, NCO, Karl Toomey, Kish SAC, Eamonn McCormack, Marlin SAC, Dave McCormack, Coach. At front; Brian Wollverson, Kish, Sinead McMullen, Marlin, Rod Hoare, Kerry Dive, Dave Jackson, NDO.

Fin-swimming became so popular and so successful in Ireland that there was a proposal to establish a Fin-Swimming Commission within CFT. The purpose of the new body would be to further all aspects of the sport and to prepare young fin-swimmers to compete at international level. Also in 1994, there was also a move at international level to have fin-swimming accepted as a new Olympic sport. The Executive of CFT felt that it was not acceptable to have a commission solely for fin-swimming, so some leading fin-swimmers proposed that a special club called 'Orca' be established, on a similar basis to the short-lived Sealions. This appeared to be an excellent proposal but here too, fin-swimming suffered from much the same difficulties as had Sealions. The vast majority of divers were simply not interested in competitions, and fin-swimming enthusiasts were not being replaced by prospective new champions. During this relatively brief period, many young divers travelled to competitions in Britain, (1985 and 1989), while others travelled to the World Championships in Berlin in 1986 and to the European Championships in Rome (1990) and Stockholm (1991).

Another popular competition, called Underwater Navigation, or Underwater Orienteering, is based on the ability of a diver to find his way about on the bottom during a dive. Being able to navigate while submerged is an essential safety skill for a diver, and the compass is used in practically every dive. The following story serves to illustrate why a compass is a necessary component of the diver's equipment. On a beautiful, sunny day in 1960, near the Hook Head Lighthouse, two divers of the Curragh club entered the sea and commenced their dive. They submerged and moved straight out from shore, intending to return on the surface, as was the common practice then. 25 minutes later and out of air, they surfaced at the end of the dive, to find that a thick fog had descended. Land could not be seen, nor any other object that would help them to navigate back to shore. This was a most serious matter. If the dive leader, Shane Gray, made the wrong decision, they might head straight out to sea. As it happened, the underwater terrain in the area consisted of long 'fingers' or ridges of rock, with patches of sand in between. The ridges ran out from shore in more or less parallel lines, while the brighter sector of the sky also gave a general indication of South. So, by surface-diving repeatedly, they could get a quick glimpse of the bottom. In this manner, keeping the brighter sky to their right, and by following the direction of the ridges, they returned safely to shore. Both divers purchased compasses at the next opportunity, as did I when told of their experience.

Underwater navigation competitions appear to be simple, but in fact they are quite tricky and require much practice. The course is laid out in the open sea or lake in depths of between 5 and 10 metres. Four 'report-points', buoyed to the surface, are placed on the bottom to provide a dogleg course in which there are three changes of direction. The 'report points' are at varying distances from each other. The course is then plotted; the compass bearings and distances are recorded and given to all the competitors before the competition. By counting the number of kicks of his fins, the diver can estimate how far he has travelled under water. Competitors travel the course individually, and at each report-point they must either take a disc, a peg, or some other device from the line on the marker. They then proceed to the next report point, using the bearing and distance given to them. The competitor who gets the most 'check-ins', and who covers the course in the fastest time, wins the competition. The national UW Orienteering Competition is held annually at Lough Owel near Mullingar.

Another offshoot of fin-swimming is underwater hockey, or Octopush, a sport which is conducted exclusively in a swimming pool. Teams of five endeavour to push a weighted 'puck' over the other team's line. They wear fins, mask and snorkel, carry small wooden bats, and have to hold their breath while under the water. It is a frantic and very demanding event that poses many problems for the referees, as the divers cannot (or at least claim that they cannot) hear his whistle while they are under the water. It is definitely not a spectator sport as all the action occurs on the bottom of the pool, moving from one side to another following the 'puck'. To the uninitiated onlooker, the surface of the water boils and bubbles during a game as if a horde of piranhas had descended on the corpse of a cow. In an early and short-lived league in the Dublin area, the Curragh Sub Aqua Club was thrown out for unfair, and should I say, un-gentlemanly conduct. It was such a lot of fuss over a little blood!  It is a sport practised only by a small number of clubs in Ireland, although it is very popular in other countries. The first Inter-Club Octopush Competition was held in Limerick in 1981. In March 1989, four English clubs competed in a tournament in Dublin, while Irish teams have travelled to England from time to time.

*       *       *       *       *       *       *       *

One of the most typical reactions of the new diver to the wonder of his first dive is to want to record his next experience with an underwater camera. It is an expression of his need to try to explain to his non-diving friends just what he has experienced under the water.

Louis Boutan, an instructor at the Faculty of Science in the University of Paris, took the first underwater photographs in 1893. Using cumbersome watertight boxes, he took revolutionary pictures in shallow water and later on others in depths down to 50m using artificial light. From such primitive beginnings technology has evolved to the point where most divers today possess a waterproof camera with built-in flash. So equipped, they have the capability to take pictures that out-do the best efforts of the professional photographers of fifty years ago. An early underwater camera called 'Calypsophot' appeared in the Sixties, but it was not a success, and was quickly replaced by an excellent series of waterproof Nikonos cameras made by Nikon. These are all-weather cameras and the various models produced can now be found all over the world and are equally effective over and under the water. In more recent years, there are cheap throwaway cameras, waterproof to three or four metres, which will produce quite reasonable pictures.

The argument still rages as to whether it is better to be a trained photographer who takes up diving, or to be an experienced diver who takes up underwater photography. From a safety point of view it is preferable that one should first be a competent diver, while from the point of view of quality photography, it probably should be the reverse.

The greatest problem for the underwater photographer is that the sunlight is filtered out very quickly as depth increases. Red is the first colour to be absorbed, disappearing by about 10 metres (in clear water) while at 30 metres blue and green are the only colours of the spectrum remaining. This applies in the best circumstances, such as when the sun is high in the sky, the water surface is calm and the water is clear. As the diver goes down, the light gets dim and the colours start to fade, until by about 30 metres, everything is a dull grey monotone. However, if he switches on a flashlight, the fish, the seaweeds and the rocks appear just as they would near the surface, the vibrant colours are restored. Therefore, for satisfactory photographs it is essential to have a good light source. As Irish waters are relatively turbid, it is probably more rewarding to specialise in close-up photography, as the less water between the camera and the subject, the less the suspended matter.

Ireland has produced some excellent photographers who have been successful at competitions in various parts of Europe. Divers such as Sean Magee, Nigel Motyer, John Costello, Tony Balfe, Ian Brennan, Billy Rafter, John Wright, and many others. The first Irish Underwater Photographic Competition was held in Killaloe in 1966, organised by the Limerick Sub Aqua Club, while the first Irish Open competition was held in 1969, also in Limerick. A series of international underwater photography competitions were held in Limerick in 1981, 1983 and 1985, organised by Patrick McCoole, himself an excellent photographer. These were very successful and of a high standard and they attracted many overseas entries. Pat McCoole and John Costello competed in the 3rd World Underwater Photographic Competition in Sicily in 1990, while Bart McMullin and Billy Nott competed at an International photographic competition in Cuba in that same year. Because of the great interest in photography amongst divers at that time, a new body called the Underwater Photographic Society of Ireland (UPSI), was formed in 1991 by Pat McCoole and others. A fine exhibition of underwater photographs was organised last March in Limerick in conjunction with the AGM and Annual Conference of CFT.

In more recent times, a novel competition has been introduced which is aimed at getting greater numbers of divers interested in the subject. Each competitor is given a throwaway camera, water proof to about five metres, and three hours in which to expend the film on whatever subject he chooses. There are many categories of photos; best subject, composition, ingenuity, best fish and best beginner. The films are developed on the spot after the dives are over, using a portable developing system that produces slides only. A panel of judges will then assess the photos and nominate the winners.

For anyone who has tried it, taking pictures under water is time-consuming, frustrating and expensive. Movie photography has all the problems of the 'stills' photographer but with the added difficulty of needing 'actors' who have to be briefed in advance as to what to do. I had always preferred movie to stills for over-water photography, so when the opportunity presented itself in 1961, I acquired an underwater housing for my 8mm Eumig Automatic camera. In July of that year, with the help of Ronnie Hurley and Adie Doyle of Limerick Sub Aqua Club and Manuel di Lucia from Kilkee, I made what I believe was the first underwater silent 8mm movie 'film' in Ireland. With the title 'Lobsters Galore', it was shot in the shallows at Myle's Creek in Kilkee. After that I made another in the Mediterranean which I called 'Deep Blue Waters', followed later by some footage in Cuba and at the Aeolian Islands.

Filming under water was always likely to bring on some humorous incidents. In May 1964, I arranged to film a group of divers from the Curragh Sub Aqua Club at Carrigahoy, close to the Hook Lighthouse, Co Wexford. Benny McLoughlin had just recently acquired a new single-hose demand valve of bizarre design and he was trying it out for the first time on this dive. It was made, I believe, by Pirelli in Italy, and in contrast to the normal single hose DVs that were beginning to appear on the market by then, the large rubber diaphragm of the second stage was on the outside, enclosing the tilt valve and springs. Benny, 'I'm a Fifty Metre Man Myself', was known to us by this most unwieldy nick name, which he acquired after a deep dive at the Club Mediterranee holiday village in Italy in 1961.

I said, "I will go in first, so give me a little time to get set. Then I want you to jump in one by one and line up on the bottom facing me. When I give the signal, I want you all to swim slowly towards me". I jumped in and wedged myself into a crevice in the rocks and filmed as each diver entered the water. Then I gave the signal and ran the camera again as they moved towards me. All was going well until Benny decided to put on an unplanned diversion! He moved off to one side and stretched out on his back on a flat rock.

Johnny King, as any good diver should, saw this action as an aberration, needing investigation. It was not normal for a diver to lie back like that on a rock or on the bottom. He might well be having a blackout. Being an excellent diver and a very strong man, Johnny zoomed down on Benny, grabbed him by the scruff of his demand valve and yanked him unceremoniously to the surface. Benny was most incensed at this unexpected end to his dive, while the rest of us were more than surprised. In those days of scarce compressed air, we operated under the assumption that only if a diver had turned blue and his eyes were bulging would we assume that he needed assistance.

When we had assembled on dry land, we had a good laugh at the misunderstanding. There was nothing wrong with Benny of course, he had merely decided to add a little extra something to the scene, but he had forgotten to warn us in advance. No harm was done - except to his demand valve. It had been damaged beyond repair and it never really worked properly again. Benny was a bit sore about that and was not at all consoled by me saying that it was only a 'Mickey Mouse' device and that he was well rid of it!

But technology brought my filming career to an early end. Television was expanding rapidly after WW2 and it was only a question of time before a TV camera was taken under water. It was discovered that the TV camera, connected to a monitor in the support vessel, could actually 'see' more clearly and with better resolution in low visibility than could the diver who was holding the camera. A television camera was used underwater for the first time in 1947 by the Americans at Bikini to inspect the conditions following a nuclear explosion. TV cameras underwater were effective, but they were bulky and required cumbersome power cables from the surface. They were quickly replaced by video cameras which were cheap, easy to place in a watertight housing powered by internal batteries, and quite economical to run. The video camera in an underwater housing is commonplace now, and it has proved to be the ideal medium for most underwater needs.

I was not exactly devastated by this development. My camera in its under water role suffered from one major drawback. It could only expose a total of twenty five feet of standard 8mm film (approximately 2 minutes of filming) after which the film had to be turned over to expose the other 25 feet. This meant getting out of the water and drying myself well to avoid dripping on the camera. Then I had to dry the watertight case, open it, take out the camera, open the camera, take out the spool, turn the film over and then retread the film. Next I had to close the camera and replace it in the housing before re-entering the water. Changing the film was difficult enough on dry land, but in rain or in a wet boat, very frustrating indeed. It did not make for continuity in either diving or in filming. Trying to film suitable movie scenes underwater has been likened to 'standing in a shower while tearing up twenty pound notes'.

With a video camera, continuity was possible. Any fleeting shots could be availed of, and it was possible to review immediately whatever had just been filmed. If the shot was unsuitable, it was a simple matter to take the scene again, providing the subject had not fled or the circumstances had not changed. In addition, like the TV lens, the video camera lens has better underwater 'vision' than the human eye and is now used extensively in deep sites for that very reason. Underwater filming is commonplace now and has become a valuable tool for all forms of research, supervision and investigation under water.

# CHAPTER 12

# DIVING SUITS

The need to stay warm and comfortable underwater has always been a challenge to designers and to divers alike. The development of dry suits for commercial divers began in the 18th century and it is not yet over. The range goes from diving suits that are heated electrically or by hot water, to the un-pressurised armoured suits, with articulated joints and internal life support and with communications equipment built into them.

All the commercial suits have one feature in common; the wearer has to be attached in one way or another to the support ships on the surface of the water. As a result, quite a large team with elaborate and expensive equipment is required to support each diver under the water. The suits are also very expensive, well beyond the range of the amateur diver. The idea of being attached to the surface is completely against the whole ethos of the modern amateur diver, or 'free' diver, as he was often described in earlier years. This term was used to distinguish the amateurs or sports divers from the professionals, who were not free, being tethered to the surface.

I do not intend to cover the development of commercial suits here, such a subject is well beyond me, instead I will deal with the dry and wets suits as used since the 1950s. Before diving suits became available, most divers in Ireland were obliged to dive in their swim togs or long underwear or in an exotic collection of old pullovers and shorts. This was not really quite as 'macho' as it may seem to the modern diver. The dives were mainly from the shore, where the water might be marginally warmer. They were also of shorter duration, and shallower, because of the small capacity cylinders then in use. Equally, because of the lack of compressors to re-fill the cylinders, it was rarely possible to have more than one dive in a day. Most divers made use of multiple layers of tight-fitting woollen garments, which did in fact give some limited protection against the cold. Some divers experimented with the type of early survival or immersion suits as used by lifeboat and helicopter crews, but they were very uncomfortable, they were too bulky, and in any case, they were prone to leaking after a small number of dives.

All over Ireland in the late 1950s, the DIY divers had started to make their own rubber suits. Indeed, a thriving cottage industry developed, using some quite ingenious methods. Tom Mason, a Garda member of the Curragh Sub Aqua Club, must have spent hours and hours in making a suit put together from hundreds of oddments of discarded foam rubber. He had to glue each irregular piece into place, but for all his effort, his suit was not very effective. Tom Shakespeare of the Irish Sub Aqua Club made a slightly more durable suit. Wearing a set of 'long johns', he had to stand upright and motionless for several hours, while his friends painted the 'long johns' with many layers of black rubber paint. He had to let the rubber paint dry, before the final torture. When it was judged to be sufficiently dry, it had to be peeled off painfully, taking most of his available body-hair with it! It was a brave attempt, but it too didn't last very long.

Should there have been a prize for the best homemade suits, the winners would most certainly have been the members of the Galway Sub Aqua Club. They produced a very respectable suit, the distinctive trademark of which was the red tape with which they strengthened the seams. To be fair, they had an advantage over previous 'inventors' in that it was possible by then to buy neoprene by the sheet. Today the suits available to the amateur diver can be divided into three main types; the wet suit, the neoprene dry suit, and the membrane dry suit. Each type has its own important advantages and drawbacks, and these are now addressed in general terms.

A new process was developed early in the 20th century, whereby rubber sheeting was produced under very high pressure in contact with an inert gas. When the pressure was released, the bubbles of gas remained trapped in the rubber. The interior of the material then looked a little like an Aero chocolate bar, except that the bubbles were much smaller. This material was used to make the first diving suits. However, the suits were soft and very easily torn when the diver was dressing or undressing. Early attempts were made to glue a fine-mesh stockinette lining to the inner side of the suit. This certainly reduced the dangers of ripping, but the stockinette itself had a tendency to start lifting at the edges after some use.

It was only when a synthetic version of rubber called expanded neoprene was produced that the era of the wet suit dawned. Expanded neoprene was much more durable than previous materials and it had good stretching qualities. The sheets of neoprene were double skinned when produced and had then to be sliced horizontally in two. The resultant neoprene material had a smooth shiny surface on one side, but the inside was still rough and easily torn. A reliable nylon lining was devised, which when bonded to the inside of the neoprene, added the necessary additional strength. This, added to new techniques for taping and stitching the seams, plus much more careful attention to cut and shape, meant that the modern wet suit had finally arrived. When used for diving, the preferred dimension for Irish conditions is of 7mm or 8mm. Neoprene suits are also used in very many other sports and pursuits, such as boardsailing, surfing, canoeing, rafting, and potholing, where the usual thickness is 4 or 6mm. The neoprene wet suit is very flexible, it usually has extra protection at the knees, the hood is attached and it is comfortable to wear for quite long periods, as for instance when snorkelling or spearfishing. Separate bootees and gloves are available as optional extras, although not all divers use them.

When the diver enters the water, a small quantity of water will get inside the suit, usually at the zip, or where the suit does not have a close fit at the wrists or ankles, hence the name. The diver's own body heat then warms up this small quantity of water, which, because it is not replaced, remains to form a protective layer to keep the diver comfortable. As the diver descends, the suit loses buoyancy because the internal gas bubbles are crushed by the rising water pressure. Once the pressure is removed, i.e. when the diver returns to the surface, the suit is restored to its normal condition.

In Britain in the late Fifties, a new suit was made by Typhoon, or possibly Dunlop, and I believe that I was the proud possessor of one of only a small number ever purchased in Ireland. Others were bought by Johnny King and Jim Motherway. They were bright yellow in colour, at a time when suits were available in black only. It was a brave bid by the manufacturers to capture a potentially huge market, and the bright colour was part of that attempt. Up to this, we divers had been given to understand that the use of a colour dye in the manufacturing process affected the durability of the rubber material. It was for this reason that divers buying a new suit, or indeed any other item of diving equipment, could have any colour they wanted, provided, like the Ford cars, they wanted black! That day has long passed, of course, and divers nowadays are as brightly dressed as parakeets.

This early wet suit, dubbed affectionately 'Old Yella' by Jimmy Flynn, had a number of defects. The neoprene was hard, it was unlined, it had very poor stretch characteristics and it was easily torn. So great care was required when dressing or undressing. It was necessary to use large quantities of french chalk or talcum powder when dressing for the water, especially when the suit was not fully dry. The talcum provided that

The author in his new yellow wet suit, Slade, 1960.

essential lubrication which helped to make the dressing process less of a hazard. After he had pulled on the jacket, the diver's head was covered in white talcum and this caused much hilarity amongst the onlookers. Divers had no problems in entertaining the crowds, but the smell inside the suit or in the car afterwards as a result of the mixture of talcum and seawater was something to be experienced, especially on a hot day. The company that produced these suits probably suffered from being too early on the market, and other man-ufacturers must have profited from their misfortunes. Some years later, before O'Dare suits were available, I became the happy owner of a fine wet suit by Typhoon, purchased in DISCO which lasted quite well even into spearfishing times. Modern lined neoprene is flexible and stretches well, and if the suit is a good fit, and properly looked after, it will last for years. Thermal efficiency does however degrade slowly over time.

Wet suits produce one important paradox. Because of the positive buoyancy at the surface, the diver must carry a considerable amount of lead weight in order to submerge. However, as the diver goes down, the suit loses its buoyancy because of the water pressure - all the little bubbles get flattened - and the diver starts to get too heavy. Too little lead and he cannot get down, too much lead and he will descend at a dangerous and accelerating speed. Fortunately, there is a happy medium, and it comes through proper and careful training. This is a good example of why all those who wish to take up diving should join a reputable club or undergo a course of instruction with a reputable commercial organisation.

O'Dare Suits is one of the most successful suit manufacturers in Europe and is based in Bray, Co Wicklow. The company won a major prize in Germany a few years ago for manufacturing the suit judged to have given the best value for money, comfort and durability. The many suits in the O'Dare range are very popular and the range caters for all the water sports, not just diving. The company was formed in 1969 by Aidan Kelly and Willie Siddall, two teenage divers, who had started diving with the Irish Sub Aqua Club in Dublin. The company is still going strong, although the two founders have since parted company. Aidan still manages the O'Dare plant at Bray while Willy now operates a very successful PADI diving school and diving equipment shop in Dun Laoghaire, where he continues to sell O'Dare suits, amongst many other makes and models.

*　　*　　*　　*　　*　　*　　*　　*

In 1959, I bought my first suit, a dry suit, from a man in County Cavan. It was a one-piece suit with built-in boots and hood. The hood had a built-in neck-seal. Entry to the suit was gained via a large opening in the chest. The chest opening had two stiff, thick 'lips' at the front, and after the suit was donned, the 'lips' were pressed together, one over

The author at Gleesk Coral Beach, Kenmare, Co Cork, June 1959.

Jim Motherway (left) and Shane O'Connor in borrowed suits preparing to dive with Alistair Gilmour (centre), at Annalong, Co Down, Oct 58.

the other. They were then turned over and the ends were brought around to the back where they were tied in position, using a long tape. It had a small tube with attached stopper on the chest for drawing out the air. The suit worked well enough but was very prone to leaks, and in particular to the 'squeeze'. It was also particularly unsuitable for spearfishing, being much too rigid and restrictive.

The most popular dry suit for sports divers in the 1950s was made from a thin green or black latex rubber material which could be worn over ordinary street clothes, thus keeping the diver dry and warm, at least in theory. It cost £12.10s.00d, a large sum at the time. The suit came in three pieces, a trousers with attached boots, a jacket and a cummerbund. The trousers were very long, reaching up to the armpits when donned. The equally long jacket reached down as far as the knees, and finally there was a wide cummerbund of the same material. There were seals at the wrists and at the neck, made of even more delicate rubber, and these had to be treated with great care. The diver was free to decide what clothing he wished to wear under the suit, but most people simply wore the clothes in which they were dressed on the day, removing only their shoes and jackets.

When putting on the suit, the diver first donned the trousers, pulling it up as far as possible towards his armpits. He then turned the 'surplus' back down as far as his knees. He next donned the jacket, taking great care when getting his head through the neck seal and when putting his hands through the wrist seals. He pulled the skirt of the jacket all the way down over the turned down top of the trousers, if you are still with me. Then he reached down and started to roll the skirt of the jacket and the top of the trousers tightly together and over each other until they ended up as a thick 'sausage' of latex around his waist. Finally, he stepped into the cummerbund and carefully arranged it over the 'sausage' in order to keep it from unrolling.

These suits were all the rage for a while but they had severe drawbacks. Firstly, the suit came without a hood, so the diver generally wore a bathing cap or a woolly hat. They also came without gloves, so the diver, if he wished, used gardening gloves, or simply went without. The suit trapped quite a lot of air inside it when it was being donned for the water, and this had to be expelled. A small rubber pipe with attached bung was provided on the chest of the suit, and you were required to suck out as much of the air as possible by this means, before approaching the water.

Also, it was better not to jump into the water from a pier or rock, or even to roll in backwards from a small boat, as divers do today. There was a distinct possibility that the air trapped within the suit would rush into the boots, leaving the diver upside down in the water, contemplating his future or reviewing his past life! The water had to be approached slowly and carefully, no dramatic entrances were advised. I have no doubt that we must have provided great entertainment for the onlookers, who would invariably congregate whenever divers appeared at the seashore. Firstly, their patience was tested as it seemed to take forever before the divers were ready. Then as the divers approached the water, they would start to perform very odd, slow movements, rather like a strange type of ballet, or the sort of exercises that Mao Tse Tsung used to require all his subjects to perform before work and during lunchtime breaks.

Firstly, the diver would stretch out and wriggle his arms to settle his clothing beneath the suit, then he would squat down carefully in order to drive as much air as possible out of the suit at the neck. Next he would suck out as much air as he could through the chest tube. Only then would the diver ease himself slowly into the water, first letting out air via a finger stuck inside the neck seal. As the water level rose towards his neck, he lifted one arm into the air, sank further into the water and finally released the last of the air via the wrist seal. This last bit was particularly tricky. If you were not careful, you might let in a gush of Atlantic water, or even worse, Irish Sea water, to ruin your Sunday best. By now the suit was fitting very well indeed, and as the diver descended, the suit became even tighter, due to the rising water pressure. In fact, if we males had underwater communication means in those times, I've no doubt that we would have been speaking in the high-pitched Donald Duck voices more usually associated with divers who were breathing helium.

In the pubs afterwards, some divers were heard to be entertaining grave reservations about the wisdom of diving under such conditions, as it was possible that their voices, or more importantly, their marriage prospects, might have become permanently affected by the squeeze! The lack of a means of compensating for the increasing pressure was the biggest drawback of these early dry suits. At about 16m, it was actually painful to move one's arms or legs. The water pressure exaggerated every fold and wrinkle in the clothing worn under the suit, pressing them into the diver's body. The first time that I experienced this squeeze was on a dive with Jim Motherway at Spanish Point in 1959. We were both wearing dry suits. When we came out of the water we found that we were covered in long red or purple weals that criss-crossed our arms, legs and body. It was as if we had been horsewhipped.

Those early dry suits were not very successful, but they were all we had then and they certainly satisfied a need. They were very fragile and prone to pinhole punctures, although they could be repaired easily with a patch just as a bicycle tube is repaired. The seals at the neck and at the wrists were very delicate and gave a lot of problems. Replacing a seal was a major undertaking with the materials then available. The suits had one small redeeming feature, however. When the dive ended, and the diver was standing on dry land, he would put his finger inside the neck seal and pulled outwards gently. The resulting whoosh of (relatively) warm air into the suit, combined with the sudden release of constriction, was almost sexual in nature. The delighted sighs of a group of divers performing this manoeuvre must have looked very dubious indeed to the onlookers.

One Easter weekend, members of the Belfast Branch of the British Sub Aqua Club combined with us for some diving along the Clare coast. The weather was appalling and we were not able to dive in the preferred places. So Derek Nelson and I decided to do some spearfishing off the relatively sheltered rocks between Black Head and Ballyvaughan, where the swell was not too bad. I was wearing my yellow wet suit while Derek was clad in his dry suit. However on the way out of the water, while struggling across the rocks, Derek accidentally poked the point of his spear through the leg of his diving suit. The water rushed in of course, ruining his brand-new corduroys that Margot Sydney-Smith had helped him to buy just that day in Galway. I can still hear her outraged voice, and see the sheepish look on his face as Derek and others tried to squeeze all the water out of his trousers, prior to their return to Belfast.

A leaking dry suit is not just uncomfortable, it is actually dangerous because if the leak is a major one, it can fill up rapidly with water, making the diver seriously overweight. The wearer depends on his intact suit for buoyancy, and unless he happens to be carrying an independent means of buoyancy, such as an ABLJ (Adjustable Buoyancy Life Jacket), he may have difficulty in regaining the surface. When Joe Burke, an Army diver was putting on a borrowed Navy dry suit for the first time at Scapa Flow, his friends warned him of the consequences of getting a major tear in his suit. "Joe", said Ben Heron and Paddy O'Grady, trying hard to keep straight faces, "If the suit fills up with water at 30 metres, you will have no option but to cut your legs off in order to get back to the surface". Joe did not like this at all and by his second dive he had changed back to his trusty wet suit.

The early dry suits had such a bad name that it was only in relatively recent times that they have become popular again. Modern technology has finally provided the high-quality suits that can stand up to severe handling while keeping the wearer dry and relatively warm over and under the water. The over-water element has become very important as divers nowadays tend to spend quite a lot of time, sometimes hours, in their diving boats before and after diving. Wind chill can become a serious safety hazard for divers in these circumstances and the dry suit gives far better protection than does the wet suit.

More importantly, when under water, the dry suit is equipped with a means of allowing air into the suit from the diver's air cylinder in order to counter the increasing water pressure. So now, the dreaded squeeze has been conquered. The diver may also decrease or increase the amount of air in his suit at will to control his buoyancy during the dive. On the way back to the surface, the diver must release some of that surplus air as he rises, otherwise he will come up too quickly. Rising in an uncontrolled manner is a serious 'no-no' of diving, to be avoided if at all possible.

The principal drawback of a dry suit is that the diver must carry considerably more weight than if he were using a wet suit, averaging as much as 15 kilos. The modern dry suits come in two main categories, one is a heavy-duty neoprene fabric, the other in a rubber-impregnated nylon membrane, which is often referred to as a 'bag'. The membrane or 'bag' is probably more durable, it can protect the diver more efficiently against the problem of wind-chill when out of water, as when in a boat, but it is not very aesthetic in appearance. It is more prone to punctures, but it is easy to repair.

The dry suit is now the preferred thermal protection for most divers in Ireland, especially those who wish to dive all year around. Despite this, many divers also retain a wet suit for use in the summer when the water may be warmer. This is because no dry suit of any design yet produced is suitable for any but the most elementary snorkelling on the surface. It is too exhausting, but more importantly it can provide no relief for the build-up of heat generated by the diver's exertions. The wearer of a wet suit who is overly warm from finning simply lets in some cooling water at his neck, an option not available to the dry suit diver who may be wearing his street clothes or a specialised felt overalls underneath. The debate as to the respective merits of the dry membrane suit over the neoprene dry suit continues to rage - divers are deeply divided over it. But at least today they have an excellent range of quality and comfortable suits from which to choose to meet their own preferences.

# CHAPTER 13

# SEARCH AND RECOVERY

Publicity and recruiting for a club during the 1950s and early 1960s was very simple. When new members were needed, all a club had to do was to appear in a public place to go diving and they would be guaranteed an audience and later an inflow of 'recruits'. Because diving was such a novel activity, editors were only too willing to publish photographs and write up the (usually exaggerated) stories of what was going on underwater (i.e. out of sight). Some of the 'tales' were bordering on those of 'the fish that got away' type, but fortunately neither the readers nor the reporters were likely to have much knowledge of the subject. The Curragh Sub Aqua Club made great use of the Leinster Leader, and the Evening Press, via Terry O'Sullivan, ex-Army himself, to publicise our activities.

Generally, there was a great curiosity about divers and diving equipment, and everywhere we appeared we would quickly become surrounded by a large and admiring throng. The smaller ones in particular would ask questions such as, "Mister, is the knife for killing sharks?" Or, "Mister, how long does the oxygen last", or "What do you see down there?" In fact, the children were especially curious and always anxious to help. At times, I felt that all I had to do was to lie down and point towards the water, and I, and all my equipment, would be carried to the very edge, if not into the water itself. Now, after 42 years of active diving I am beginning to wish that some of those same children, or more correctly perhaps, THEIR children, could come along to help me in and out of the water, now that I have need of them!

An unexpected aspect of our new-found leisure pursuit was that we started to get calls from people who had lost property in the sea, rivers or lakes, such as outboard motors, cameras, false teeth, wedding rings, and so on. Small objects were obviously more difficult to locate, but we did recover one set of false teeth, mainly because they had fallen out at the foot of the steps on the wall of a small harbour, thus reducing the area to be searched. In general, small items like these were unlikely to be recovered as we had neither the equipment nor the experience to deal with such matters. We received many calls from around the country for outboard motors. While the owners always knew exactly where their outboards lay, we rarely, if ever, had any luck at the locations specified by them. Our luck was mixed, we found some and failed on many.

A more interesting request came our way in 1960. Someone had definitely seen a cannon on the bed of the River Boyne and she could put us right on the spot. We went out to the site of the battle on a beautifully hot and sunny summer's day and we snorkelled and dived at all the locations given to us. We employed a magnetometer, an electronic device that uses the local variations in the magnetic flux of the earth to indicate the presence of metal objects on the bottom. It was made by diver Paddy Ghent, one of whose hobbies was electronics, and it may well have been the first one ever used by divers in Ireland. The magnetometer had to be towed in an inflatable behind a rowing boat in order to keep it away from other distracting metals such as the divers' aqualungs. At the end of the day we had managed to accumulate a large collection of bicycle wheels, prams and old teapots, none of which could have in any way been associated with the Battle of the Boyne.

\* \* \* \* \* \* \* \*

All the clubs were experiencing a big increase in the number of calls from the public for diving assistance. Clubs rarely charged for their services, at most they would accept a donation to club funds. We generally saw such requests as an opportunity to have a day's or a weekend's diving in a new location. However, there was a much more serious side to being a new and scarce resource in the Ireland of the early 1960s. More and more, the sports divers were being called upon to search for the bodies of people lost in drowning tragedies. Up to this time, the only divers in Ireland were the professional 'hard-hat' divers employed by the Board of Works or some of the Harbour Boards. The Defence Forces, the Gardai or other Government agencies had not yet developed their own specialist diving teams.

Before this, searching for bodies had been conducted in a primitive and time-honoured manner, using ropes and grapnels. The grapnel was a four or five-pronged implement not unlike a small anchor. It was thrown into the water and then drawn back in the hope that it would snag on the body, which would then be drawn back to the shore or riverbank. Searches had been conducted in this manner for centuries, it was very much a hit-and-miss process, and the process could go on for quite a long time. Only in cases in which a car had gone into a harbour might a harbour diver be called upon to recover the car, and hopefully the occupants as well.

All this changed with the development of sports diving clubs across the country. The Gardai quickly realised their potential and began to request the help of any divers living in their areas, usually to assist in search and recovery operations. Divers are rarely called upon to make rescues, as the tragedy would have happened and the lives would have been lost long before any divers could get to the scene. Divers are more usually called upon to carry out search and recovery missions. It was an informal process and often it would not be the Gardai themselves who called on the services of the local divers but someone 'who knew someone who knew a diver'.

One of the earliest calls to us in the Curragh Sub Aqua Club was to search in the Liffey at Athgarvan near the Curragh in April 1960, for a man who had been seen falling into the river. Soon after, we got another call to the Barrow at Monasterevan, Co Kildare for a missing child. We did not succeed in either case. These searches presented us with a serious learning curve as we had no precedents to work from, so we came to formulate a few rules to guide us in search and recovery operations.

We realised that it was unhelpful if not downright dangerous, to rush in to the water and start searching merely to make a gesture of support to the grieving relatives. All the relevant information had to be collected and assessed, and thorough preparations made in advance. On arrival at the site of a tragedy, the first problem was to cope with the distressed relatives and friends, many of whom felt that all we had to do was to jump in and find the body. Next was to find a reliable witness, if there was one. Then we needed to talk to the Gardai present to find out what were the circumstances of the event as they knew it. Finally we needed to talk to anyone present who had a knowledge of the river, canal, lake, or sea and its currents, depths and possible underwater obstacles.

We decided that, where possible, the minimum group should be a team of three; one diver in the water, one on land or in the boat, ready to assist, and one non-diving person on dry land. Usually, we found that it was safer to put down one diver at a time attached by rope to a companion on the surface. In later, more organised times, we would use the terms 'Stand-By Divers' and 'Shore Marshals', but such practices and titles were still well in the future. Until we had improved in experience and equipment, the best we could do was to go through the motions of searching on the bottom, and then go home, saying that we needed more equipment or needed to re-fill our cylinders. Most of the time, it was a fairly straightforward exercise, but sometimes there were surprises, as the following story illustrates.

$$* \quad * \quad * \quad * \quad * \quad * \quad * \quad *$$

In October 1961, the Curragh Sub Aqua Club was hosting a sub aqua Gala at the Army Swimming Pool when a call came in for divers to go to Athy, as a child had fallen into the river. Johnny King, myself and Ronnie Hurley, of Limerick, agreed to leave the Gala and travel down immediately, as we had full air cylinders. When we arrived at the scene of the accident, I was very taken aback to see that the river was a raging flood, brimming at the top of the containing wall. It was obvious to me immediately that this task was beyond our abilities, experience and equipment and that all we could do was to make a token gesture towards recovering the body.

We were offered the services of a boatman whose small wooden boat looked to be anything but suitable for the job, and he himself looked distinctly uneasy about taking divers on board. Unusually, the boat had a canvas sun canopy supported on four slender aluminium posts. These posts were to prove to be very important in the drama about to unfold. Johnny and I got changed as quickly as possible; Ronnie was to act as shore marshal. Johnny King was to dive first, attached to a rope that I would hold onto from the boat, prepared to take over from him when he had finished. We set out into the racing water and Johnny submerged. Almost immediately, it was obvious that Johnny was being carried along very rapidly by the current.

About two hundred metres down stream from us lay a salmon weir that incorporated a narrow wooden catwalk, about two feet above the water, stretching from one bank to the other. In what seemed to have been no more than about three minutes, Johnny, having let go of the rope, popped up at the weir, clinging for all he was worth to a support pillar of the catwalk. So I asked the boatman if he could circle back and make a pass close to the weir while I threw the rope to Johnny. My plan was to haul him bodily off the weir and to retire upstream to consult with him as to the wisdom of continuing.

We did not get close enough for the rope to reach Johnny on the first pass, and I could sense that the boatman was less and less happy about my request. The outboard engine did not appear to be working properly, or perhaps it was not powerful enough for the job. As we made a second pass, the engine died, or the boatman had a sudden loss of confidence, - I could not see as I was up at the bow, watching Johnny. All I remember was hearing - "O Jesus, we're finished." The engine cut out and the boat was hurled onto the weir. The flimsy looking aluminium posts now came into their own as they jammed me, and the boat, between the weir and the wooden catwalk.

I found myself pinned to the catwalk at chest level. I screamed at the boatman, "Get out fast, the boat won't hold". At the same time, I was busy putting my fins, mask and snorkel up on the catwalk. Almost as soon as he had scrambled over me onto the catwalk, the framework of the canopy collapsed and the boat was whisked away across the weir, turning over as it went. I was now free to scramble up on to the catwalk and to go to the assistance of Johnny. The boat was recovered eventually about a mile down stream, while we were all shaken but unharmed. In fact, Johnny or myself would probably not have come to any great grief if we had gone over the weir, as we were in diving suits, but the poor boatman would have needed our very close assistance if he was to have survived.

Needless to say, all further diving was abandoned, we apologised for our feeble efforts, and it was a thoughtful little group that returned to the Gala in the Curragh that evening. The tale we had to tell was received in silence by the assembled divers. It had been a sharp object lesson to us of the folly of diving in such conditions. We put that lesson to good use in later search and recovery operations.

As the general public began reading of our diving activities, the calls for assistance began to come in more frequently. On a wintry evening in 1960, I got a phone call from Johnny King, "A truck has fallen into a quarry in Ranelagh, in Dublin, and the driver is feared drowned, can you meet me there?" So I went as quickly as I could to the quarry where a shocked and depressed group of workers were standing around in lightly falling snow, looking down at where the truck had disappeared. Somehow the body of the driver had been recovered by some brave individual before our arrival, so it was only left to us to dive under the truck to attach a wire cable to the rear axle. The water was bitterly cold and we could work by touch only as the water was totally black. It was not a pleasant experience, as we could not be sure of the stability of the truck.

About this same time, a group from the Club searched for the body of a little boy who had fallen into a quarry, somewhere in the Finglas area. Micky Lynch actually found the little body, and he was not the better of it for a long time afterwards. Norman O'Byrne, Mick Duffy and I conducted a most disagreeable search, looking for the body of a child who had fallen into the River Dodder. It was like diving in an open sewer, the river being full of refuse of all kinds. We could only move slowly and with great caution along the bottom in total blackness, relying on touch only, afraid to get hung up on a rusty car or a tangle of barbed wire. We were not successful and the body was found a day or two later, further downstream near where the Dodder enters the Liffey.

*     *     *     *     *     *     *     *

On Sunday, 29 June 1969, approximately 45 divers were involved in a spearfishing competition at Kilkee, Co. Clare. The competition was one of a number held to determine the composition of the Irish team to travel to the world spearfishing championships in Italy. As we were finishing up and preparing to head for home, word came out that there had been a major boating accident in north Clare, and that as many as nine people had been lost. We were all deeply shocked, but aware that even if those on the spot had known about our presence in Kilkee, we could not have arrived in time to be of any use. However, we talked about this at Kilkee before we dispersed and some of us agreed to meet at New Quay early on the following morning, as we were in possession of full diving cylinders.

The Redbank Oyster Fisheries Company operated from a number of buildings close to the pier at New Quay, a tiny village on the north coast of County Clare, facing out onto Galway Bay. A short time before this incident the Company had taken delivery of a new boat. It was a flat-bottomed boat designed to operate in the shallows of the lagoon, where the oysters were reared. It would normally have a crew of two to three. On Sunday 29th of June 1969, a special gala day had been organised to celebrate the arrival of the new vessel. The vessel was first blessed by the parish priest, and the owners then proceeded to take groups of spectators out in the new vessel for short trips in the Bay. A group of schoolgirls, who had been away playing a camogie match, arrived just after the skipper had called a halt to the trips for the day and had tied up at the pier. They pleaded with him to take them out, and he reluctantly agreed.

Unfortunately, many others climbed aboard for that additional trip. It transpired later that possibly as many as 49, mostly young people, had climbed on board without the notice or approval of the owners. The weather had worsened, and when the boat was being turned around to return to the pier, some water came aboard. All the passengers rushed to the other side, to get away from the water. The boat, being virtually flat-bottomed, turned over immediately, throwing most passengers into the strong tidal current. The vessel started to drift rapidly with the tide in the direction of Galway bay. The horrified onlookers were galvanised into action, and some quite extraordinary acts of heroism followed. Anyone who had access to a boat immediately set out and started to pick up struggling survivors. Three men set out in a dilapidated rowing boat, using planks of timber and the top of a biscuit tin to propel themselves to the scene where they rescued several victims. A young girl from New Quay, who had been on the vessel, was a strong swimmer. Along with a number of others, she became trapped under the hull of the Redbank in an air pocket that enabled them to breathe. She found her way out from under the hull, and then went back several times to save a number of others by bringing them out to one of the rescue boats. Most others managed to swim to shore, but when the counting and checking began, fear and dread swept over the crowd. Eight were unaccounted for, mostly young people. Worse, a girl who had been rescued, died in the ambulance on the way to Ennis Hospital. A night of the most unremitting gloom and horror descended upon this small community.

When the alarm was raised in Galway, the Gardai requested a helicopter from the Air Corps and contacted George Ryder, a prominent member of the Galway Sub Aqua Club. George, who had just returned that afternoon from a dive in Carraroe, went immediately to Renmore Barracks and boarded the helicopter which carried him out across the Bay to where the upturned Oyster Fisheries boat was drifting. George, who had never been in a helicopter before, had to jump into the sea from about twelve feet. Operating without a backup diver, he dived into and under the boat. After about ten minutes he surfaced and confirmed that the boat was clear of bodies. He was recovered by the Aran Islands Lifeboat, and from there he was lifted into the helicopter and brought back to Galway. The Aran Lifeboat, the Galway Harbour Pilot Boat and many fishing boats, local and from the Aran Islands, joined in the search. Members of the Red Cross, Civil Defence and many civilians arrived also and began to search along the shores. These activities at least were of some consolation to the grieving relatives.

At about 10.30 on Monday, Fergus Marshall, Shane Gray, Billy Nott and myself arrived at the pier in New Quay. There was a little group of local people standing around on the pier, staring out at the water in stunned silence. The oyster beds lay in a huge and very shallow lagoon, which stretched away to the East for more than a mile. The lagoon was connected to Galway Bay by a channel that was about 1,500 metres long and 100 metres wide. The channel was, and still is, a most dangerous stretch of water, as the tide rushes in and out at a remarkable speed. On those occasions when the tide comes into conflict with a strong wind, the resulting short steep waves are very nasty indeed, and that stretch of water is for none but the most experienced boatmen.

I did a quick 'recce' of the area around the pier, and questioned one man as to where exactly the Oyster Fisheries boat had turned over. He pointed out the spot in mid-channel, only about 50 metres out from the pier. He also told me that eight young people were still missing. The boat had turned over in mid-channel at a time when the tide was racing outwards from the lagoon. The diving task was clearly way beyond the capabilities of our small and ill-equipped group and I felt that it was extremely unlikely that our efforts would yield results. We did not have a boat to cover us, nor did we have a compressor to re-fill our cylinders. In any case there were too few of us to be of serious value. I explained this to some of the bystanders, in an attempt to dampen their hopes in advance.

The tide was close to being fully out, so I decided that the best we could do was to take advantage of the slack tide and do a swim-line search over and back across and at right angles to the channel. As we prepared for our dive the number of onlookers increased and we noticed that they had become more animated. Clearly they were expecting great things from us, while we knew from past experience that we were unlikely to succeed at the first attempt, if at all. Underwater searches are generally long and tedious affairs, and require great care, preparation and patience.

We lined up at the water's edge, just up-channel of the pier, holding onto a light rope, each diver at approximately arm's length from the next. We swam along the bottom across the channel and surfaced in the shallow water at the other side. Moving downstream by about 75 metres, we made a return sweep back to the South side of the channel, emerging on the seaward side of the pier. We were surprised by the relatively clear water and by the lack of obstructions on the bottom, but we did not recover any of the missing bodies.

As we changed into our clothes, I found it very difficult to say that we were leaving, that there was no more we could do for now. The disappointment on the faces of the onlookers who had clustered around us was obvious. All we could do was to offer our sympathies and to say that the Garda Diving Unit would be coming along soon, maybe tomorrow. I did not know it then, but we were all to be back before the end of the week to participate in what turned out to be one of the longest and most widespread search operations of its kind seen in Ireland up to that time.

*   *   *   *   *   *   *   *

A word about search techniques is appropriate here. I had learned about the swim-line and other techniques from reading the report of Sydney Wignall, from Wales, an experienced amateur underwater archaeologist. He had spent a number of years researching the Armada wrecks in Spain and in London. As a result of which he launched a determined and eventually successful search for the best documented of the wrecks, the Santa Maria de la Rosa. This vessel was known to have foundered in the sound between the Blasket Islands and the mainland. I met him in Dublin before he left Ireland and was absolutely delighted when he gave me a copy of his report.

The chief diver for the group in the search for the Santa Rosa was Lieut-Commander John Grattan, on leave from the British Navy. Born in India, he had been awarded an OBE for his work with a team of divers on bomb and mine disposal at Malta in the 1960s. He is a direct descendent of Henry Grattan, who had gained for the Irish people a great improvement in political freedom after 1782. Grattan became commander of the Deep Diving and Recovery ship, HMS Reclaim in 1968. Over the three summers that it took to find the wreck, he trained all the divers, most of them amateurs, who had volunteered for varying periods to support the operations. The

140

Report contained details of the quite extraordinary number of swim-line searches that had been conducted, and which he had meticulously recorded on a marine chart. The Blasket Sound was an area of very strong tidal movements and he made clever use of the tides in order to extend the coverage of each swim, by swimming in the direction of the tidal run. The quest was successful eventually, but only as a result of dogged persistence and determination by all concerned. There is an interesting film available of some of their dives.

On a swim-line, any number of divers can be used at one time, at least in theory. John Grattan used up to ten divers on a line, but I found after some experience that five or six is about the optimum number, as it gives greater control. However, it means losing a little to the width of the strip of sea bottom that can be examined. The divers start off by lining up on the surface, facing the direction of intended travel and holding onto a rope. A marker buoy is placed in the sea by the boat cover team to indicate where the swim-line started. When the divers submerge, all at the same time, each diver positions himself along the rope on the bottom, at such a distance that he can just see the diver to his left and to his right.

The centre diver of the group tows a marker float, attached either to his weight-belt or to his elbow. This has two purposes: one is to enable the cover boat team to follow the divers by watching the marker float; the other is to allow the centre diver, when an object of significance is discovered, to mark the location by detaching the float and tying it to the object. Equally, he could also take off his weight belt and use that as an anchor to mark the spot. All the divers would then surface to be recovered and to plan the next move. The centre diver and the two end divers carry compasses and follow on the pre-planned compass course, endeavouring to keep the line of divers at right angles to the line of advance. The two outer divers also have to keep an outward pull on the line throughout the dive in an attempt to prevent bunching at the centre. In addition to all the above, each diver has to clear his ears, maintain correct buoyancy, check regularly on the quantity of air remaining in his cylinder, watch his buddies, and at the same time, keep a look out for the object of the search. They were very busy divers!

A number of simple signals have been devised for communication between divers. The dive lasts until the first diver runs out of air, (or until a diver has some other problem which requires him to surface), in which case the dive ends and all surface at the same time. The place where the dive ends has to be marked then, to enable the director of operations to decide where the next swim-line should begin. Because of the changes of tide, it is often was the case that a swim-line has to start where the

141

previous one ended and to swim in the opposite direction. Because of the medium in which divers operate, there must be a fair amount of overlap between searches to allow for drift, the accuracy of the compass reading, and so on. Finally, all swim-line dives have to be recorded on a chart to avoid duplication of effort, and to facilitate forward planning.

It is possible to cover a swathe of sea bottom as long as 1,000 metres on just one dive, depending on the strength of the current. The width of a given swathe depends on the underwater visibility and the interval between the divers on the line, so it can vary with each dive. On one dive, a Garda swim-line actually covered a distance of 1,800m, starting near the pier and ending far out in Galway Bay. Because the water was fairly clear at New Quay during the time we were there, and because the sea bottom was fairly free of heavy seaweed or rocks, it was possible to declare with reasonable certainty that a given swathe of sea bottom had been searched and cleared.

We were aware however that we were working in a three-dimensional environment. Apart altogether from the clarity of the water, divers have quite a limited view of their surroundings. They can see best to their front and beneath them and to a fair degree to their right and left, but they have a major blind spot above them and to their rear. It would be quite easy to pass underneath an object and to fail to see it if it was floating in mid-water. To complicate our endeavours at New Quay, because of the strength of the currents in the channel, and because of the length of time since the tragedy, we had to assume that we were probably dealing with 'moving targets'.

In general, while the swim-line search is a fairly 'low tech' technique, it works quite well in most situations, and has served us well over the years. There are many other search techniques, one of which is where the diver is towed behind a boat on an underwater sled, by which large areas can be covered in a short time. This technique requires that the water be very clear, and that the object being searched for would be very large, such as a ship or boat. Another method of search to be used under water is the circular search. It is the best technique for looking for small items in a limited area. Providing that the location is accurately known, it has a good chance of success. There are also many rope techniques for searching rivers, ponds and small lakes.

In general, these other methods require greater training and the divers concerned should have some experience in using them. The swim-line technique is most suited to amateur sports divers as it requires of them much the same skills that they apply to their normal diving activities.

*    *    *    *    *    *    *    *

The combined Army and Garda diving team at New Quay:

Standing, Gardai, from the left: Tom Knott, Charlie Byrne, Willie Scanlon, Denis Motherway, Jim Crockett, Paddy Morrissey, Sgt Niall Bracken, Andy Breen and Frank Treacy.

Kneeling Army: Billy Nott, Fergus Marshall, Mick Moriarty, Shane Gray, Paddy Ghent, Des Hearns, Dave Betson. Seated; Manuel di Lucia, Kilkee. Not in photo, Fintan Mullowney.

On Tuesday 1st July 1969, the Garda Sub Aqua Unit, under Inspector Leo Gillen and Garda Sergeant Niall Bracken, arrived at New Quay and they commenced search operations immediately. However, by Wednesday it had become obvious to Sergeant Bracken (the senior Garda diver, who was in charge of diving training at the Garda depot at that time) that the task was far too big for the number of divers available to him. He asked for assistance from the Defence Forces, and with the help of the T.D. for the area, Dr. Bill Loughnane, a number of divers, myself included, were asked to volunteer for diving duties at New Quay.

The Army did not have professionally trained operational divers at that time, nor did the Navy, but there were up to forty experienced sports divers in the Army who could be called upon, using their own personal diving equipment. I was designated to be in charge of the Army group, and our ready response to the request was made all the easier because we knew many of the Garda divers through their involvement with CFT. Comdt. Griffin from I Bn was our Liaison Officer. By Thursday, 02 July, 1969, a combined force of 10 Army and 8 Garda divers were in position and the underwater search was ready to begin in earnest.

The task was huge, the area to be searched had been extended to several square miles - beyond the channel itself - to include much of the eastern shores of Galway Bay. In addition, we had to search the area of the oyster beds, which lay inland and in very shallow water. The speed and force of the water rushing in and out of the oyster beds was such that it was easy to imagine how bodies would be carried quite some distance out to sea or even back into the oyster beds, well away from the scene of the tragedy.

We established our camp on a flat empty space behind the Fisheries building, setting up two eight-man tents: one for sleeping in and the other for meals, briefings, de-briefings and conferences. The Garda divers were a little beyond us, in an assortment of privately owned tents. They had established their own catering arrangements, buying food locally and cooking it themselves on the site. I had organised for our meals to be sent out to us every day from the Officers Mess at Renmore Barracks.

The tragedy had occurred at a time before inflatable diving boats were commonplace in Ireland, so, at my request, the Department of Defence had contracted Manuel di Lucia of Kilkee, and his boat, to work with the Army divers for the duration of the search. Manuel's boat was a hard-hulled gull-winged fibreglass boat, while the Gardai had their own small inflatable. The combined team was broken into two sections, mainly because we had only two boats, and we started to carry out a series of swim-line searches, moving always with the tidal currents. When one section of divers came ashore to rest, to eat, and to refill their cylinders, the other group was under water doing another swim-line search.

After a day or two, when we had not located any bodies, we began to fear that the bodies must have been washed out into the Bay. So we started doing swim-lines parallel to the shore in the outer reaches, to the North of Aughinish Point. We also instituted snorkel swim-line searches over the oyster beds in the very shallow water where aqualungs were not required. So we were very crestfallen when the first body was found by shore patrols on the rocks near Aughinish Point, principally because we had not found the body ourselves. However, this discovery served to confirm my earlier decision to widen the search, as we were now reaching a time when bodies would normally be expected to surface. I also decided that more help was required so I requested a helicopter on a daily basis, in order to extend the coverage of our searches. The pilot would land the aircraft precariously on the end of the very small pier, it being the only suitable landing spot locally, to take one of our team aloft. The helicopter was used to patrol the shorelines and it filled a valuable role in providing extra coverage and expert eyes to the search.

I was on board one morning when we spotted a girl's body on the surface. At that time the Air Corps method for lifting a body was by way of a specially designed scoop, made of aluminium and netting, about two metres long and with high sides. It was carried in a slung position on the side of the aircraft and had to be jockeyed into position by the winchman before being lowered. The pilot, in this case, Lieut. Fergus O'Connor, positioned the aircraft over the body, while the winchman, Airman Alec Dunne, now Sergeant, instructed him to manoeuvre until he had lowered the scoop into the water behind the corpse.

Then he instructed the pilot to move forward, until the scoop was underneath the body. They succeeded at the first attempt and having lifted the body, the pilot then headed for the shore. He had to find a remote location on the shore, where there was a laneway to give access for the ambulance. It had been the policy that any bodies recovered would be landed at a point well away from the sight of any immediate family members. As I was the only non-crewman on board, I was expendable! He set the scoop down first and then landed beside it to let me out. It was a very unpleasant 30 minutes for me, sitting beside the body in a remote and silent part of the foreshore. As with all bodies which have been in the sea for some time, its condition was quite disturbing. All I could do was to say a few private prayers for her and her family and hope that this particular task would fall to one of the others next time. I returned to New Quay in the ambulance and rejoined the other divers.

The Navy appeared in the Bay early one morning in the shape of the corvette, LE. Cliona, and we were delighted to see them. A launch arrived at the pier shortly after, carrying Lieut. John Kavanagh, who wanted to know what he could do for us. At that time the Navy had a number of officers who had been trained as Clearance and Ships Divers, but they were unable to practice their skills because the necessary equipment and additional trained personnel had not been provided*. I suggested to Lieut. Kavanagh that he could take on the task of searching the Bay from Black Head across to the North-

* NOTE: Today the Navy has a highly effective and extremely professional diving unit, with excellent equipment and training. They are frequently called upon to perform all manner of tasks far removed from their naval ones. In April 1999, the Minister for the Marine presented an award of 'Appreciation for Meritorious Service' to the Naval Diving Section for its work in search and recovery over the years. The Army Ranger Wing and the Army Corps of Engineers also have diving teams who are trained and equipped to a very high standard.

East towards Kinvara, in case any bodies surfaced beyond our range of search. With only two small boats available to us, we could not spare either boat to do long surface searches out in the Bay. The small boats were needed to transport divers to and from the dive sites and, more importantly, to give them close safety cover. I should point out here that while in the days immediately after the tragedy, there had been a large number of local fishing-boats, as well as the Aran Islands Lifeboat, actively involved in the search in the Bay, most of them had returned to their fishing or other duties by this time.

The Cliona was not able to come into the shallower waters, where we felt that the bodies were most likely to be found, because the corvette had a draught of 16 feet and much of Galway Bay where we were operating was fairly shallow. But they were able to cover an area further out in the Bay that was beyond our capabilities, and thus filled a vital gap in the search. We had by now instituted a new system of joint Garda/Army boat patrols starting at 06.00 daily. Manned by divers who were equipped to dive should it be needed, one boat at a time would do planned sweeps of the shoreline. These patrols continued throughout the day crewed by a rotation of personnel. The other boat continued to be used as safety cover for the diver swim-lines.

All during the above, the Red Cross and the Civil Defence continued to provide foot patrols along the shore, and an ambulance and team was stationed at the pier. Also, from time to time, mainly at the weekends, small groups of divers arrived from the Galway Sub Aqua Club and I was only too happy to employ them in doing searches in various places where we felt that a second look was warranted. After about ten days, the bodies were being recovered more frequently, until eventually only two were missing: a young girl and the youngest victim, the son of the postmaster, whose house was just opposite the pier. Now that all the bodies but two had been recovered, the tension and the pressure began to build, both amongst the divers and amongst the people in New Quay, as everyone desperately wanted to find the remaining victims.

As luck would have it, I was on a 'Dawn Patrol' (as I had christened the early morning boat patrols), at about 05.45 on 12 July, in the Garda inflatable with Garda Frank Treacy and Capt. Fintan Mullowney. Just around the headland at Aughinish Point, to the North of where the channel opened into the Bay, we spotted the body of the little boy floating on the surface. We put a rope around the body to hold it against the boat and we towed it gently and slowly towards the shore. Fintan went ashore first to call the attention of the Civil Defence patrol on the cliffs above, and to tell them to bring down a stretcher. Fintan and I then put the stretcher under the body and lifted it up gently, and struggled across the rocks to the shore. Fortunately, the sea was quite calm just then. We passed the stretcher over to the Civil Defence team, who threw a blanket over it and carried it up the low cliffs to the ambulance. That morning in the boat, the three of us, all family men, had been very affected by the sight of the little boy, dressed in his Sunday best, lying face down in the water.

We now concentrated all our efforts on the area running to the north from Aughinish Point, but even though we found a girl's shoe underwater, we had no luck. On the 16th of July the last body was found on the rocks by shore searchers near the Point. At long last we could relax, the job was done, all eight bodies had been recovered by a variety of means, and we felt pleased at a good job well done. We were also very relieved because for a while it had looked as if we were getting nowhere. It had become very difficult to continue to radiate an air of confidence and assurance in the presence of the grieving relatives. We broke camp; sent our tents, furniture, eating utensils and bedding equipment back to the QM of the Ist Battalion in Renmore Barracks, Galway; paid our mess bills to the Officers Mess; said goodbye to our Garda and local friends and dispersed to our home stations.

* * * * * * * *

I am glad to say here that the two groups of divers worked together in a happy spirit of co-operation and in a very friendly manner. We mixed and shared all the diving chores without any problems or complaints. For a diving and boating operation lasting nearly three weeks, all had gone remarkably smoothly, with no diving illnesses or accidents. However, there had been one incident that might have been very serious. On Friday 7 July, a team of six army divers were returning from a swim-line search outside the channel, in the boat being piloted by Manual de Lucia.

Niall Bracken and I were strolling along the road, discussing the next moves to be made, when we suddenly saw the boat flip over backwards, throwing all the occupants into the water. This happened well out in the rough water of mid-channel, a good 800 metres from where we were. This was a great shock to us, but an even worse one for an elderly woman who happened to be cycling nearby. She also saw the incident and fell off her bike, requiring treatment for shock and scratches. She was convinced that she had seen yet another major boating tragedy, so soon after the first one.

Our first reaction was to count heads - we were relieved to see seven bobbing in the water. Our next reaction was to take bearings on where the accident had happened, so that we could start the recovery of equipment. We scrambled all available divers on shore - they were all Garda divers - to go out immediately. They were quickly on the scene and picked up the divers, who were unharmed, and brought them back to the shore. They then towed Manual's upside-down boat to shore where he immediately removed the engine and took it to a garage to strip it down and to cover it in oil. It was functioning satisfactorily by next day.

Happily, every item of diving equipment on board the boat was recovered in a protracted series of dives lasting late into the evening. The depth at the site was ten metres, and the search was made easier because the bottom was flat and sandy. The only item not recovered was the toolkit for the engine! This remarkable recovery feat came about because of a happy accident. The Army divers had been using a 30 metre long rope that had an inflated float attached at one end. It was the personal marker buoy belonging to Billy Nott, which he had been using for spearfishing competitions. (By this time, regulations required each spearfisherman to tow a personal marker float during competitions. This had been introduced as a safety measure). Billy was the centre diver on the line and the marker buoy had been attached to his weight belt. When they had finished their dive and were all back in the boat, Billy had simply discarded his weight belt on the bottom of the boat, with the line and float still attached. When the boat was swamped at the stern by a large wave, everyone and everything was thrown into the sea. The weight belt sank to the bottom and after a short time, even as Niall and I were watching anxiously, the buoy struggled to the surface. It remained in place, providing a perfect datum marker for the subsequent recovery.

However, there was a lighter side also to our operations. We could not dive at night, so we would leave two divers on watch at the camp while the rest would go to Kinvara for some 'R and R'. We were very aware of the suffering and anxieties of the relatives who were watching everything we were doing, and this put its own pressure on us. But there was also a need for us to get away sometimes. It was Manuel di Lucia who had the bright suggestion, "I will contact my good friend Brendan O'Regan at Shannon Airport, and I am certain sure that he could get us tickets to one of the banquet meals". The Shannon Free Airport Development Company was promoting medieval banquets in a number of old castles in the region in the interests of tourism.

Both Niall and myself felt that this should be good for morale and we approved. Shortly afterwards, Manuel announced that we had been given tickets to the medieval banquet at Dunguaire Castle in Kinvara. The banquet was to start at 8pm and in the best traditions of diving, we had started the warm-up process in our favourite pub. So we were in giggling mood when we approached the Castle, although because of who we were and what we were doing, we did our best to appear serious and even glum. However, our very best intentions were ruined just as soon as we came to the entrance to the Castle.

We were confronted at the gate by a young man in tights and puffed-out brightly striped pants. He greeted us in 'Ye Olde Englishe' referring to us as 'merrie gentlemen'. He did not realise it, but he had hit the nail on the head, we were exactly that, we were 'merry'! The giggling started and it got worse and worse as the evening wore on. The meal was excellent and most enjoyable, with plenty of meade. In retrospect the meade was not a good idea either, as it did not mix very well with the 'black stuff'. We were in the company of a large group of mainly American tourists who were taking everything in. The entertainment, which started and continued during the meal, was an English-language version of the Midsummer Court by Brian Merriman, a Clare poet of the 17th Century. For anyone who knows this epic and important work, it is full of suggestive remarks, dealing with the complaints of a group of women who were bitterly disappointed at the inadequacy of Irish men as lovers!

Our American cousins seemed to be a little bemused by our reactions to the play, not quite knowing how to deal with us. They assumed that we were members of a football team, as we were all fairly large and had an 'outdoor' look about us. I was starting to feel distinctly embarrassed and beginning to wonder, not for the first time, about my future in the Defence Forces. The actors were clearly not used to this treatment, because what to a foreigner might appear to be culturally interesting, to an Irishman with too much 'refreshment' aboard, it was ridiculously funny.

The attempts of our divers to suppress the laughter gave way, as the evening rolled on, to outright guffaws and loud retorts at the suggestive remarks of the players, who were dressed in the style of the 17th Century. The sight of sixteen large males in giggling mood would put off any actors, but to give them their due, they stuck to their tasks in the best traditions of the stage. When the show and the meal had ended, and the others had left the castle, I felt that it was my duty to apologise on behalf of the group. So I went back into the Castle and sought out the six or seven artistes in their backstairs changing room. I asked for their forgiveness and said that we were all suffering from the strain of a very unpleasant and prolonged task. I said that we were merely letting off steam, and that I hoped they would understand. I was greeted in total silence and by frozen faces, so I turned away and followed the others, hoping that that was the end of it. To their credit, it was.

The entire diving operation at New Quay was a great exercise in diving and it strengthened relations with the Garda divers. Both the Gardai and ourselves learned a great deal which we applied to many other search operations in subsequent years.

* * * * * * * *

In August, 1970, some pilots from the Air Corps were working for a film company, flying modern replicas of World War 1-type British and German biplanes. On Tuesday 18th, they were filming over Wicklow Bay. The director and the camera crew were in a helicopter, and the five or six aircraft involved had been instructed to dive towards the helicopter, one behind the other. On the second run in, something went tragically wrong and the leading aircraft collided with the helicopter, killing all four on board the two craft. Both aircraft plunged into the bay, and local boatmen quickly picked up the bodies of the director, the cameraman and the helicopter pilot. However, there was no sign of the body of the Air Corps pilot or of his aircraft.

The Garda Diving Unit was called immediately, but they were already engaged in a search in the West so the call went out once more for army volunteers to report as soon as possible to Wicklow. I was designated to be in charge of the operation while Captain Jimmy Flynn was to be the Liaison Officer to DFHQ and in charge of logistics. It shows the spirit of the time that a number of civilian members of the Curragh club took time off from work and volunteered to join us. One member of the Garda Sub Aqua Club, Frank Treacy, also arrived. The Curragh Sub Aqua Club provided us with their compressor, a very valuable asset, as there were no compressed air sources in Wicklow at that time. This was familiar work and I quickly organised teams to prepare for swimline searches, working from the pier at Wicklow Harbour. While this was being set up, I went out with a boatman who claimed to have seen where the aircraft had fallen.

I did a few quick spot dives on oil patches. On the second dive, I landed on the remains of the helicopter. There were no bodies but I did pick up a gold watch, a set of dentures, and most importantly, a large can of film, which following development, apparently provided valuable evidence to the crash investigators. However, none of the other oil spots were significant and nowhere was there any trace of the pilot or his aircraft. So the long slow process of methodical searches was set in motion. As there was a weak but distinct tidal run in the Bay, we were able to make use of it to cover quite long search runs.

Presently, the corvette, LE Maeve arrived in the Bay, commanded by Comdr. Liam Brett. He very kindly offered to take all the divers on board, an offer that I was very grateful to accept, as it got us away from the throng of onlookers on the pier. His EO happened to be Lieut. Peadar McElhinney, who himself was a diver. He had been trained in Britain as a Clearance Diver and he had the kind of qualifications that made divers like ourselves feel like the amateurs that we were. Members of the Garda Diving Unit arrived later and were integrated into the search operation.

Even though the object that we were searching for was large, a wrecked aircraft, there was the distinct possibility that the body would not be in or even close to the wreck. For this reason there was a possibility that the operation could well be a drawn-out affair. But fortune was on our side. By now we were operating in great comfort from the corvette and getting great support and advice from the EO and others. On the 21st of August, on the third swim-line dive, Shane Gray, who was on the other end of the line from myself, came across the wrecked aircraft. By signalling on the rope, he brought us all in around the sad sight.

It was particularly poignant for Shane, as he himself had been a qualified pilot in the Air Corps before leaving and transferring to the Army. It was obvious to us that it would not be possible to remove the body from the aircraft, so everybody surfaced, leaving a marker float attached to the wreck. A local trawler skipper was then asked to lift the wreck using his onboard winch, which he did, cables having been attached by our divers. The wrecked aircraft was hoisted up and placed on the deck of the trawler, with the body still in the cockpit. The trawler then was brought alongside the Maeve to await the arrival of the coroner. Our job was over.

It had been a useful exercise for us divers, a tragedy for the families involved, and yet another example of the relationship between the military and the civilian members of the Club.

\*     \*     \*     \*     \*     \*     \*     \*

In the autumn of 1973, a prominent Dublin businessman went missing in the Wicklow Mountains near Glenmalure. His car was found and many large-scale searches by Civil Defence and Mountain Rescue groups were conducted over a period of months, but without success. Some friend of his eventually suggested that the small lake, called Art's Lake under Lugnaquilla, Ireland's third highest mountain, should be searched. He approached the Minister for Defence who agreed to provide a helicopter to the Curragh Sub Aqua Club to conduct a search on a Saturday in November.

We were only too happy to oblige, so we had arranged to rendezvous with the helicopter at the car park in Glenmalure. The weather was very poor, but despite low clouds and a strong gusting wind, the Alouette arrived from Baldonnel and landed at the carpark. There the pilot consulted with us and made his plan for the airlift. He decided to take up the cylinders and the weight-belts first, and as I was not diving, I travelled on that first lift. (At that time I was on stand-by to serve with the United Nations in Israel and I was not willing to dive, just in case I picked up a heavy cold or worse).

The landing spot at the top of the ridge was soft and very steep. The pilot could touch down his nose-wheel only, holding the aircraft horizontally while myself and the crewman hurled the cylinders and the weight-belts out of the aircraft onto the boggy ground. I then jumped out and rolled away quickly, and waited for the others to arrive. I was in the perfect position to watch the helicopter as it landed at the car park far below me to pick up the divers. It then lifted back up the slope, the noise increasing to a numbing high-pitched scream as it came right down beside me. The divers in their diving suits threw themselves dramatically and with abandon from the aircraft and rolled away, in accordance with the crewman's instructions.

Most of the divers were civilians, and one, Tom Mason, our Club Diving Officer, was a Garda. High on adrenalin, they took to this novel diving transport like ducks to water. Having made three lifts from the car park, the helicopter left us for Baldonnel for the duration of the dive, to return after ninety minutes as I had requested. The dive itself was uneventful, the lake was shallow, and the water was very cold and dark. We found nothing of interest and the return airlift from the ridge to the car park was carried out without difficulty. The body of the missing man was found some months later on a remote slope of the mountain. This again was a great experience for all those involved, and it helped to reinforce the strong bond between the Club and the Defence Forces that has existed since the Club was formed in the Curragh in 1958.

Circumstances in 2000 are such that very few divers, particularly in the Dublin area, are ever called upon to take part in events as described above. It is the last thing in which a new diver could expect to find himself involved. A sports diver learns to dive so that he can enjoy and explore the sea, not to take part in such unpleasant work. Despite this, I am satisfied that if the divers of today were called upon, they would respond willingly.

While divers in the Dublin area are not normally called upon to assist the State, it is still a common occurrence elsewhere in the country. In cases of drowning or suspected drowning, where there is a suspicion of a body in a lake, well, or at the end of a pier, the Gardai would often call on local divers before they look for the official Garda Diving Unit. Sometimes they would have no option as the Diving Unit might well be on another search operation. Many such calls seem to occur during bad weather or at night. Whenever divers were asked to help out, they willingly responded and gave of their best efforts, time and money. They were not paid, they were rarely given even minimal

Galway 'Rapid Reaction" group, c. 1960
Dr. Jim Doyle, Peadar Canavan, Peter O'Beirn, George Ryder and Kerry McConn.

expenses, nor would they have looked for such either. Much more seriously, they were not covered by insurance. Yet divers have always felt that it was their civic duty to react to requests for assistance.

Galway Docks has been the scene of very many accidents, mainly where cars were driven or have fallen into the sea. In the early 1960s, members of the Galway University Sub Aqua Club, were being called out at frequent intervals by the Gardai to dive into the docks to recover bodies or vehicles. They became so efficient at this that they felt that it might even be possible to get to the scene quickly enough to save lives, as opposed to merely bringing up the bodies. So they agreed to form a small 'rapid reaction' group in conjunction with the Gardai and they planned and trained with that aim in mind. They had to ensure each night that their cars were packed with their diving gear, that their cylinders were filled, and that they were ready for the call. And they very nearly succeeded, because on one occasion they dragged a man out of his car and up on to the quay wall, to discover that he was still alive. Unfortunately, despite the best efforts of the ambulance crew and doctors, he died later. They were very proud of their little team and they worked very well with the Gardai and the Corporation, who were most appreciative of their actions. While they had turned out on numerous occasions and risked their lives and personal diving equipment in the service of others, they never looked for payment for their services. Their principal concern was to get insurance cover for taking risks on behalf of the State.

However, neither the Corporation, the County Council, nor the Departments of Justice or of Local Government would agree to give them insurance cover. So reluctantly they were forced to give up the 'rapid-reaction' project in order to protect themselves, although members of the Club still respond to Garda requests to this very day. The situation has not changed. All over the country, divers are being called upon to assist in the search for missing people, and they willingly give of their services. The relatives are most appreciative, as are the local politicians and Gardai. However, the State has never arranged to introduce legislation to protect the divers upon whose services they are so happy to call.

The number of searches and recoveries conducted by amateur volunteers are legion, and unfortunately many are unrecorded. Some are well publicised, such as those three divers of the Kilkenny club, John and Bill Wyse and John Ryan, who rescued four canoeists on the River Nore in 1978. They received an award under the "National Rescue Award Scheme", presented by Fergus O'Brien, TD. In 1986, Manuel di Lucia received a similar award for his part in the rescue of a young woman in particularly difficult conditions in Kilkee Bay. It was an appropriate award as Manuel had been the instigator of one of the first voluntary Sea Rescue Centres in the country, at Kilkee, which was opened officially only a month later. The funds for the Centre were raised by voluntary local efforts, and the example of Kilkee was followed at many locations such as the one at Achill Island, County Mayo in 1987. This latter was destroyed in January 1991 in one of the worst storms experienced in the area from many years.

The same willingness to risk life, limb and personal property is shown all over the country by other organisations such as the Mountain, Cave, Cliff, and Coast Rescue; parachute groups; the 60 or more voluntary Sea Rescue teams around the coast; not to mention the long-established Lifeboat stations. There is no good reason why amateurs should continue to take the risks and to tolerate the circumstances under which they work, but they do, and their willingness was and is being exploited by the State. It is surely not beyond the power of the State to devise a scheme whereby once divers, members of a Sea Rescue unit, or others, are formally called out by Gardai, they can be covered by state insurance for the duration of the call-out. CFT has, to its credit, ensured that divers are covered by its own national insurance policy in situations where such divers have been called upon officially by the State. However, this is a third-party policy only and it does not cover loss or damage to personal diving equipment or more importantly diver injury or loss of life.

Michael Heffernan, family man, amateur diver, long-time member and leader of the Grainne Mhaoil Sub Aqua Club in Ballina, Co. Mayo thought nothing of saying yes when called upon. With others of the Rescue Team, he went out in the dark on a stormy night to try and save a number of people who were known to have become trapped at the back of a sea-cave. He lost his life in attempting to swim through heaving waves to bring hope to the small group. One of the group was already dead, and the others were no doubt wondering if they would ever again see the light of day. Fortunately, they were rescued.

The memorial to Michael Heffernan at Lackan Pier, Co. Mayo. Photo by Eddie Bourke.

For all the mostly unrecorded searches and recoveries, willingly and unselfishly carried out over the years in hazardous conditions by divers across this island - for all the hundreds of hours spent underwater by these amateur volunteer divers – Michael Heffernan surely must be the very epitome of the spirit that drives them to these unselfish acts, and he must be remembered for his sacrifice.

The sacrifice of Michael Heffernan and the bravery of Club-mate Josie Barratt, and Garda Divers Ciaran Doyle, David Mulhall, Sean O'Connell and others have been acknowledged by the State. Dr Michael Woods, Minister for the Marine made the presentations at Dublin Castle on Friday 27th of February 1999. In October 2000, a very fine life-sized bronze statue of Michael Heffernan in diving suit was unveiled at Lackan Pier, near Killala, Co. Mayo by the Memorial Fund Committee - the first such statue ever to be unveiled in Ireland.

# CHAPTER 14

# UNDERWATER WORK EXPERIENCES

Happily, not all calls for our services and developing expertise involved the search for bodies. There were many tasks presented to us that were far less serious and much more congenial. One of the earliest involved the recovery of a yacht that had sunk in Dun Laoghaire as a result of a very bad storm in November 1961. The owner was known to Johnny King and we agreed to raise it for him, something we had only managed with much smaller vessels up to this. The yacht weighed about eight tons, and it was lying on its side on the bottom in 15 feet of water, near the West Pier, where the last of the Lightships had been anchored.

Having surveyed the wreck, we set about preparing a number of large home-heating oil tanks, which were going to do the lifting for us. All the tank openings except the large inspection ports on the top were welded shut; then brackets and cleats were welded on to the tanks to hold the heavy-duty lifting straps in place. We acquired a large quantity of webbing and heavy u-bolts, to be made into slings for lifting the yacht. Johnny King had a catamaran that was ideal for carrying large and awkward loads, being essentially a large flat floating platform with a fifty-horse power outboard motor at the stern.

So on the 18th of November, Johnny King, Larry Bradley, Hal Jackson and myself went out in bitterly cold weather to start the lifting operation. To our surprise, the visibility underwater was not too bad, so we were able to see what we were doing most of the time, except when we stirred up the silt. First, we lowered the two tanks, one at a time, by partly filling them with water. The tanks were positioned, one over the bow and one at the stern, and secured in place by means of the straps and 'u-bolts'. We then tightened the straps as best as we could and surfaced.

The tanks were positioned so that the large inspection ports were facing downwards. We proceeded to bring down some spare cylinders of compressed air and started to release the air into the tanks. For a long time nothing happened, but then the straps began to tighten. We made sure to be out of the way in case any tank should decide break free and to take off suddenly for the surface. Eventually the yacht broke from the bottom, and rose sluggishly towards the surface. It did not come right up to the surface of course, only the lifting tanks, the mast and some other portions of the superstructure became visible, the yacht being suspended beneath the water by the slings. We then started to tow the yacht very slowly towards the Coal Harbour until it grounded in shallower water. We then had to wait for low tide, when we dived again to shorten the straps once more. When the tide returned, it again lifted the yacht. We repeated this process a number of times until we finally brought the yacht close enough to the quay wall to be reached by a large mobile crane, hired by the grateful owner. Mission accomplished.

*   *   *   *   *   *   *   *

Another and more unusual request was received by the Club in the Autumn of 1963. For years, the Island Golf Club at Malahide had been depending on a well for all its fresh water needs. Over time, the well was unable to meet the increasing demand, and also the water was turning brackish, particularly during the summers. The Golf Club urgently needed to tap into the public supply. Now, despite its name, the Club is not situated on an island, but rather on a long spit of sand dunes. It was accessed by road from the north, and by ferry from Malahide, a much shorter distance across the Sound. The nearest public water supply to the Golf Club lay directly across the 400 metres of the sound on the coast road at Malahide itself. Their problem was either to pay for a long and presumably expensive water supply to be brought in from the North, or to find some means of getting the water across the Sound from Malahide. It so happened that the President of the Golf Club was also the managing director of Unidare, a large company that specialised in all forms of plastic piping. John Hailes, a prominent member of the Curragh Club, also worked at Unidare. The MD had been informed that John was a diver and he asked him if the Curragh Sub Aqua Club could help.

Unidare would provide the 1-inch plastic piping and the County Council would make the connection across the road to the water system. It remained up to us to do the bit in the middle. When we surveyed the sea bottom, which was about 15 feet deep in the centre of the Sound, we discovered that it was clear of obstructions, rocks or weed, and we assumed that it would be easy to dig a trench with our knives. But we were wrong. Under the inch or so of sand and silt, there was a layer of hard-packed dark marl that proved to be very difficult to dig and to shift. This was quite a setback, but ever the optimists, we struck a deal with the Golf Club and set to.

Johnny King, always the practical one, had an idea. "We will plough a furrow across the sound, using a farm plough". We all laughed first but then said it was worth trying. By coincidence, I had very recently seen an old-fashioned plough, of the horse-drawn type, in a garage on the outskirts of Kildare town. So Johnny and I went down, bought it for £5 and brought it back to Malahide. We tried to pull the plough, first using Johnny's boat, and later, using a borrowed tractor. Neither method moved the plough even one metre.

Eventually we acquired the loan of a hand-operated winch and 1,000 feet of steel cable and set it up on the Malahide side of the channel. Shane Gray, Jimmy Flynn, Shane O'Connor, Mickey Lynch, Martin McHale, Eric Gregan and many others were waiting and ready to get to work. As quickly as we could, we placed the plough at the water's edge on the golf club side of the sound and attached the cable from it to the winch, which was on the sand on the opposite side of the Sound. Johnny's catamaran had come into its own again for the duration of the operation.

I was first in to start the ploughing job, complete with aqualung on my back, holding on to the handles of the plough. The team on the winch were given the signal and started winching. Each time the long lever on the winch was moved through about 100 degrees, approximately one metre of the cable was wound on to the drum. It would have been a slow process at that rate of movement. But as it turned out, we did not get far at all. The plough just could not be held in its conventional and necessary attitude in relation to the sea bottom. Once the strain was applied, the plough simply tipped over on its nose, and no combination of the strongest and heaviest divers in the group could prevent this happening. Back to the drawing boards.

As usual it was Johnny who solved the problem. He took the plough away to be modified. He arranged to have a curved metal skid, on a long tubular bar, welded at an angle on to the front of the plough. This had the effect of preventing the plough from doing a nose-dive when the strain was applied. The modification worked very well, and it was only a matter of patience before the furrow was ploughed and we were ready for the pipeline.

Approximately 1,200 feet of 1-inch pipe on a huge wooden reel was then delivered to the site by Unidare. We pulled the pipe across the Sound, using the catamaran. This was an easy task, as the pipe floated. But when we tried to pull the pipe to the bottom, it stayed on the surface no matter what we did. So we had to fill it with sea-water to weigh it down, and even then we had to go along the pipe underwater and place additional lead weights, supplied to us by Unidare, on the pipe at intervals. As the pipe was put in place in the furrow, divers, working outwards from both sides of the Sound at the same time, started to cover it in. This proved to be easier than expected because they were able to backfill with the loose material displaced by the plough. This would not have been possible with sand or silt, but because of the heavy, almost plastic nature of the marl, it worked quite well.

The work was interrupted by a storm at one stage, which broke the pipe at the deepest part of the channel, where we had not yet buried it. It snapped as a result of being tugged violently to and fro. Fortunately it was repaired very easily in situ by two divers, using a simple repair kit provided by Unidare. The entire operation lasted for nearly three weeks as we were only working on Wednesdays and at the weekends, as we all had to look after our day jobs as well.

No doubt the golfers must have had great misgivings at our antics. They had placed their trust in an amateur group who appeared to be simply having great fun at their expense. On a personal basis, it was a very difficult time for me too. I was pre-occupied with trying to move into our new, and as yet incomplete, bungalow, at Kilcullen. The water was switched on in a ceremony at the Golf Club, on Friday 25th of October. We got great praise and publicity for our work, and more importantly we got a fat check for Club funds, which enabled us to buy our first heavy-duty, trailer-mounted compressor. The pipe supplied fresh water at 240 gallons per hour to the Golf Club for more than twenty years. At an early stage in our efforts, I had dubbed the pipe-laying project 'Operation PLUTO' (Pipe Line Under The Ocean), after the line laid across the Channel to supply the Allied landings in Normandy in 1944 with petrol. But when Tom Mason heard this he 'harrumphed'; "if you ask me, I think it should have been called 'Operation Mickey Mouse'". Perhaps he was right!

*　*　*　*　*　*　*　*

The Emerald Star Line was a Guinness company that operated a fleet of 'self-drive' cabin cruisers on the Shannon. Some of these vessels were concrete-hulled. In August 1965, one of this class of vessel was driven up on the rocks on a small island opposite the Hodson Bay Hotel on Lough Ree, north of Athlone. Having been approached by the insurance assessor, Tom Stopford, of Dalkey, a small group of us agreed to recover the cruiser and to deliver it to the repair yards at Shannon Harbour. When we inspected the cruiser, on Thursday 2nd September, we discovered that the port side had been badly damaged. The hull consisted of a number of over-lapping layers of a fine wire mesh onto which were sprayed many coats of concrete. This method of construction provided a strong hull that required minimum maintenance. We found that a large section of the concrete had been fractured, and in many places, it had disappeared altogether, leaving the wire mesh exposed. The damaged area was about ten feet long and, measuring from the keel outwards, about six feet at it's widest.

Johnny King, Shane Gray, John Hailes and I set to work, mixing cement and smoothing it into place underwater. This would not work with conventional cement, but we were adding a quick-setting chemical, which ensured that the mixture set very quickly. Two worked in the cabin, mixing cement and two worked in the water spreading the cement by hand. A handful at a time was passed to a diver who then ducked down and plastered the cement by hand over a section of the damaged hull. It was slow and tedious work, while above water, we were being assaulted by midges, but we persisted. John Weaving, a renowned river and canal expert, who himself lived on a converted former Guinness barge, advised us on many aspects of the work, and on the subsequent journey down the river.

After a fair number of hours, clocked up over about two weeks of Wednesdays and week-ends, we felt confident enough to hire no less than three water pumps, one very large, the other two of modest capacity. We also hired a local boat to tow us down river to Shannon Harbour. But first we had to move the cruiser about 500 metres across the Bay to the pier at the Hodson Bay Hotel. It was with great excitement that we watched the cruiser rise up, and even though the water was still pouring in through the damaged areas, the pumps were able to keep it afloat until we tied up at the pier. The major test was still ahead of us though, as we had undertaken to deliver the cruiser to Shannon Harbour, on the Grand Canal, some miles downstream of Athlone.

On the following Saturday, we started the pumps, which were strapped to the deck. The cruiser rose up and stayed up, while the towing barge took us out into the channel and down the lake towards Athlone. It was tricky work trying to coax the cruiser to follow the towing barge into the lock without incurring further damage. We had to contend with the swift current, a strong wind, and the extremely narrow entrance to the lock itself. All was going well for us, and we started to relax as we got into the wide, deep and smooth stretches of the Shannon below Athlone. We were still in our diving suits, and where there is a strong wind, a diver in a wet wetsuit can get chilled very quickly. So we huddled out of the wind in a dry part of the cruiser, drinking hot tea and other stronger beverages from flasks. But we had started to relax too soon. A new emergency hit us - all the pumps stopped working at the same time!

Water pumps had one very annoying feature. As soon as all the available water was pumped out, the pump would come to a halt. It was a simple but slow process to prime the pump with water and to start it up once more. In our case, this would normally not be a problem, as the two other pumps, working together, were more than capable of keeping us afloat. But now all three had stopped and we were in big trouble. We were still moving downstream under tow, aided by the flow of the river, but we were also moving in another new direction. We were moving towards the bottom of the river! Rarely have four divers moved so fast. Our bad language burned up the ozone and probably some parts of the deck. The pumps had fortunately been placed on the deck, and not down below, where the rapidly rising water would have prevented us getting at them. So it was possible to work on them, and the water we used for priming was very close to hand, and getting closer by the minute! We managed to prime the pumps and get rid of some of the water just in time to prevent a disaster. The emergency passed and the rest was 'plain sailing' to Shannon Harbour on the Grand Canal where we handed the cruiser over to the boatyard for repair. We were later informed that it was repaired and put back into service within months, to the satisfaction of the owners.

An interesting aspect of this recovery was that, shortly after we had started work, another similar cruiser had gone aground further up Lough Ree from our location. A well-known personality in Athlone who owned a powerful launch, proposed to Emerald Star that he would recover this cruiser using different means, and that he would not take forever "like those f—-ing divers at Hodson Bay". He was given the job, and he did recover the cruiser, but he hauled it off the rocks by brute force, and it became a total write-off.

*     *     *     *     *     *     *     *

In 1963, Irish Lights decided to replace the Lightship on the Kish Bank, outside Dublin Port, with a new design of lighthouse that had been proven to be effective in Scandinavia. It was designed as a manned station. Lighthouses are usually constructed on rocks or headlands, but this new concept involved placing the lighthouse on the sea bottom, in this case on the Kish sandbank, at the approaches to Dublin Bay. Irish Lights awarded the contract to Christiani-Nielsen, a Danish company that had much experience in this field. In essence, the design involved building a structure in a number of hollow telescopic sections, one inside the other, on a circular base. The entire structure would then be floated out to the Kish Bank and placed on a prepared position on the seabed. Huge quantities of sand and water were then to be pumped into the base under great pressure, forcing the inner tower sections upwards to their planned height. Finally, thousands of tons of boulders were to be placed inside and outside around the base to help keep the entire structure in position on the seabed.

The work began inside a caisson in the Coal Quay at Dun Laoghaire Harbour. After the initial work on the base had progressed sufficiently, the engineers removed the caisson and allowed the circular base to float. Through Johnny King, we were approached to provide diving services to the company. The first diving task involved us in some of the preparatory tests in Scotsman's Bay while the construction continued in the harbour. The engineers built a one-tenth scale model of the final design and they needed to test it in the sea. I had not been present in Scotsman's Bay for the early tests of the scale-model, which weighed about five tons, but clearly something had gone wrong, because it was now on its side on the bottom and our task was to recover it. Because of his involvement in the salvaging of some of the German wrecks in Scapa Flow, ex-RN Commander Gibney, who lived in Dalkey, was contracted to Christiani-Neilsen to recover the miniature Kish for the engineers. He hired a trawler and a barge, with which he intended to lift the model, and he needed divers to attach the lifting cables. Jimmy Flynn, Johnny King, Shane Gray, Martin McHale and I made up the diving team, not realising just what was ahead of us.

On 28th August 1963, we met Comdr. Gibney at 06.45 in Alexandra Basin in Dublin Port, boarded the trawler and set out for Scotsman's Bay, towing the barge behind us. Our first dives were made in order to shackle the lifting chains to the miniature Kish, which was lying on its side in about 35 feet of water. Like all tasks associated with the sea, what appears to be a simple job from the surface, turns out to be quite difficult underwater. Jimmy and I dived first, and we found that the lifting chains were some distance away from where they should have been, i.e. almost on top of the unit. We had to put the chains over our shoulders and carry them the ten or fifteen metres along the sea bottom to the model. It was heavy, exhausting work, made more difficult because we were wearing fins, which meant that we had to walk backwards.

After putting the chains on the lifting eyes, we were very glad to get back on board the trawler for a badly needed rest. There we discussed a condition known to divers as 'beating the valve'. This is not a medical term, but a diving one. We were not worrying about our hearts, we were talking about our demand valves. To beat your demand valve meant that you were breathing so heavily underwater that the demand valve simply could not supply you with enough air. The DV is only a mechanical device and its capacity to deliver air is limited by its design. It is potentially a very dangerous situation for a diver. When the condition arises, the diver should, if he has sufficient air and bottom time remaining, stop what he is doing to rest and wait until his breathing rate returns to normal.

Once we had the chains in place it was a matter of sitting around for most of the morning, waiting for the tide to lift the barge and the scale model to which it was attached. By now I had started to call the mini-Kish 'Sputnik' after the Soviet satellite. The tide came in and all that happened was that the barge started to list more and more dramatically by the bow, but there was no shifting Sputnik. We did many more dives, at one stage to untangle the chains, which because of the movement of the barge, had become wrapped around the model. We were eventually forced to retire, defeated, to Alexandra Basin, after 14 exhausting hours of frustration and about five dives each. However, we were assured that we would be called upon again.

On 5th September, we were back at Alexandra Basin where we slept on board the trawler, as we had an early start next morning. Because of the tide, we had to depart at 05.30, with the first dive at 08.30. The sea was considerably calmer than on the previous occasion, but we still had to endure another very difficult day. All our efforts were devoted to getting the model of the lighthouse into an upright position, so that the 'hydraulic ram', the most important central part of the model, could be recovered. The engineers needed it badly for evaluation purposes. At 14.00 we finally got the 'Sputnik' into an upright position, only to find that three of the many heavy bolts which held the 'ram' in position could not be budged. They had been strained when the scale-model had fallen over. We put a marker buoy on the model and retired yet again, defeated and exhausted, again each of us having made several dives.

We returned to the fray on 17th October, leaving the pier at Dun Laoghaire at 04.45. We towed the barge out and were in place and diving by 09.00, but this time the Commander had hired a powered winch. At 16.00, probably because of all our swearing, the model finally yielded up the much-prized centre section, and we went home tired but jubilant. As in most underwater work, persistence had paid off once more.

Meanwhile, back at the construction site within the Coal Harbour, it had become obvious to the engineers that, each time the tide went out, the now-floating circular base settled back on the bottom and was suffering structural damage as a result. They became very concerned about the damage, and felt that they needed divers to carry out regular inspections of the underside of the base. Having proved our worth in the recovery of the vital hydraulic ram, we were approached again to take on this new task. Johnny King, Jimmy Flynn, John Hailes, Shane Gray, Eric Gregan, myself and others, depending on availability, took turns in carrying out inspections of the sides and underneath of the base.

All during the period of time that we were involved with Christiani-Nielsen, we were also busy with the laying of the water pipeline to Malahide Golf Club. It was an indication of just how much demand there was for diving skills at that time, and how few divers nationally were available to meet the demand. Divers from the Irish Sub Aqua Club and the other clubs were also occupied with various diving tasks across the country around that time.

It was a weird sensation to be diving under a floating concrete structure that weighed as much as two thousand tons. The water was quite shallow under some parts of the base, which added to the strangeness of the dive, and it meant that we had to be wary of the tide. One should not be at the wrong end of the base when the tide went out! While it was bright at the edges of the base, the light faded as we moved in towards the centre and we had to use lights to search for cracks. When we found any, as we did, we had to measure them for depth, direction and length, and then we had to plot their locations relative to a datum point. It was very easy to become disoriented under the base, as after a short time, what had been a flat, featureless 'ceiling' became the 'floor'. Because it was usually too dark to see without a light, the exhaled bubbles, on which a diver normally relies to indicate 'up', were not easily seen or sensed. The bubbles in any case were not free to ascend vertically, they were being deflected away by the concrete 'roof'.

The sound of the work in progress above us was very loud. We could hear the pounding of the cement mixers, the cranes, (there were several mounted within the unit), the compressors and the pumps. It was impossible not to imagine that at any moment, some heavy machine might be dropped from a crane, to come crashing through the concrete onto one's head.

Johnny had an underwater camera with which he took pictures of the cracks. On one occasion, we were asked to release large quantities of sawdust under the cracks to assist the engineers to locate them from 'top-side'. After each dive we had to report our findings and measurements to the engineer on duty. Because we were discovering damage on the underside of the unit, and because they themselves could see some of this from inside the structure, the engineers decided to move the base to a safer location. We carried out a number of inspections of the harbour floor for them, to determine the suitability of two proposed locations. One of the proposed locations was where the lightships were moored on the West Pier, and the other was at the end of the Coal Quay pier, near where the ice plant is situated today. They decided eventually that the end of the pier was better for their needs. That move solved the problem of the regular groundings at least, and work proceeded apace. But then the inevitable occurred.

Anyone who has experience of diving work will realise that there is at least one emergency or major setback built in to every operation where the sea is involved. Equally, anyone who knows Dun Laoghaire Harbour will know of the serious flaw in its design. Whenever a severe north-easterly gale blows, the inner harbour is exposed to the full force of the wind, and the waves come marching in from outside, to cause mayhem in the Coal Harbour. The lighthouse project emergency arrived with a vengeance in the form of a storm-force NE gale. On the 4th of December 1963, I got a call in the evening to come up to Dublin immediately; all divers were needed to help with the effort to save the base.

We changed into our diving suits on the pier at about 9.30 at night, watching all the feverish activity on the unit. It apparently had started to crash against the pier wall, cracks were appearing all over the structure and there was real possibility that it would become a total loss. We were provided with an inflatable and a huge quantity of oakum, which had been prepared in advance for us. We were told to select a section of 'wall' and to get on with the work. What followed was a remarkable experience, and it is very vivid in my memory to this day.

Johnny and I dived first, moving right up to the wall of the base, where we started to push long strips of oakum into the underwater sections of the bigger cracks, while Shane and Jimmy worked from the inflatable, stuffing the over-water sections. It was difficult enough trying to stuff oakum into the cracks that could be seen, but when it came to following a crack underwater, it became dangerous because everything was in motion. The waves were smashing against the base, and after a short time in the water, it seemed to me that it was the base itself that was heaving up and down, not myself and the water. It was a most disagreeable sensation. The company had brought in extra manpower, as well as additional floodlighting, pumps, and other machinery in an attempt to save the base, and the noise was horrendous, made worse by the howling gale. As my head was alternatively under and over the water, because of the waves, the sound in my ears was rising and falling in intensity, and the intense floodlighting appeared to be flashing on and off like huge disco lights. Under the water, the noise was so much louder than anything we had experienced to date, because of the additional machinery. It has remained in my memory, rather like a scene from Dante's Inferno, assuming that Dante could have envisaged such a hellish scene set in a modern context.

We worked for a chaotic and exhausting four hours or so, changing around from time to time. Johnny lost a brand new underwater light, the inflatable got punctured, and we did what we could, but   eventually we had to give up out of sheer exhaustion. The other workers continued with the struggle until morning while we were informed that we were required again first thing in the morning. To our relief, the latter was cancelled before we left the site near midnight. But the result was inevitable: while the base had remained afloat, it had been so badly damaged that it was decided to abandon it and to start again from scratch to construct a new one. The abandoned base was then used as a platform on which the new one was to be constructed. When the engineers were finished with it, about a year later, the old base was towed down to Greystones Harbour, where it was sunk to form an extension to the existing pier. That is why the extension to the pier there has such an unlikely circular shape.

The new lighthouse unit was finished without further disaster, and it was towed out to the Kish Bank, sunk in the pre-prepared position and the remainder of the work was completed in situ. It was the first and only lighthouse of this design to be erected in

Ireland and it has continued to guide and protect shipping into and out of Dublin Port ever since. It is now an unmanned automatic station.

*   *   *   *   *   *   *   *

Another more bizarre task was presented to us in May 1970 when I received a phone call from an official in the Waterworks department of Dublin Corporation. They were having problems with the flow of drinking water to the city through the aqueduct from the Treatment Works at Ballymore Eustace. Over the years, there had been a build-up of deposits on the inside of the pipeline and this was placing a restriction on the volume of water that could be passed down to the rapidly growing city of Dublin. They needed to get rid of these deposits and they needed divers to do the job and to ensure that the pipes were being cleaned properly. In addition, the Corporation officials wished that the cleaning work would be completed without interruption to the supply, a stipulation that complicated things for us. So Jimmy Flynn and I went out to do a reconnaissance, already mentally committed to taking on the job.

However, when we had a look into the pipe at the first siphon just below the Treatment Works, we began to have some doubts. The pipe was made of concrete, about six feet in diameter, and there was no illumination apart from that supplied by the open manhole. The flow of water was impressively dark, swift, and silent. They did assure us that they would reduce the flow during the periods we were in the aqueduct, and they also assured us that the water volume could not be increased by accident while we were inside. The Corporation had previously prepared a heavy four-wheeled trolley, onto which were attached two flexible metal 'hoops', designed to press outward in all directions under tension against the inner walls of the pipe. A series of ordinary household scrubbing brushes were fixed onto the metal 'hoops', arranged end to end in continuous lines. It was a simple idea but it worked very well.

The first siphon at the head of the pipeline was like a small room, big enough to facilitate the placing of the trolley in the water. Once inside, the trolley could not be removed again until we had reached the end of the line near Blackchurch, where again there was a large siphon. The aqueduct ran across country from Ballymore Eustace, for a total of approximately 12 miles, with access manholes at irregular intervals along the line. The intervals ranged from as little as 100 metres to over 700 metres, the average distance being in the region of 500 metres. The access manholes were narrow and had metal rungs for climbing vertically up and down, and some of them were well below ground level.

Jimmy Flynn speaking to Micky Lynch prior to resuming work in the pipeline, with an official of Dublin Corporation.

Having decided to take on the job, we set up a Standard Operating Procedure (SOP) that, not surprisingly, placed a great emphasis on safety. One of the first tasks was to get ourselves covered by insurance. Next, we provided ourselves with underwater lights and helmets, and we arranged to have portable radios, one at each of the opened manholes. Some of the manholes had not been opened for years and the Corporation workers had to search for some of them before they could be dug out and opened. We arranged for four divers to take part: Mickey Lynch, Jimmy Flynn, John Hailes and myself. We had decided that two divers would proceed along the aqueduct pushing the cleaning trolley, while two other divers had to be in place at the bottom of the rungs at the next manhole downstream. Movement was not to start until they were in position and gave the go-ahead. They were there to provide assistance to the divers in the pipeline, should it be needed.

The principal problem was that it would be very difficult, if not impossible, once inside the pipe, to walk back upstream against the press of the water. Finning or swimming was certainly out of the question. We had to carry underwater lights with us also, as once we moved away from the manhole at which we had entered the pipeline, it became totally dark until the next open manhole came into view. It was not a place for anyone who suffered from claustrophobia. We did not use aqualungs, as there was not a need for them, but we kept four filled aqualungs on stand-by, two at each opened manhole, in case they were needed. We did carry our fins, masks and snorkels with us, attached to our weight belts. The trolley did not require much pushing by us, as we had originally feared. Once we grabbed on to the trolley, the water pressure on our bodies was enough to provide forward motion at something less than walking pace. Fortunately, all went smoothly, and no serious emergencies arose during the two weeks of the operation. It was easily the strangest 'diving' operation any of us had ever undertaken, but it worked and we left yet another satisfied customer.

Looking back at those events, we were very amateurish, but very lucky also. We certainly took many risks but we never experienced any serious problems. Tragically, a diver from another club lost his life in the lake at Poulaphouca around that time.

We learned as we went along, and in the spirit of diving that still applies today, we shared our experiences with our friends in the general diving community. Today, the Health and Safety at Work Act would rightly prohibit amateurs like us from taking on tasks of the sort described here, and that is as it should be. However, it was great fun while it lasted. But with age comes caution and the following saying is often quoted in diving circles. *'There are old divers and there are bold divers, but there are no old, bold divers'!*

# CHAPTER 15

# THE ARMY DIVING GROUP

When the Curragh Sub Aqua Club was established in 1958, most of the members were commissioned officers of the Defence Forces. As diving continued to develop in Ireland, many of these individuals became very involved in the organisation and administration of sports diving and also featured prominently in competitions held at national level, such as spearfishing and fin-swimming. These individuals were also involved in many search and recovery diving missions through the country, thus gaining a high profile and a good reputation for the sport within the Defence Forces. It was as a direct result of individual Army divers' enthusiasm for the sport, that the Army Athletics Association formally accepted diving as one of its recognised sports in 1964.

In 1961, Shane O'Connor and myself, both Captains at that time, were required to submit a report on an underwater capability for the Forces to the Director of Training, Defence Forces Headquarters (DFHQ). While it was well received, nothing transpired from our proposals until another report was requested of me in July 1979. It remains a source of great pride and satisfaction to myself, Shane O'Connor and others that the professional diving elements existing today in the Defence Forces may have had their origins, at least in part, in the formation of the Curragh Sub Aqua Club back in 1958.

A United Nations mission called the United Nations Truce Supervisory Organisation (UNTSO) was established at the end of the Israeli War of Independence in 1948. The function of the Mission was to supervise the borders between the new Israel and the surrounding Arab states. From the beginning, UNTSO proved to be very popular with Irish observers as families were permitted to accompany them. The Headquarters was in Jerusalem with subsidiary local HQs in Cairo, Damascus, Amman and Beirut. For those officers who were divers, it was the perfect opportunity to dive in the Red Sea, easily accessible by road. I was lucky to be posted to serve with UNTSO in January 1974 for a tour of eighteen months. At my first station at Tiberius, I experienced some very pleasant snorkel diving in the Sea of Galilee. I was very surprised at the large numbers of fish to be seen, mainly the St Peter's Fish, right off Ron Beach in Tiberius, where hundreds of people were swimming and sub-bathing.

After three months working the Observation Posts on the Golan, I was transferred to UNTSO Headquarters in Jerusalem from where I managed to visit Eilat on a number of occasions over the following months. In addition, a friend of mine, Conor Craig from the Belfast Branch of the British Sub Aqua Club, made contact with me. He was working as an instructor at the Royal Jordanian School of Diving in Aqaba, Jordan. In April 1975 he invited me and my family to stay with him for a week's diving. The diving conditions at Aqaba, a few kilometres from the border with Saudia Arabia, were much better than at Eilat. At that time, there was a smaller population on the Jordanian side of the Gulf, less shipping traffic, while the tourist industry was not as well developed as it is today. To a great degree, the reefs were in pristine condition and the fish and other marine creatures were present in great numbers and varieties.

During my time in Jerusalem, I also took the opportunity to visit the Dead Sea near Jericho. I had been warned of the dangers of accidentally drinking the water, and I was told to take an extra-careful shower afterwards to wash away the corrosive water. I had taken along my fins, mask and snorkel with the intention of inspecting the sea bottom. The first surprise for me was that the water smarted and stung all the orifices of my body and every minor scratch on my skin. Although I did not allow the water into my mouth, on my lips it tasted like the salts, such as Epsom Salts, that are taken for stomach upsets. Also, such was the buoyancy of the water it proved to be impossible to reach the bottom even in the shallows, without wearing my weight belt, which I had managed to leave behind me in Jerusalem. By carrying a large stone and struggling furiously, I managed to reach the bottom at about four metres, where I hurriedly grabbed a few small stones before being dragged back to the surface by the powerful buoyancy.

\*     \*     \*     \*     \*     \*     \*     \*

It was only when units were sent to Cyprus in 1964 to serve with the United Nations Force in Cyprus (UNFICYP), that sports diving for all ranks really became popular. I served in Cyprus as a staff captain in the HQ of the 41st Battalion for six months from October 1964 and I was lucky to manage some diving and a lot of snorkelling. Captains Shane Gray and Ronnie Gallagher were also on the island, both serving with the 3rd Infantry Group, another smaller Irish unit whose tour on the Island overlapped with that of my own. We joined forces on a number of occasions to dive on the South coast near the British Sovereign Base at Dhekelia. I wrote an article for my club magazine afterwards about one of my dives. The article is reproduced here and it gives a flavour of the conditions we experienced in the Mediterranean.

'It was a beautiful sunny Sunday morning in November 1964 as I left Wolfe Tone Camp in Famagusta and headed south for Dhekelia some 16 miles away. I had planned to meet Shane Gray and Ronnie Gallagher there at the Club Rooms of the Dhekelia Special Branch of the British Sub Aqua Club. We were in receipt of a standing invitation from the committee of the Branch to dive with them on Sundays. Shane or Ronnie failed to show up, however. It was late in the season for those acclimatised to the island, but to me after only four weeks, it was as warm as the best summer at home. Only two members of the Branch, Taffy and Deirdre arrived. We collected our aqualungs and headed off for Cape Greco, a large headland that forms part of the SE region of the Island.

We waded out over the low rocks and sank gratefully into the tepid water, not requiring our diving suits. As the coast was very low-lying in this area, we had to snorkel straight out on the surface for about 350 metres before it became deep enough to warrant submerging. The first impression, as always in the Med, was that of a large empty room. The sun sparkled in the ripples of sand on the bottom, very bare due to the lack of vegetation. Visibility was excellent as we arrived on the bottom at about 15 metres, still heading out from the shore. After a short while, that initial impression of emptiness was altered, as I realised that there was a good variety of marine life, once I discovered where to look. Many small multi-coloured fish darted around, some of them looking like versions of our own Atlantic wrasse. We saw several small grouper, one of them being about 10/12lbs, (4kg). We came to a flat 'plain' at about 20 metres, well silted over and with a lot of eelgrass, the most common Mediterranean seaweed. Here and there could be seen a number of small pinna shells, and I picked one up as it was empty. As I was looking at it more closely, I noticed that there was a very small octopus trying to climb out over one of the shell halves.

I forgot all about the others and the dive and watched my hitchhiker intently. He could hardly be more than three inches across and he was two-toned in colour. Half of his body was brown, copying the brown of the shell, while the other half was white, to reflect the white of the mother-of-pearl inside. He was clinging on for dear life as he was moving through the water at what was, for him, an unaccustomed rate of knots. By turning the shell over, I was able to prevent him from escaping, by using the pressure of my forward motion to force him back against the shell. He was a perfect miniature octopus and he had that appealing air of innocence that all young creatures possess. I thought of other divers who captured octopuses and who had persuaded them to perform 'dances' by stroking their tentacles. But whether this little fellow could perform or not, I never found out.

The octopus is supposed to be one of the more intelligent animals in the sea, possessing several near-human traits. He shows his emotions by changing colour, and he constructs a home fitted with a hall-door made from a suitable seashell, a flat stone or a broken shard of pottery. Other random octopus thoughts crossed my mind as we approached the shore and the water became shallow: the unpleasant 'octopus-wrestling' competition held annually in the United States, where the winner in 1964 had landed a 200lbs monster; the extremely pleasant meal of octopus under the olive trees at the Club Mediterranee camp at Palinuro in southern Italy in 1961.

Having reached the point where I would have to stand up or else scrape my knees, I decided to release my passenger. He puffed out the most perfect little cloud of 'ink' and shot off, jet propelling himself frantically into the safety of a large rock. The 'ink' had a remarkable clinging quality to it. It tended to linger in the water in streamers, some of which clung to the blade when I waved my diving knife through it. The moment of return to reality could not be postponed any longer. Regretfully, I stood up into the warm afternoon sun and re-assumed the crushing burden of the aqualung, my weigh belt and gravity. I picked my way clumsily over the rocks, back to my companions.'

\*    \*    \*    \*    \*    \*    \*    \*

In August 1968, Captain Shane Gray, who was back in Cyprus again serving with the 10th Infantry Group, organised a diving course lasting one week, for some members of his Unit. He brought the class, which included the chaplain, Fr.Colm Matthews and one Australian member of the United Nations Civilian Police (UNCIVPOL) to the sea for many excellent dives at Kyrenia, on the North coast of the Island.

Since 1970, an infantry battalion has been maintained in South Lebanon as part of the United Nations Interim Force in Lebanon (UNIFIL) mission. There was also a smaller detachment provided as part of the Force Headquarters located at Naqoura on the coast, just North of the Israeli border. Not surprisingly, tours of duty at either location have been popular with divers. Each battalion usually contained some qualified divers, who took every opportunity to visit the Red Sea at various locations from Eilat south along the Sinai coast to Ras Muhammed.

The opportunities were very limited for diving during my tour of duty with the 46th Battalion, 1979/80, but I did manage to make one dive in a very unusual location. In November 1979, I led a group of divers from the Battalion across the border into Israel at Rosh Haniqra where we rented cylinders from a dive shop nearby. On advice from the proprietor we dived Northwards along the shore towards the border. We ended up going underwater into one of a number of caves almost directly under the heavily defended official crossing point between Lebanon and Israel. I kept thinking to myself as we approached the caves that an excitable sentry above us might easily decide that we were raiders and might start to drop grenades on top of us.

The caves can also be approached from the road above, and they are a much-visited tourist attraction. When we surfaced inside the main cave, some tourists were a little startled and apprehensive, but when they heard the Cork accent of Captain Tony Fogarty, they relaxed and started to ask us about Ireland. A lot of laughter was caused when Tony tried to convince them that we were leprechauns on our diving holidays. It is not given to very many to dive beside and under a hotly disputed border post, a post that had often been attacked by the PLO and other groups. The dive was otherwise ordinary and uneventful except that we noticed that there were far more fish to be seen in the water than at locations further up the Lebanese coast. We put that down to the fact that fishing was not conducted Lebanese-style, with grenades and explosives.

In 1985, I was fortunate to be posted to the HQ of UNIFIL as the Camp Commandant of Camp Command, the small composite unit of Irish and Ghanaian soldiers that provided logistical support and local defence to the Force Headquarters. The Camp itself is right on the water's edge, close to and on the northern side of the crossing point between Israel and Lebanon. In the UN Camp I was very well placed to take full advantage of the warm Mediterranean. There was a small natural lagoon at the water's edge within the camp perimeter, only about 200 metres from my room. The depth was right and the water was normally calm and warm.

The lagoon had been partially 'improved' over the years by UN personnel, to permit of swimming, wind-surfing, and to give access to the open sea beyond. I went there regularly for both swimming and snorkelling, and it was only a matter of time before I was approached by some Irish soldiers who wanted to learn how to dive. As there were some divers in the Battalion also at that time, we decided to run a number of courses at Naqoura. Captain Richie O'Neill and Sgt A. Donnelly were the instructors for one course in which one of the Battalion medical officers, Captain Charles O'Malley, took part.

I organised another course for Irish soldiers who belonged to the UN HQ in Naqoura. I borrowed extra basic equipment from Welfare stores, through the good offices of Commandant Dan Duffy, the Force Welfare Officer. I also borrowed some aqualungs from divers in the battalion at Tibnin, and ran the course using the lagoon for instruction and practice. The course was very much a part-time one, the training sessions were held on Saturday mornings, and they were subject to many interruptions. However,

I very much enjoyed the process of bringing my class up to the stage where they could go on their first aqualung dive.

When the big moment came, several nervous divers took their turn to submerge with me outside the lagoon in about three or four metres of clear water. Everything went well until I came to the last individual. He had performed properly while he was under the water and when we came to the surface at the end of the dive, I told him to follow behind me back into the lagoon. Now, it so happened that the weather had changed since our dive had started, and the surface water was fairly choppy. For reasons unknown to me, he panicked when he saw the conditions, which to be fair, he had not encountered before, and had not been expecting. By the time I had travelled the short distance to the inside of the lagoon, I heard him shouting for help.

I promptly ditched my aqualung and raced out to where he was. He was trying to climb up on a rock just below water level, and he was being buffeted by the waves. As I got close up to him, he unexpectedly lunged at me and threw his arms around me. He knocked my snorkel violently out of my mouth, and also my denture, which I had been sporting since a spearfishing competition long ago in Wicklow, and to which I was very attached. (In retrospect, I was obviously not sufficiently well attached!) I brought him back without difficulty to the safety of the lagoon. He was shaken but unharmed, and also not a little embarrassed.

We completed the course by bringing the group to Eilat for some long weekends in September 1985 and in January 1986. All those who had passed their preliminary tests at Naqoura were able to round off their training by diving in the beautiful conditions of the Red Sea. Despite his unpleasant setback, the individual concerned in the incident above did a number of dives to 20 metres without any difficulty and greatly enjoyed the experience.

After my diving incident at Naqoura, I went around the headquarters for a few days whistling while I spoke, and trying not to smile too broadly. By good fortune, I was due home on leave shortly afterwards, and I was able to get an emergency replacement set through the good offices of our family dentist in Dublin. It was an embarrassing episode, I got a lot of stick about the loss of the denture, and one of my NCOs even composed a poem about the episode!

It was only during my tour of duty at Naqoura that I finally managed to dive at Ras Muhammed, which lies at the very southern tip of the Sinai Peninsula. It was for many years the Mecca for all divers, especially those from Northern Europe. In the group with me were Sgt Pat King, Sgt Joe Cunningham and Sgt John Mellet. We drove directly from Naqoura to the border at Eilat in a UN vehicle, and from there by Egyptian taxi to

Sharm el Sheikh. That Friday evening we dived under the lighthouse at Ras um Sidd and were thrilled by the experience. The following morning we travelled with others by 4WD vehicle to Ras Muhammed at the very tip of the Sinai Peninsula, having to surrender our passports to an Egyptian soldier at an isolated checkpoint about five kilometres from our destination.

At the dive site, we snorkelled out for about fifty metres and then dropped down into the wonderfully clear water. Heading out and around a small island, we moved along the side of a beautiful reef, surrounded by hordes of colourful fish. Accustomed to being fed by divers, they eagerly followed us along. I had brought some sandwiches from the Cookhouse at Camp Tara, which we had neither the time nor the desire to eat on the long journey down. So on the dive I was carrying some very stale cheese and egg sandwiches in the pocket of my ABLJ - my life jacket.

I saw a large grouper of about 15 kilos, and I held out a sandwich to attract his attention. To my surprise, an even larger grouper, which had been lurking unseen behind me, flashed over my shoulder, grabbed the sandwich and vanished. It happened in a split second, so fast that I did not even see him taking the sandwich. It was only when back on dry land that I discovered he had skinned the thumb and first finger of my right hand, even though I was wearing a diving glove. He must have taken the sandwich and my hand into his mouth and spat my hand out again, all in a split second. I was annoyed at first, but when I thought of the age and the composition of the old Army sandwich, I decided that perhaps we were quits!

After this excitement, we continued on the dive. To our great disappointment we did not see any sharks, and our dive leader told us afterwards that the presence or absence of sharks appeared to depend on the sea temperatures and currents. The strong sun cast long slanting, flickering rays around us that seemed to converge into a black blob in the depths far below us. I was aware that we were suspended over an immense drop as the reef continued downwards for about 700 metres beneath us. It was a sobering but thrilling thought. We were, in fact, diving along part of the Great Rift, an enormous crack in the surface of the earth, big enough to be visible from space.

As more members of the Forces took up diving, and in particular, as more of the ORs (Other Ranks), became involved, it was only a matter of time before the call for the formation of a Defence Forces club was heard and answered. In 1975, at a meeting in Dublin, the Army Sub Aqua Group (ASAG) was formed and a committee elected. Shortly afterwards, ASAG, as it was then called, applied for, and were granted membership of CFT. While its membership was confined to members of the Defence Forces, it was the expressed wish that the club would function, and be regarded, as a normal club in every way possible. The numbers grew very rapidly, to the extent that regional groups had to be established in each of the four Commands (military districts). In the same year, 1975, diving was recognised officially as an adventure sport by the Defence Forces Council for Adventure Training (DFCAT). DFCAT itself was a new body, set up to encourage all adventurous activities such as canoeing, mountain walking, rock climbing, parachuting, orienteering and diving. These activities were encouraged because it was correctly assumed that involvement in any of them would have an important influence on the development of the character and leadership qualities of the participants.

Following official recognition by DFCAT, and with the background history of search and recovery missions as outlined elsewhere, DFHQ commenced a modest programme for the supply of boats, engines, compressors, and some specialised electronic equipment for ASAG. From an early stage, the ASAG policy had been laid down that individuals were required to purchase their own personal diving equipment. The rationale here was that if divers bought their own equipment, they would be certain to take great care of it. This was an important safety factor, as club equipment shared and used by different divers is less likely to be properly maintained. At the same time it would an indicator of the intentions of the individual to become a diver, because anyone who paid up to £800 to purchase personal equipment had to be serious about diving.

It has been the custom in the service to award badges to personnel that reflect their particular skills or qualifications. The badges are worn on the uniform like the service ribbons that give a general indication of the experience of the wearer. The Defence Forces does not have a parachute unit but a considerable number of enthusiasts have undertaken to train as parachutists with the support and encouragement of DFHQ. Having completed a requisite number of jumps they were then awarded 'wings' to indicate their qualifications. Some years after the establishment of ASAG, divers felt that a similar badge should be awarded to indicate diving expertise and a proposal was made to DFCAT. This proposal was eventually accepted and production of a suitable badge commenced. The design was to be in solid silver, depicting a killer whale (Orca) with a sword superimposed, and it was to be worn on the right breast. The design was taken in part from the logo of the Curragh Sub Aqua Club. Each badge bore a serial number and the award of the badge was recorded in the official military personal file of each recipient. I was very flattered and honoured when I was the recipient of the very first badge, Serial No.1, presented to me by my diving comrades. It is one of my most treasured possessions.

The establishment of ASAG and the decision of the Department of Defence to support it by purchasing equipment was responsible for the saving of at least one life. The first boat, complete with outboard engine, to be supplied to ASAG was a Caligari, an Italian-made inflatable. We were all very anxious to try it out, and on New Year's Day, 1976, we launched it at Sandycove Harbour. On board were Frank O'Donovan, Tony Fogarty, myself, and Joe Ahern. The day was sunny but quite cold and the wind was fresh to strong from the North-West. We headed straight out into Scotsman's Bay, full of admiration for our newest and most prized acquisition.

To our astonishment, out in the middle of the Bay, we came across a young woman in the water, hanging on to her wind surfer. Although dressed in a wet suit, she seemed to be completely exhausted and could barely manage to speak to us. We told her to get in, but she could not, so Tony Fogarty jumped into the water to help her aboard. We recovered her board and sail, putting them across the bow, and returned immediately to Sandycove. Thus the Caligari had made a most fortunate start to its career, by affecting a rescue. It was a lucky craft and gave great service for many years afterwards.

*　　*　　*　　*　　*　　*　　*　　*

Because DFHQ officially recognised diving, ASAG was permitted to run training courses and training camps each year. The basic courses were run as required in the Commands by the local committees. Divers who needed to upgrade to higher levels were then tested by outside examiners, usually during the weeklong training camps. CFT provided the senior examiners, normally two civilians, to test the military divers. ASAG had more than enough Moniteurs (Examiners/Instructors) within its ranks to do the tests, but in keeping with the strictures of CFT, all examiners had to be from an outside club. This very important principal has ensured that over the years the level of examination was of the highest order.

After some trial and error, it became an annual practice to hold one trainee camp and one advanced diver camp per year. These camps have been extremely popular and contribute in no small way to the fact that diving is one of the most popular and successful of all the adventure training activities fostered by the Defence Forces. The weeks are very intense, with diving morning and afternoon interspersed with theory lectures and practical work. It gave the trainees a great opportunity to become experienced and competent divers in a short time. The camps were based on military posts ranging from Duncannon, Co. Wexford right around the South and West coasts to Dunree, in Co. Donegal.

Above
Apprentice John Greensmith receiving his fin-swimming trophy from Brig-Gen Jim Beary at Sandycove, 1978. ASAG Chairman Comdt Des Hearns also pictured.

Right
Sgt Pat King diving under Fort Leenane, Co. Donegal, 1976.

Unloading on the beach. L. to R.: Jim Walsh, Ritchie Wall, Gerry Gallagher, Pat King and Mick Beary, May 1990.

Since 1983, the Trainee Camp has been held at Bere Island in Bantry Bay. The island provides all the elements that are required for beginners: calm sheltered waters that are practically immune to gales, all the depths necessary for the various grades and tests, while all sites are within easy and safe reach of sheltered landing places. There is also a fine public car ferry run by the Murphy family, which facilitates the taking of military vehicles onto the island.

The trainee camps concentrate on rounding out the training of the new divers and preparing them for the Club Diver test (CMAS 2 Star) as laid down by CFT. Training and testing is also provided in subjects such as Life Saving, First Aid, CPR and oxygen administration, boat handling, outboard engine maintenance, compressor operation, underwater navigation, interpretation of marine charts, with a big emphasis on general fitness.

The days in the training camps are long, the standards are high, and there is very little time for relaxation. The CFT examiners also are kept very busy during the weeks, having to cope with far more aspirants, and for a wider range of subjects, than they would ever meet in a given club anywhere else. The weeks spent with the Army divers have come to be a highly valued 'perk' for each National Diving Officer and his or her assistant.

Because most diving is conducted from small boats today, a great emphasis is placed on the production of competent boat handlers, or cox'ns, who were required to undergo stringent tests in all aspects of the duties of a cox'n. One element of the early tests was called the 'crash stop', where the diver must demonstrate just how efficiently he could bring his boat to a dead stop from full speed. In 1976, a group of divers from the Eastern and Western Commands travelled to Galway to undergo boat-handling tests conducted by members of the Galway Sub Aqua Club.

On a cold winter's day at Salthill, I was in an inflatable being driven by Pte Charlie Henniger, from Limerick. Also on board was Sgt Joe Cunningham and the examiner from Galway, Peadar Canavan. Joe and I had already passed our tests so we were relaxing. Joe Cunningham was sitting up at the bow enjoying the scenery when the order 'crash stop' was called. It is possible that Joe did not hear the command, but he most certainly was not ready.

Charlie Henniger was a very strong man and when he put the helm hard over, cutting the throttle at the same time, the nose of the boat lifted up into the air, spun around dramatically and the boat came to a dead stop. I happened to be looking forward at that moment and I saw Joe go straight up into the air, performing a back roll before crashing into the water. The bewilderment on his face when he surfaced told us that he had no idea how he found himself in the water. He was unhurt and we laughed at his experience for quite a while afterwards. The 'crash stop' test is no longer included in the Cox'n examinations.

The Navy has always been extremely helpful and co-operative with ASAG, and from time to time, they provided instruction at Haulbowline for certain advanced training courses. Frequently, the Navy has provided a vessel to take out the Army divers on day trips to such places as Tory Island, Crow Head, and the Aran Islands. Their divers do not participate in the Army training camps, as their system of training is entirely different to ours. Navy divers regard the free diving concept as very dubious indeed.

At an early diving camp in Lahinch, the Navy liaison officer was Lieut. Jerry O'Donoghue, himself a qualified Clearance Diver. On one morning dive, I happened to be in the diving boat off Mutton Island, Co Clare, which was being piloted by Jerry. We had six boats strung out along the northern sides of Lime and Seal Rocks, over a distance of about 1,000 metres. Each boat had at least four divers under water at the same time, a total of 24 divers. Two more divers were each boat, one of whom was acting as stand-by cover diver, the other being the cox'n.

Jerry, dressed in his Navy lifejacket, surprised me by speaking out loudly, to no one in particular, 'You are all mad, this is crazy, this is not the way to go diving.' His own training and experience was telling him that this was all wrong, and he was probably wishing that he was somewhere else, as tragedy was most certainly about to strike! Normally, one navy diver at a time was under water tethered to an attendant in the diving boat above. Another diver, fully kitted up, would be on standby, ready to go to his assistance. What may not have been obvious to Jerry however was the strong safety framework in existence beneath the apparent chaos.

All divers had been assembled on shore before the dive and thoroughly briefed. They were given the weather forecast for the area and they were told where they were going to dive. They were informed about any potential hazards such as currents, tidal conditions, and so on, which they might encounter. They were also given the telephone numbers of the nearest doctors and hospitals. They were all told in which boat they would travel, when and with whom they were to dive, how deep they could go and how long they could stay down. In addition, each boatman and assistant boatman, (who would take over for the period in which the first boatman was under water), had been nominated, usually on the basis of experience. All divers have been trained to keep an eye on their fellows at all times. The boatmen were required to keep an eye on the other boats, prepared to assist any of them if required. Finally, all the boats were fully equipped with diving flags, spare fuel, tool kits and spares for the engines, anchors, marker buoys, medical kits and distress flares. In more recent times they would also carry portable radios.

*　　*　　*　　*　　*　　*　　*　　*

On 20th of September, 1978, an Air Corps aircraft crashed into the Shannon, not very far from the Airport. The two occupants, the pilot and a civilian, had been engaged in a survey of birds on the Shannon mudflats when they crashed in the centre of the channel. They were very lucky that it was low tide, because it was only a short struggle to the exposed mudflats. Had it occurred at high tide, the mudflats would have been covered, and they would have faced a long and dangerous swim to safety. I was Chairman of ASAG at the time, and I felt that this would be a good opportunity to demonstrate our capabilities to find and to lift a large object from under the water.

My request however might not have been accepted, but for the fact that the Harbour Master at Limerick was making a lot of noise about the obstruction to his shipping channel! To my delight, and with not a little apprehension too, I was given the go-ahead to recover the aircraft. It was perfectly possible that we would fail in our attempts or that some accident would befall us, and that my name and reputation, and that of ASAG, would be ruined. However, I had full confidence in our collective experience and abilities, so I hired three lifting bags from Marine Sales, as ASAG did not possess such items then. The Air Corps flew us and all our equipment, including a compressor, from Baldonnel to Shannon, where we immediately moved to board the Airport Rescue Launch.

The team consisted of myself, Frank O'Donovan, Tony Fogarty, all from Dublin, and we were joined by Dave Hyland, Willie Byrne, Pat O'Brien and Bobby Magee, from Limerick, all experienced and keen divers. The airport authorities had also seen an opportunity to exercise their boat crew, and had offered us the use of the Airport Rescue Launch. The Airport launch was beautifully fitted out for all eventualities, including fire fighting, and it provided great comforts for us divers. They took us up-river to where they had put down a marker buoy to indicate the approximate location of the Cessna.

I went down first to do a recce, and I approached the bottom very gingerly, in almost total darkness but in slack water. To my relief, my first contact was with the tail section, immediately recognisable by its shape. Once I knew where I was relative to the aircraft, it was easier to make my way around. Working by touch only, I explored the cockpit area, and out along both wings for a short distance. The plane was upside down in 6 metres of water, and it appeared to be relatively undamaged. I surfaced then and made our plans to attach the lifting bags.

A lifting bag is a very simple construction. It is like a small hot-air balloon, made of heavy oiled canvas or nylon, with a number of strong ropes running from metal eyelets around the narrow opening of the bag. The ropes come together at a heavy ring or shackle. When the bag is attached securely to the object to be lifted, one diver holds the bag above the object to which it is attached while another diver releases air from his mouthpiece into the open underside of the bag. He continues to release air into the bag until it starts to fill, straighten up and to take the strain. More air would then provide the necessary lift.

Where too much air is released into a lifting bag, it will not burst - the excess air simply escapes under the open underside. Divers have to be careful of the object being lifted though, because it could take off suddenly for the surface, carrying all before it. In a controlled lift, usually in deeper waters, and where larger airbags are in use, there will be a valve fitted at the top. A diver will ride up with the bag, opening the valve if necessary to release air and slow down the rate of ascent. In large and very heavy jobs, air would be pumped down from a compressor, but such a technique was not necessary on this occasion.

Working in pairs, we placed two lifting bags at the nose of the aircraft, one on each side of the cockpit. Then we placed a smaller one just forward of the tail. While this was going on, two other divers recovered the No.88 VHF radio from the cockpit. It had been underwater for 48 hours, and we were impressed to find that it still worked. 90 minutes after we had started, the Cessna rose to the surface in an ungainly upside down position, and the launch crew took over. They placed a towline on the wreck and started off down the river, heading for a slipway at Walls Point, where the Air Corps recovery vehicles and crew were waiting.

Once on the move, we retired down below for a 'cuppa'. Unfortunately, in navigating the channel, which was still quite narrow in places as the tide was only starting to fill, the Cessna got snagged on the anchor chain of the Slate Buoy. Try as they could, the launch crew could not free it, and the aircraft sank once more. It was too late to dive again and we needed to re-fill our cylinders, so we retired to Sarsfield Barracks in Limerick until morning, much to the irritation of the Harbour Master. However, next morning we lifted the Cessna promptly and it was delivered into the hands of the recovery crew at the slipway without further difficulty.

The aircraft was a write-off, not just because of the structural damage, but because the aluminium would have been adversely affected after immersion in salt water. But at least the shipping channel was cleared. It was a valuable experience for the divers, while it is not often that divers are flown to their diving sites in such luxury. A set of lifting bags was purchased for ASAG shortly afterwards, and they have been used to good effect on a number of occasions since.

\*     \*     \*     \*     \*     \*     \*     \*

In October 1976, one of the longest and most difficult murder investigations ever carried out in the State by the Gardai ended in a very detailed search of a lake in Galway. From information received it was believed that the body of the missing woman had been dumped there. The lake was Lough Inagh, about 5 by 1km in extent, and it is to the west of Galway between Maamturk and the Twelve Pins. The depth of the lake ranged down to 20m, and at the centre, the silt was so deep that a four metres long iron probe could not touch solid bottom. The Garda Diving Unit was called to do a search of the lake, and they quickly realised that they needed many more divers. Civilian members of the Galway Sub Aqua Club and Galway University SAC had been helping them also, but they were not available on a full-time basis. The Gardai requested assistance from the Defence Forces, and a group of seven Navy and seven Army divers commenced operations on 3rd October 1976.

Captain Fergus Marshall was in charge of the Army group and Lieut. Danny O'Neill commanded the Navy divers. Conditions were very difficult, divers had to work by touch only, as once the silt was disturbed it became impossible to see anything. Diving continued from 4th to 10th October, when the body was finally located by divers from the Galway Sub Aqua Club. The searchers had been checking on the lake bottom in narrow strips, using a long metal bar, (there being no visibility whatsoever), and it was the good luck of the Galway group to find the body on their particular dive. A total of 20 Army divers had been rotated through the operation over the seven days of the search. They spent 160 hours, and the seven Navy divers over 50 hours, underwater, working up to 12 hours per day. It was a very successful but demanding exercise, and it helped to cement the strong and effective bonds between the divers of the Gardai, the Army, the Navy and members of amateur clubs.

*     *     *     *     *     *     *     *

On Sunday 18th of October 1987, the Army Sub Aqua Group participated in a Civil Defence Exercise which simulated a passenger aircraft crash close to Dalkey Island, Co. Dublin. Eighteen Army divers, with three inflatables, and the Navy with two inflatables, were involved in searching for and recovering the forty simulated bodies in the sea near the Island. The bodies were simulated by weighted and partly filled black plastic bags scattered in a wide area around to the South and East of the Muglins. The diving boats were also required to ferry Civil Defence personnel and equipment to and from the Island, where Civil Defence had set up a camp in order to be closer to the scene of the crash. Firefighting pumps were ferried over also to help in tackling a fire that had been arranged there. Other equipment, tentage, bedding etc. were also carried to and from the Island. Later on, divers acting as crash survivors, were placed in hazardous situations on the rocks, to be recovered by Civil Defence Rescue teams and by Air Corps helicopter.

Other operations conducted by Army divers at the request of the Garda Siochana included a search for the Carrig Una, which was lost off Rathlin O'Beirne Island, Co Donegal, 23rd November 1976. On the 25th of November, Army divers under Comdt Frank O'Donovan travelled to Malinmore, but could not dive due to severe weather and returned to Barracks. They returned again to Malinmore on 1st of December but were prevented once more from diving because of the weather. A group of nine divers under Lieut. Jim Kiely conducted a search for a body in the Silver River at Kilcormac, Co Offaly on 24th and 25th of February 1977.

Also, at Carrig-on-Shannon on 6th of September 1978, Comdts Nott and Smith recovered the body of a child. At Keel, Achill Island, Co Mayo, from the 2nd to the 4th of October 1978, Comdt Fergus Marshall and a group of divers were airlifted to dive under difficult conditions for a missing person. At Creevey Pier, Co. Donegal, on the 13th and 14th of October 1978, Comdt Fergus Marshall and a small group were airlifted to dive on a stolen vehicle that had been driven into the sea. At Portumna, Co Galway on the 31st of March 1979, Comdt Harry Smith and a group of divers dived in the Shannon, searching for a missing person. Many other searches and recoveries were undertaken by Army divers over the years but unfortunately they were not recorded.

\* \* \* \* \* \* \* \*

After two years of planning and preparation by Commandant Pat Sweeney and Lieutenants Dave Dignam and Peter McNally, and after two years of saving by everybody, 25 members of ASAG left Dublin on the 18th of June 1988 for a week of diving at Scapa Flow in the Orkney Islands. This was the first time that a diving group, composed of Army and Air Corps divers ranging in rank from Private to Lieutenant-Colonel, had travelled outside of Ireland with the approval of DFHQ. Because it was the first diving venture abroad, it was very important that it would be successful. As a result of the detailed and careful planning, and because of the commitment of all concerned, it was a total success, and it set the pattern for many more similar trips afterwards.

An opportunity to visit the warships that were scuttled while at anchor there in 1919 would be irresistible to any diver, but to military divers, it was an essential experience. Many Irish civilian divers have visited Scapa before and since, but for the ASAG personnel, this was a very special and memorable occasion. The Islands are beautiful. Their history is compelling, especially for military people, and the islanders might as well have been Irish, so welcoming were they. They even spoke with Donegal accents! The weather was perfect; we were there for the longest day of the year, 21st of June, which by coincidence, was the same date that the scuttling took place in 1919. The attitude to pub opening and closing hours made us feel perfectly at home, and the prices were most attractive.

The diving was great even if the water was definitely colder, and our two trawler skippers really knew their stuff. In Ireland we would have used inflatable boats to give close diver cover. They did not operate in this manner, and they were so good that we did not even miss the smaller boats. Most of the wrecks were buoyed and we were able to descend and ascend directly with minimum loss of time, and with a substantial saving in air

The author on board the Evening Star alongside the Shalder at Scapa Flow, June 1988.

consumption. We explored all the principal wrecks. 72 ships had been at anchor when the scuttling commenced but only 54 of them went to the bottom. In subsequent years all but seven were raised; these were abandoned for a variety of reasons, mostly because of depth.

On my first dive, we arrived onto the reddish sea floor that had the normal compliment of coloured sea anemones, crabs and small fish. I put down the reddish colour to the proximity of the rusting wreck. It was only when my eyes got accustomed to the gloom did  I notice that there were lines of rivets under us. I realised that we were not on the sea bottom but on the flank of a huge ship lying on its starboard side in 24m. The rows of rivets marched off into the gloom in regimented lines, and one was left with the impression of an enormous structure.

The wreck was that of the light cruiser SMS Karlsruhe, 5,354 tonnes, which had been built in Wilhemshaven in 1916. It was a most impressive introduction to the week's diving, and I never really got accustomed to the sheer scale of some of the vessels. Of all the dives we did during that week, my strongest memory is of a dive with Dave Betson on the remains of the SMS Brummer, which had been a fast mine-laying cruiser of 4,308 tons. It is now lying on it's starboard side and much of the superstructure, bridge, lights, masts were reasonably intact. But it also has suffered some damage, no doubt as a result of the salvage attempts.

Dropping down the shot line, Dave and I found ourselves   on the port side and we quickly moved across and down to reach the deck. As we moved towards the bow at a depth of 30 metres, we came across one of the gun turrets and, taking great care, I worked my way inside. It was not a totally enclosed turret, but was partly open at the rear. Using my flashlight, I was able to move into a position more or less where the layer would have taken his station. The layer is the member of the gun crew who has to set the range and direction on his gun sights before levelling all the bubbles of the instruments. When he has completed these tasks, the gun is 'layed', i.e. ready to be fired. All the handwheels, used for elevating and traversing the gun, were still there, although the optical sights themselves were gone.

Aboard the Evening Star on the way to the dive site, Scapa Flow.   L.to R. Dave Dignam, Phil Lane, Paddy O'Grady, Joe Burke, John Wade, Joe Minogue and skipper Malcom Fouldes.

The breech was open and when I shone my flashlight up through the barrel, I could see that it had been colonised by many sea anemones. Considering the years that have passed since it arrived on the bottom, the gun, of approximately 15cm, (6in.) was still in surprisingly good condition. Being a gunner myself, I could picture in my mind's eye the German gunners as they drilled, shouting and cursing as they endlessly practised loading and firing, doing their best to be faster and more accurate than the crews of the neighbouring turrets. I was reluctant to leave that turret, but at 34 metres, there was not a lot of time if we were to avoid prolonged decompression stops on the way back to the surface.

An unusual dive was made in shallower water, to the remains of the UB116, built by Blohm and Voss in 1918, a submarine that had been raised in 1919 and sunk again in its present position in 26m. In 1975 it was found to have a live torpedo in one of its tubes which when detonated in situ by the RN almost totally destroyed what was left of the submarine. The debris field on a sandy bottom however, is still clearly that of a submarine with many of the main pieces clearly identifiable.

Most of the wrecks are in an advanced stage of collapse and have become progressively more dangerous with the passing of time. We obeyed the rules of John Duncan of the Scapa Flow Diving Centre on the Island of Burray, who asked us not to go inside any of the hulls, and not to take souvenirs. John had provided us with two diving boats: the Evening Star, and the Shalder. The latter had a compressor on board, so that the empty cylinders were re-filled promptly, ready for the next dive. At our comfortable quarters at Burray, we were made most welcome by all those with whom we were in contact during what had been a most successful week. Divers of the Army Sub Aqua Group, now the Army Diving Group (ADG), have been to other diving locations since then, such as Cuba and Malta. In 1998, they went back again to Scapa Flow, but this time they drove in an Army bus through Northern Ireland to Stranraer and out by ferry to the Orkneys.

# CHAPTER 16

# RECOMPRESSION AND THE DIVER

A diver does not have complete freedom to do as he pleases when he is underwater. In even the simplest dive, a diver is subjected to the laws of physics and physiology. New developments in materials and higher cylinder pressures mean that a diver today can dive to greater depths for longer periods. The accumulated wisdom and experience of all the scientists and divers of the past enable him to enjoy safe and enjoyable sojourns underwater.

Each dive must be carefully planned in advance, taking into account the depth, the quantity of air available in the cylinder and the time that he wishes to spend under the water. There are a number of air diving tables available internationally to divers. If these tables are followed carefully, the diver will not suffer any decompression problems. In 1964, having considered the options available, CFT adopted the US Navy Air Diving Tables, which were in use by amateur divers in many countries of the world at that time. The Tables contain a graph called the NDC (No-Decompression Curve). The NDC is a graphical representation of the factors of time and depth that, if followed, ensures that a diver would not suffer an attack of the 'bends'. No-decompression diving is the recommended option for amateur sports divers - it is the safe way to dive. However, if a diver wishes to execute a dive that exceeds the limits of the NDC, he must plan carefully for decompression stops on the way back to the surface. These stops are essential in order to allow the excess nitrogen to be exhaled before arriving at the surface. He must carry sufficient air to permit this and he must be extra vigilant in case something goes wrong during the dive.

In the early years, a diver had to consult the Air Diving Tables to plan his dive and then memorise the details. As the dive progressed, he would consult his depth gauge and wrist watch and use his knowledge of the Tables to make any necessary adjustments. Some divers would carry a waterproofed set of the Tables with them for consultation as the dive progressed. It was the standard practice then, as it is today, to stay within the 'No Decompression Curve' and to do a precautionary safety stop at 3m before finally surfacing.

Although the US Navy Tables have served Irish divers very well, factors such as improved training, higher cylinder pressures, larger cylinder capacities and better thermal protection permit Irish sports divers to stay down for longer periods at greater depths than ever before. As a result of these modern developments, some doubts began to be expressed in the late 1980s as to whether the US Tables were still suitable for amateur divers.

Dr. Albert Buehlmann of the University of Zurich first came to international attention when he became physiology adviser to Hannes Keller who had used mixed gases in deep diving experiments in Zurich in 1959. I was fortunate to have been present at a lecture given by Dr Buehlmann to the 2nd World Congress of Underwater Activities in London in October 1962 in which he outlined the results of his early work on this subject. Over the years he produced a new set of air diving tables that were judged to be more appropriate and much safer for amateur divers. After much debate and investigation of the various new systems that were available, CFT decided to change to the Buehlmann Tables in 1993. Some, but not all, national federations had already made the change over to Buehlmann Tables by this time.

CFT has kept up with the latest technical advances in mixed gases diving also, requiring the adoption of the specialised diving tables appropriate to the gases. The mixed gases now available to amateur divers provide a number of additional advantages over air. The more popular mixture is that of nitrogen and oxygen, called Nitrox for convenience. The use of Nitrox does not allow the diver to go any deeper than if he were diving on air. It simply gives him a longer stay under water. The use of a mixture of the gases, nitrogen, air and helium, or Trimix for short, is a much more technical subject and it requires careful training and a proper support team when diving operations are in progress. Trimix has the advantage of enabling the diver to go much deeper and to return to the surface more quickly than he would if he were using conventional gases and dive tables. Courses have been devised and run, and certificates awarded, by CFT to divers who wish to use these new techniques. Not all divers use, or are willing to use, either Nitrox or Trimix gas mixtures, preferring to stay with the traditional compressed air.

*   *   *   *   *   *   *   *

Divers can be afflicted with a number of unpleasant ailments, but the diver ailment best known to the general public is the 'bends', or decompression sickness. In the past, sponge divers were the principal sufferers. Equipped with the early diving helmets, they dived too deeply and for far too long. They knew little or nothing about what was happening to their bodies under pressure and they often ignored all safety precautions. As a result, when they surfaced, they were often 'bent over' by the pain in their joints. A more recent and well publicised example of this effect occurred during the building of the Brooklyn bridge in New York. During the construction of the towers, the engineers had to build caissons deep within the riverbed, and to keep out the water they were pressurised. Very quickly workers were complaining of pains in their joints and the 'new' disease was christened 'caisson disease'. They were suffering exactly what divers would suffer if they came up without decompression stops. When the engineers were celebrating the completion of one of the foundations, the Mayor of New York and other officials were invited down to see the work where they were treated to champagne. Much to everyone's disappointment the champagne was flat, and some people drank a lot in an attempt to get the desired effect, but to no avail. However, when they returned to the surface, those who had drunk well but not wisely fell around the place, drunk to the world. The pressure was 'lifted' and the bubbles and the alcohol had the delayed affect.

In simple terms, a diver incurs the 'bends' if he stays too long at depth and rises to the surface too quickly. In this case the additional nitrogen in his blood will promptly change from a dissolved into a gaseous form. Because of the relative size of some of the bubbles, they may collect in the bloodstream at the 'choke points', usually at the joints. This phenomenon can be illustrated by rapidly opening the screw cap of a soda water bottle. With the release of the pressure, the carbon dioxide in the soda water, which had been dissolved and invisible, changes immediately into a gaseous state, and becomes visible in the form of bubbles. The effects of the 'bends' range from the mildest of itchiness under the skin in one small location, through severe pain, to death (very rare), depending on how foolish or how unlucky the diver is.

Putting a diver in the recompression chamber has the effect of causing the nitrogen to re-dissolve back into the bloodstream. The nitrogen can then be eliminated through the lungs. The diver must be brought slowly back to normal surface pressure and full health. The treatment process can range from hours to days, depending on the severity of the case. Most treated divers will recover fully, but in severe cases, or where there was a delay in starting the treatment, there may be permanent disability.

If a diver stays within the time and depth data shown on the Dive Tables for the NDC, he will not be in any danger from the 'bends'. But there is always the possibility that he might make an error or forget to consult his instruments. Elsewhere I referred to the problem of nitrogen narcosis where a diver's mental processes as he descends may be affected adversely. However, advances in technology have made things very much easier for the diver today. He can carry a powerful specialised computer on his wrist that will supply him with accurate and constantly updated information as the dive progresses. The latest computer has been reduced in size to resemble the shape and size of the average wristwatch. The newer models even permit the diver to connect the wrist computer to his PC when he gets home so that he can download all the details of his dive. The dive record may then be printed out for study by himself or for use in the instruction of others.

191

In the 1960s, the Galway Sub Aqua Club was being run by a very talented mix of professors, doctors, surgeons, accountants and business people. They were very much to the fore in advising CFT on many aspects of diving science, marine biology and medicine, contributing greatly to the establishment of the high standards that exist throughout the Irish diving community today. Peter O'Beirn, Jim Doyle, Peadar Canavan, Nigel Mathers, George Ryder and others suggested that CFT should mount a campaign to have a recompression chamber installed at the Regional Hospital in Galway. A recompression chamber is a large structure, usually with two compartments, in which a diver suffering from decompression sickness or other diver ailments is placed for a length of time under pressure. The pressure in the chamber can be arranged to simulate the approximate pressure conditions that the diver would have been subjected when he first encountered his problem underwater. At that time, there was only one recompression chamber on the island at the time, located at the hospital in Craigavon in Northern Ireland.

Medically, such a chamber is called a hyperbaric chamber, and apart from treating diving illnesses, it has many other medical uses for the treatment of certain conditions where the increased oxygen pressure can have a beneficial effect on the condition of a patient. Similar chambers are very popular in some countries for the treatment of sports injuries.

There is one major hazard associated with the operation of a recompression chamber, namely the high risk of an oxygen-enhanced fire such as the one that killed the three astronauts in their Apollo spacecraft on the ground at Cape Kennedy. The astronauts were breathing 100% oxygen at the time of the disaster, but the pressure in the recompression chamber also means that the oxygen content of the air, while far from 100%, it is much higher than that of atmospheric air and it can ignite easily. Therefore, all danger of a spark must be eliminated and those entering the chamber must remove keys, coins, and matches from their pockets, and remove their shoes before entering the chamber.

Now, it is one matter to install a Chamber, expensive as it would be, but it is an entirely different and difficult matter to provide for the trained operating staff. Once a chamber is declared to be open 'for business', there has to be a qualified treatment team on 24 hour call, ready to respond immediately to any emergency. Generally two technicians are required to operate the chamber from the outside, while one member of the team has to enter the chamber with the patient. He has to remain with the patient to carry out medical treatment or provide other assistance as required. This individual is in effect undergoing the same 'dive' as the patient, and once inside, he cannot leave until the treatment is completed. The Galway divers were quietly confident that they could produce the trained voluntary personnel to run the chamber.

The campaign for a chamber to be installed at Galway Regional Hospital, (today the University Hospital, Galway), was a great success. Sports divers everywhere contributed by raising a significant proportion of the cost, a Chamber was delivered in December 1974 and it was officially opened for business in 1975. It has two compartments and it can treat up to eight sitting patients or two stretcher cases at a time. It has treated many divers with complete success, not a few of them visitors to Ireland. It has of course been in regular use in hyperbaric cases. In more recent years, the Navy has installed a similar chamber at the Naval Base in Cork. However, it is not a totally shore-based facility, as the chamber is taken to sea whenever there are diving operations or training exercises in progress.

Small groups of sports divers are invited from time to time to visit the Chamber in Galway to undergo a 'dry' dive, usually to 50 metres. Such volunteers must possess current 'fitness to dive' medical certificates and should be free of head colds or ear problems. They are usually allowed to bring their depth gauges or dive computers into the chamber with them as it is an excellent opportunity to check on the accuracy of the instruments. The divers sit in the larger inner compartment and if any individual experiences an ear-clearing or other problem, the 'descent' can be halted by the outside operator. The diver with the problem can then be moved into the small outer compartment and brought 'to the surface' quickly.

When the 'dive' starts, the compressed air rushes noisily into the chamber and the divers must make sure to clear their ears very rapidly as the pressure mounts. The temperature rises also and divers may find themselves perspiring heavily. After a few minutes, when the simulated depth of 50 metres is reached, a blissful silence descends, in which the divers are preoccupied with their thoughts and their computers. Then one person will speak and everybody is immediately convulsed in laughter. He will sound like Donald Duck, as his vocal chords are affected by the high oxygen pressure. To the onlookers outside the chamber it sounds as if they were all having a great party.

Under such pressure, the divers in the chamber are also affected by 'nitrogen narcosis', or 'l'ivresse des grandes profondeurs' (rapture of the deeps) as Cousteau called it. All divers who breathe air under water are affected by this condition, even though general fitness and frequency of deep diving can delay the onset of the 'narks', (Navy slang for nitrogen narcosis). The condition becomes more evident as the diver approaches 30 metres or more. It affects his decision-making abilities and he may feel drunk or giddy, and he is likely to do something very foolish. Fortunately, the 'narks' dissipate as the diver ascends and there are no harmful, lasting after-affects.

Cpl Joe Burke and other divers in the Navy Recompression Chamber at the Naval Base, Cork Harbour.

As there is very little time available to an air-breathing diver at 50 metres, the return to the surface must begin very quickly. As the pressure reduces, the chamber becomes cold, damp and unpleasant, and the divers are quite relieved to get out of the chamber and to warm up. In theory, no diver should exceed the diving table limits, but human nature being what it is divers do make mistakes, even with computers. Fortunately, the numbers of divers who have been treated in any of the chambers in Ireland is very low, and nobody has yet died here of the 'bends'.

For quite some time, CFT has been raising funds to renovate the chamber in Galway and have been appealing to the Government for support. In early summer 2000, the hard work and dedication of the volunteer divers of Galway and the efforts of the officers of CFT were rewarded when the Department of Health accepted their proposals and sanctioned a sum of £250,000 towards the purchase and installation of a new Recompression Chamber at University Hospital, Galway.

# CHAPTER 17

# DIVING IN IRISH WATERS

The island of Ireland lies in the path of the Trade Winds, the winds that once brought the clipper ships back to northern Europe from the Caribbean and the Far East. The same Trade Winds also carry the dying hurricanes of the Caribbean across to us at frequent intervals. The Trade Winds are restless at the best of times, and as with any other island, winds of some kind are the norm on most days of the year. We are also affected by the winds of the Spring and Autumn equinoxes while the jet-stream, well known to modern aircraft pilots, roars across the Atlantic from West to East at very high altitude. Usually passing to the north of the island, it creates problems for us when it wobbles southwards from its normal path.

Our island lies along the same approximate latitude as Moscow or Edmonton in Saskatchewan. The winter snows and extremely low temperatures experienced in those locations should also apply to us, but thankfully, they do not. We do not often say thanks to the Weather Clerk, but we should, because the warm Gulf Stream in the Atlantic works it's magic on us by giving us a temperate climate. Mind you when I said something like this to some of my diver friends last year, they said "give us the stifling heat of the long summer, we can always learn how to dive under the ice in the winter". Because of this happy situation, diving is an all year around activity in Ireland for many divers, although there is a noticeable lack of fish and other undersea life in the coldest winter months.

Irish divers do not mind the cold or the rain, they can dress appropriately, neither do they need sunshine, although it is a pleasant bonus. Strong winds create the biggest problems for Irish divers; if there are strong winds then there are large waves and diving is out for all but the most determined or the most foolhardy. Ireland is not a small island, it is in fact the world's twenty-fifth largest. So even if we had motorways linking all the best dive sites, it is not really feasible to drive in a day from one coast to the opposite coast in order to avoid a troublesome gale. But there may well be a change underway in the climate here. Our scientists tell us that the temperature of the seas around us is rising slowly. Certainly unusual fish are being sighted more often, while storms appear to be more frequent and more severe.

The best conditions for diving are usually found at locations well away from big cities, from the estuaries of large rivers, from regions of heavy shipping traffic, and where the coast is steep and rocky rather than flat and sandy. Such locations suffer little natural silting and minimum human pollution, and happily the west and southwest coasts of Ireland fulfil most of these requirements. Sometimes after a prolonged spell of very heavy weather there can be a localised reduction in the clarity of the water, caused by the run off of rain water from cliffs and highlands. The 'red tide' appears to be a more frequent event while the plankton bloom affects the water clarity towards the end of summer most years. However, we are especially fortunate in having a large number of small islands and isolated large rocks off the coasts where the water is relatively free of pollution. When the weather conditions are right, diving in these locations can be better than anywhere else in Northern Europe.

While a diver will not see the profusion of large and small brightly-coloured fish that are found in tropical waters, he will see, especially if he takes the time to look closely, a wide and interesting variety of fish life in Irish waters. A diver who rushes around underwater, trying to cover as much of the terrain as possible, will miss out on many of the smaller wonders of the underwater world. I believe that it is far more rewarding to take things slowly and have a careful look round. In rocky sites, particularly on the West coast, where the living conditions are more suitable lobsters, squat lobsters, crawfish, smaller crustaceans such as the Norway lobsters – also known as Dublin Bay prawns – and shrimps of many sizes and shapes can be seen.

It is not unusual to see squid or octopus, or even other more exotic fish such as John Dorys or sunfish. Sunfish are shaped like very large rugby balls with two large floppy fins, one dorsal and one pectoral. Trigger fish, fish from the tropics, are often seen. Roger Fitzgerald once shot one during a competition in Kiklee. Sea urchins and the smaller spiny urchins are in abundance, as well as a great variety of starfish, sponges, sea anemones, and other plant-like animals. Sometimes, where there is a concentration of the many species of sea anemones, the diver could get the initial impression that he had wandered into a garden, such is the profusion of colour and shape.

Even the East Coast at Dublin can provide some wonderful experiences. I remember bringing a visiting German diver on a dive to the Muglins, off Dalkey Island, Co Dublin. He was astounded at the profusion of sea life that he had seen in just one half-hour. He said that where he and his friends dive they see nothing like that during a whole season of diving. He was most enthusiastic about a location that we divers from the Dublin area take so much for granted. When visibility is good around Dalkey Island and the Muglins, it can be like visiting a large aquarium, such is the variety of the sea life to be experienced there.

Although it is a less frequent occurrence today, a diver may be lucky enough to meet with up a large shoal of pollack, mackerel or even herring in open deep water. It is a wonderful experience, to be in mid-water at the centre of a circling wall of glistening fish. The fish have the capacity to remain at a safe distance from the diver, without even one fish accidentally breaking ranks to come closer. It is a strange sensation to be the object of so many thousands of eyes, an experience for which divers are always grateful. In locations like the Saltee Islands or at Sceilig Michael you may often see birds such as guillemots or puffins passing by as they hunt for fish, paying no attention whatsoever to the divers. With their wings partly folded they can move around underwater with astonishing speed and agility. The observant divers will come to know and value the presence of the many varieties of fish that they see regularly in their natural habitats, and that greatly enhances the experiences of their dives.

Like many divers, I have come to appreciate fish for what they are, with their colours, their shapes and habits. I now try to get as close to fish as possible, by moving slowly and holding my breath as much as it is safe to do so. It is not uncommon to see a small fish come right up to the diver's mask and to remain looking into his eyes. He is probably not interested in the diver, he is more likely to be looking at his own reflection in the glass of the mask. On a recent dive on the south side of Puffin Island in Kerry, I came across a small group of crawfish, known to the Americans as spiny lobsters, at a depth of about 25 metres. Lying head down on a steeply sloping rock face, I moved slowly towards the largest and reached out my hand carefully. He, or she, I could not tell, did not move. As I lay motionless, the creature used one long delicate red feeler to touch my wrist and arm, obviously trying to understand what he was seeing but not showing any fear. I looked at his black, bulging eyes set on their short stalks and tried to imagine how he was picturing me. Clearly he did not see me as a threat, although he was naturally quite wary and ready to flee.

On another dive with Pat Sweeney outside Lonehort Point on Bere Island in Bantry Bay, we came across a number of large prawns that were marked in a manner I had not seen before. They had three white stripes across their claw arms, and I called them sergeant prawns because of this! By moving carefully, Pat was able to get his hand under one and to lift it up for better examination by both of us. The prawn showed no fear whatsoever, if anything it appeared to be as curious about us as we were about him. In many locations around the world there are cleaner fish and shrimps that make their living by cleaning the gills and mouths of much larger fish. They eat the lice and other parasites that are attached to the larger fish. It is possible that these prawns too have such a purpose and perhaps it saw us as customers! Simple encounters like these make a dive memorable and add enormously to the satisfaction.

In 1999 I had the good fortune to visit the beautiful new aquarium, the second largest in Europe, built in Lisbon for Expo 98. At the lowest level, it is possible to stand in one of a number of viewing 'bulges', where one can look across the tank and up at the surface. It gives the vivid impression that you are inside the tank with the fish and sharks, as the water is now on three sides of you. Having just taken up position in one of the 'bulges', I looked up to see a number of large silver-coloured fish wheeling by in single file in mid-water. I immediately felt a thrill of recognition and delight - I felt as if I had just met with some old friends. It was a strong and unexpected emotion, and I was quite surprised by the empathy I felt with those beautiful creatures, denizens of the open sea, wheeling endlessly around in the confines of the tank, large as it was. I felt sorry for them and their predicament, even though they were at least safe from the hazards of their normal environment, where 'eat or be eaten' was the normal way of life.

Irish territorial waters form, in theory anyway, a haven for all cetaceans, and it is often possible to see examples of these wonderful creatures at close quarters. The warm-blooded, air breathing mammals such as dolphins and porpoises are the most common sightings. Occasionally there are sightings of killer whales (orcas), which despite their names, are neither whales nor ruthless killers, they are the largest of the dolphin family. While divers do not often see sharks, many species live in Irish waters. The harmless basking sharks are still seen occasionally on the west coast, and one was even seen in Dublin Bay about three years ago. Divers frequently have encounters with seals. Old bull seals can be aggressive when protecting their harems, but they will leave a diver alone if they do not feel threatened or provoked. A mother protecting very young pups should best be left alone also, but young seals can be very inquisitive about divers and will often come close to have a good look.

On the Muglins, a rocky island on the outer side of Dalkey Island, in Dublin Bay, a family of seals has been living for many years. Because many of the clubs in the South Dublin area dive there every weekend throughout the year, the seals have become completely bored with seeing divers and they generally take no notice of them. The young seals though, being very curious creatures, will often investigate groups of divers. Many a diver has been surprised to feel a tug on one of his fins, and when he turned around, expecting to see another diver, he would find himself looking into the large, sad, dark eyes of a seal. It is generally accepted amongst divers that this may well be one of the ways in which seals greet each other, by means of a gentle tug on the other's fin. It is also not unusual for a diver to be able to touch a young seal, if the diver approaches slowly, and in a non-threatening manner.

A few years ago, while on a dive with Mary Taafe and Rosaleen Maguire near the landing stage at the Muglins near Dalkey, in Dublin Bay, I received a tap on the arm. I turned back to see a young seal lying draped across a rock, as if he was reclining on a settee. He was watching us with great interest. Other divers in the Club in the past had managed to make contact with seals, but I had never had

Cillian Gray with seal pup at Dalkey Island, Aug 1986. Photo: Sean Breathnach, SUBSEA.

such an opportunity. So I felt that this was my chance. Slowly I turned around and reached out my hand intending to stroke his head. I was also trying not to exhale too heavily, in case I scared him away. He showed no unease at all, and as my hand neared his head, he opened his mouth slowly. For reasons not clear to me even today, I put my hand into his mouth. He closed his mouth slowly over my hand and I could feel his teeth grip my fingers, but tentatively, as if assessing if my hand was edible. To my relief, he opened his mouth and I slowly withdrew my hand. I reached out again, and the same thing happened once more. Then he obviously decided that he had seen enough, there was nothing here worth eating. Perhaps he did not like the taste of my rubber glove, or maybe he just needed to go to the surface for air. The young seal then turned and moved off in that effortless manner that makes us divers feel so clumsy and graceless by comparison.

In June of 1999, I was diving with others of my Club on the Coningmore Rocks, south of the Saltees. These Rocks are home to a large colony of seals and we were expecting to see some of them during our dives. When I rounded a large boulder, at a depth of about 18 metres, I saw a curious sight. Three seals were in close proximity to another group of our divers. One seal in particular was paying close attention to Siobhan McGlinchey, following her around and nipping at her fins. Although she kept backing away, the young seal persisted and she could not to shake him off. Her two diving companions were merely looking on in amusement, as they knew that Siobhan was in no danger. I zoomed down and put my nose up against that of the seal, getting a very close look at his large canine teeth. When he suddenly realised that he was now outnumbered five to one (his companions had disappeared), he retreated and vanished from our sight. Siobhan had been wearing bright pink fins and we decided afterwards that it probably was the colour that attracted him.

"Why do you go diving, what is it like, do you see sharks, what is the knife for, how deep can you go, how long will the 'oxygen' last?" These questions are still asked of divers today just as they were forty years ago, and the questioners are not always children. There is a natural curiosity about the underwater world that films and TV have not yet dispelled. There is no easy answer to any or all of those questions. Different divers will give different replies. People take up diving for very many reasons, but most likely from a combination of factors such as curiosity, exploration, challenge, love of the sea, or quite simply, peer pressure. It may even be that a diver is reverting to childhood. Children, who have a natural affinity with water, are not allowed to get wet, so perhaps for some, this is a subconscious revenge against the disciplines of childhood. For many budding divers it may well be the technical attraction of the specialised equipment, or the detailed, progressive training or even the diving discipline. It may the attraction of boating in inflatables or RIBs. For others it may simply be a macho thing in order to impress a member of the opposite sex! There are probably as many reasons why people like to go under water as there are divers.

I still enjoy hugely the training of new divers, in watching their progress, and in preparing them for the sea. I have always enjoyed coaching in the pool, and in helping beginners to get over their own particular hurdles. I take great pleasure from the wonder and excitement they display in their introduction to the underwater world and in their euphoria and sense of achievement at the end of their first open sea dives. I have always been a 'team player', preferring the team environment to my own individual efforts, whatever the activity. Diving is a team game, admittedly a very small team, normally just two divers, following what we call the Buddy system.

The dive leader, usually the most experienced diver, will be responsible for his companion before, during, and after the dive. He makes the decisions and is expected to be able to keep them both out of harm's way and bring them safely back to the boat or to shore. At the same time he too is equally dependent on his fellow diver should he get into difficulty himself. This is an aspect of diving that is emphasised during training and for which all divers have to be mentally prepared. On one occasion after the death of a diver in a freak accident in Dublin Bay, a Trainee Diver in my Club asked what would be my priority in the event of a life-threatening situation underwater. I answered without hesitation that my priority would be the saving of the life of the Trainee, at the cost of my own, if that was necessary. I believe strongly that, having undertaken the responsibility for the safety of another underwater, I was duty bound to do my utmost to ensure that my charge would survive.

For me the attraction of the typical dive is to drop into the water and to feel the release from the burden of gravity and the clammy constriction of my diving equipment. To drop down the side of a rock face, seeing the fish, shellfish and to admire the colours of the seaweeds. To be able to see the bottom long before I get there. To listen to my breathing and to the sounds made by my life-support system, the demand valve. To clear my ears on the way down, adjusting my buoyancy to the changing pressure, to exchange signals with my buddy. To come to a stop on the rocky bottom, checking each other's depth, air contents gauge, and elapsed dive time. To look up past my exhaust bubbles and see the underside of the boat where I know that other members of the team are watching and waiting.

To realise that I am 'on the edge' - to experience the thrill of danger, yet feeling confident in my ability to survive. To follow the instructions of the Diving Officer as to the time permitted and the maximum depth to be achieved, as given in the briefing before hand, and within these limits, to follow my own dive plan. To rise up towards the surface as the dive nears its end, moving slowly and exhaling fully, watching my buddy carefully, in that most dangerous part of the dive, the return to the surface. To notice the increase in brightness, to feel the water getting warmer, to feel the pressure easing, requiring yet another adjustment to my buoyancy. To pause for three minutes at 3 or four metres below the surface as a decompression safety measure. To surface, to check my companion, to look around for the diving boat, to exchange OK signals, to inflate my life jacket and to settle back into the embrace of the water, waiting for the pick-up. To check finally that both of you are OK after getting back into the boat. To discuss the dive and what each saw and to explain any aspects that could not be understood under water by means of hand signals, whether standard or unorthodox. To experience that strange sense of euphoria, of achievement, of survival, that gives meaning to it all.

Under the water, a diver quickly realises that his five senses, taken for granted on dry land, are radically altered by the new environment. His sight is affected, everything is enlarged or appears nearer than it really is, and he suffers from a form of tunnel vision caused by the diving mask. He is rarely able to see further than about 20 metres around him. Because sound travels very much faster in water, it is quite difficult to decide the direction from which sounds arrive. This is important, as he must be able to judge the possible danger caused by the approach of a surface craft. (Diving boats fly the International 'Code A' flag which means that there are divers down and   approaching vessels must reduce speed and veer away). The sense of smell will be of little use to the diver while taste is very limited in its usefulness, except perhaps to give the diver a warning if the air in his cylinder is contaminated. A diver's sense of touch however, is extremely important as a diver must be able adjust any part of his equipment by touch only. Even touch can be impaired as the fingers lose much of their sensitivity when gloved, or when they are immersed in cold water for any length of time.

No two dives can ever be the same. It is accepted wisdom amongst divers that it is possible to dive in the same location twice on the same day and yet to experience an entirely different dive. It may be that the tide has changed the conditions, or that a fish or dolphin is sighted, or perhaps that you or your buddy has had to cope with an equipment problem. The fact is that all dives have some element or factor that makes each one different and memorable from any other. It is part of the fascination of diving, the unexpected incident or the  continuing change in the underwater environment.

Every diver will have his own list of favourite diving locations, and when I look back at my diving experiences, I recall some of my own. Slieve League in Donegal, under that immense cliff where the underwater rocks at the base of the cliff are as big as houses. Or the O'Doherty Rocks off Malin Head, where despite the ferocious tidal runs, it is possible to dive safely within an interconnected network of 20 metre deep channels. Or the 1,000 metre long Grundel Rock off Mutton Island, Co Clare, where the sheer underwater cliff face drops to depths of 60 metres. Because the reef does not break surface, it must be approached underwater on compass from the west.

Or Kilstiffen Reef, at the outer end of Lahinch Bay, where can be found a narrow 30m chasm, formed as if a giant hot knife had sliced into the reef. On the bottom at the inner Eastern end there is a large cave. Or the 'flying buttresses', as I called them, on the same reef where at a depth of 20m, can be found three large slender natural stone arches quite close to each other, looking as if they had been put there by an architect to support the face of the reef. The dramatic dives to be had on the O'Berrity Rock, north of Kilkee Bay, the Buachaill Rock on the outer side of Inish Turk, the Seven Stags, 1,500m out from Portacloy, in North-West Mayo, or the grandeur of the north face of Sceilig Michael in Co. Kerry.

I savour especially the more recent experience of August 2000, at the end of a very enjoyable dive with Mick Schultz under the southern cliffs of Puffin Island, also in Co. Kerry. On reaching the surface at the end of the 39 minute dive, my eyes fell on a beautiful and unexpected scene. The sun had come out and the calm blue sea reflected the blue of the sky. The cliffs of the island towered above us on our right hand side, and away to the west, the three dramatic and progressively larger rocks, Lemon, the Little

Sceilig and Sceilig Michael were lined up and highlighted against the horizon like three progressively larger pyramids. Every detail was sharp and clear. The little wavelets around us sparkled and flashed like brilliant jewels in the midday sun and I could hear the calling of the numerous seagulls as they wheeled above us. I experienced that feeling, common to many divers at the end of a wonderful dive - I simply did not want to leave the water and climb back into the diving boat.

Diving is a risk sport - that cannot be denied. To be suitable for diving, a person must have sound basic health, be able to swim, and to pass an annual medical examination that lays great stress on sound lungs and heart. Because the diving conditions in Ireland demands it, it is essential that an individual submits himself or herself to a course of instruction in a responsible and well-organised club or commercial diving centre. However, for the large numbers participating, and for the length of time diving has been practised in Ireland, the sport compares more than favourably with other outdoor activities. The organisation is very structured, the preparation is excellent and it is tightly controlled. In the first printed individual logbook of the Curragh Sub Aqua Club, we included an extract from 'The Aran Islands' by John Millington Synge which we felt summed up what should be the correct attitude of a diver to the sea. *A man who is not afraid of the sea will soon be drownded, because he will be going out on a day that he should not*. I believe firmly that because of the conditions in which they have to operate, and because of the quality of the training and examination they receive, Irish divers are among the very best in the world and when the weather is right, diving in Irish waters is simply superb

# CHAPTER 18

# THE OCEAN ENVIRONMENT

All divers dream of diving in clear, warm, blue, deep water, where the fish are friendly, the scenery is superb and the normal rules of physics and physiology do not apply! There is no such place of course, but some locations come close to the ideal. Places like some of the islands of the Caribbean, the Indian Ocean, the Great Barrier Reef in Australia, the Red Sea or the coasts of Thailand or Belize. The Mediterranean used to be included in the list of wondrous destinations, but not any more.

The Med still has beautifully clear, warm, blue water. The gales are relatively rare, the diving facilities are excellent, and the onshore attractions are superb. The problem is that in most diver-friendly areas of the Mediterranean, the waters are empty. The fish have left the coastal areas; they have been driven away by over-fishing, too much boating and by pollution. There are of course, some exceptions to this, where reservations or sanctuaries have been established, and where all manner of fishing or interference with the environment is strictly prohibited.

It is easy to imagine the effects on the fish population of the steady increase in the numbers of people fishing from the rocks, or from their small fishing boats. Worse still, the increase in the number, size and efficiency of fishing boats, or more correctly of the fishing fleets, has undoubtedly had a devastating affect on the fish population. There has been a remorseless rise in the number of power boats, jet-skis, water-ski tow boats, and para-glider boats on the water. We must not forget the huge increase in the number and size of car and passenger ferries, naval vessels, and submarines, all of which must seriously affect the fish populations. We can imagine the damage caused by the ultra-low frequency radio waves generated by all kinds of submersibles and scientific buoys, both static and drifting. We can understand the disturbance caused to fish by the construction of yet more bridges and harbours, as well as the drilling for oil, minerals or the detonation of explosives in the interests of science.

What can the race memory of the whales, dolphins and other mammals tell them about their circumstances? For seemingly endless centuries, the oceans echoed only to their own songs, their 'conversations', or to the natural noises of the other entities that lived there. Sound carries faster and for much further than in air. How do the warm-blooded air breathing mammals in particular cope with the deafening increase in noise created by mankind and his water borne activities? Have we given enough thought to the damage that we are causing? How can we humans even begin to compensate for the effects that our activities have wrought on the denizens of the sea? No matter how well intentioned are the laws relating to noise, or dumping at sea, or to the control of fish stocks, the reality is that the remorseless rise in the human use, and abuse, of the oceans continues at an ever-increasing rate.

The fishing fleets, with their accompanying factory and supply ships, have found that their very efficiency at catching fish has resulted in diminishing returns from the 'traditional grounds'. They have been forced to move to new fishing grounds along the African coast or even as far as Antarctica. No doubt they will inevitably experience the same diminishing returns there in the not so distance future. By the time the owners and the financiers of these great fleets come to realise that they are not getting enough return for their money, the damage will be done. Many of the fish that we take so much for granted now may well have disappeared for all time. At best, it will take many generations before their numbers can return to the levels that were experienced around the turn of the 19th century.

From the earliest times, all the vessels that have ever passed across the oceans have dumped their rubbish overboard. The routes that some ferries have been travelling on for years could probably be traced to and from their destinations by following the rubbish trails on the sea bottom. In modern times, the naval carrier fleets, each the equivalent of a small city, have been moving over and back across various parts of the oceans for many years now. It is said in jest that it is only a question of time before a ship will run aground on a tin can reef! To be fair, the modern Navies and merchant fleets do have rules about such matters today, and do their best to bring all their rubbish to the next port for disposal on shore. But it was not always so. Hazardous wastes have been dumped at sea by all the industrialised nations, but while the sea can cope with a lot, can it cope with another 100 years of the same or even increased abuse? Since the arrival of the nuclear powered submarine, a number have been lost to accidents while other 'retired' submarines are just dumped in the sea. Their nuclear reactors will continue to spew out radiation for the next 1,000 years.

Good diving sites, like all other tourist sites on land, are quickly 'explored to death'! In the era of cheap mass travel, once a good diving site has come to the notice of the world diving community, the masses descend on it. By doing so, they destroy the very 'un-spoiled-ness' of the area which attracted them to go there in the first place. It is a problem that applies to the over-water scene too, but for the underwater environment, the damage can be long term or even permanent, and worse because it is less obvious.

In September 1961, I spent three weeks with friends from Belfast and the Curragh on a diving holiday at the Club Mediterranee village at Palinuro in southern Italy. Towards the end of the second week, we were told that we were going hunting for coral. The coral in question was the relatively rare red coral, only to be found in deep waters. We were told to go to a blacksmith in the village to get our 'coral hammers'. Each hammer looked like a small and lighter version of a geologist's pick. I still have it, with my collection of shells and corals. Yes, I did collect shells long ago, but not today. The dive was to 160 feet (roughly 50 metres) and I laughingly described it afterwards as 'The Battle of the Coral Sea'. We had to search for the corals as they were small and difficult to spot under the overhanging rocks. I remember noticing that many of the polyps were extended collecting food, looking like little white flowers in the dark water. I managed to collect a small plastic bag of red coral for my troubles, as did all the others. We were informed at the time that it was getting more and more difficult to find red coral in the area - was it any wonder! I would be horrified today if I were to see divers causing such depredation, as would many of my friends. I have no doubt that 'Club Med' have long ago banned such activities.

The Independent World Commission on the Oceans, established in 1995 under UN auspices, reported at the 'Expo 98' meeting in Lisbon that 77% of the pollution of the sea is estimated to come from land sources. The Commission spoke of a crisis in the oceans that may be a threat to the survival of the human race. Cousteau said once that if the oceans die, humanity dies. The population of the earth is rising inexorably, and we are guilty of destroying the very environment that we enjoy.

I have been diving for over forty years, and I can say from my own observations that here in Ireland, the numbers and the sizes of fish and shell fish have diminished noticeably in many of the popular dive sites. The water quality has deteriorated also. When members of the Curragh club first started diving regularly in the sea, Howth was our usual destination. Diving from the steps beyond Balscadden, we had many enjoyable explorations of the rocky seabed. However, just about that time, a new pumping house was built at the car park, as the second-last stage of a new and very large North Dublin sewage scheme. The final stage was the long underwater pipe that was designed to take the sewage from the pumping house "far out into the tidal movement, where it would be dispersed harmlessly" - words used in praise of the design at the time.

It was not very long after the inauguration of the scheme, that we found ourselves pushing 'turds' (brown trout!) out of our way on the surface near the rocks at Balscadden. In addition, we had to endure the smell from our diving suits as we drove back to the Curragh. The pipe and the tides were clearly not co-operating with the engineers. We promptly gave up diving there and moved to Bulloch Harbour, on the South side of Dublin Bay. Diving in Bulloch was very pleasant, with plenty of fish, shellfish and reasonably clean healthy seaweeds. However, yet another pumping station was built on the rocks behind the pier. A fifty metre long under water pipe was laid down to discharge the macerated, but otherwise untreated, sewage of the Dalkey/Killiney area into the "strong tides where it would be dispersed harmlessly". Now where had we heard that before? In no time at all, we had a situation similar to that at Howth.

It had failed on the North Side and it did not work at Bulloch Harbour either. Ask any dedicated beachcomber, he will tell you that the sea has a habit of returning to land most of the objects thrown into it. Even the heavy military projectiles that were dumped in the Beaufort Dyke between Ireland and Scotland many years ago have continued to supply the coasts of Antrim, Down and Louth with dangerous debris right up to the present day. The condition of the seaweeds in the Bulloch Harbour area deteriorated noticeably, and we felt that we could no longer dive there. The shellfish however, scavengers like almost everything else that lives in the sea, seemed not to suffer, most likely because of their new source of food!

In 1968, there was a complaint from a member of the public that the discharge pipe was broken and that it was not doing its job properly. I was asked by Dun Laoghaire Corporation to dive at the outfall and to check its condition. Ted Spendlove and myself dived on the 28th of August 1968 and inspected the underwater section of the discharge pipe. The pipe ended in a multiple opening, looking rather like the base of a giant rocket motor. This design was presumably to assist in the dispersion of the effluent. When I inspected it, having to look deeply into each of the four openings, the only exit that was operating was the uppermost one, while the rest of the pipe appeared to be undamaged. The effluent was pouring out and streaming to the surface to the eagerly awaiting sea gulls. The other exits were undamaged, unblocked, and under-used. With some reluctance, the Club abandoned Bulloch Harbour as a dive site shortly afterwards.

In the Seventies, when cruise liners called to Dublin, they would anchor in Scotsman's Bay. After a liner had departed, following a two or three-day visit, we observed a large increase in sewage in the area. We speculated that these ships probably emptied their effluent into the sea during their stay or before departure. We could not prove or even check on this matter, because at that time it was not uncommon for the sewage plant at the West pier at Dun Laoghaire to overflow, allowing the effluent to spread along the shore in both directions. Fortunately this plant is no longer in existence, and cruise liners no longer anchor in Scotsman's Bay. Or when they do, the modern cruise liners, or indeed aircraft carriers, with populations the size of small towns, are required by maritime law to have holding tanks for their effluents which are then discharged onshore when in harbour.

But once on the high sea, by the same international law they are permitted to discharge their effluents without treatment, as are the multitudes of cargo vessels, fishing boats, pleasure and working vessels. On the river Shannon the cruise boats can discharge their sewage at certain piers, but elsewhere they presumably discharge directly into the river. If so, considering the remorseless rise in the boating numbers, how long can that practice continue before the situation becomes intolerable?

However, where there is a will there is a way, and the State and the various Councils around Dublin Bay seem determined to improve matters. It is only fair to say that those divers who have been diving in the Dublin Bay area for many years are agreed that there appears to be a slight but noticeable improvement in the water condition. It may be that the major sewage treatment scheme of recent years is finally beginning to have an effect on the clarity of the water and the cleanliness of the seabed in Dublin Bay. However, it will take many years before the accumulated sludge will have completely dissipated.

Most Irish divers, initially unconcerned about conservation and about the need to protect that very thing which gave them such enjoyment, have in more recent times become very aware of the problem. They have consciously become protectors of their favourite dive locations and new divers in training are encouraged to protect and respect the underwater environment from which they receive their enjoyment. Even the feeding of fish by divers, enjoyable as it is, and widely practised as it is, creates its own problems by interfering with the local environment. Spearfishing as a sport is not practised here anymore, and as a result of the good work of the Scientific Commission of CFT, there is a general and voluntary code of practice whereby divers do not collect shells, kill fish or disturb in any way the undersea condition.

In 1974, I was fortunate to dive at a few locations just outside the city of Eilat on the Sinai shore. It was my first dive in the Red Sea and it was a great experience, taking place as it did before the great mass movement of divers of later years, or indeed before the expansion of Eilat itself. Even my eldest son John, ten years old then, still talks with enthusiasm about his snorkelling there with me. After a gap of twelve years, I dived there again and I was horrified to see the changes that had occurred in that relatively short time. The political situation had brought the Egyptian border to within ten kilometres of Eilat, and this had the effect of compressing the boating, fishing and other sea-based activities of the residents into a very small area. The pollution of the sea floor and the condition of the corals was shocking. The sea floor was littered with tin cans, rubber tyres, concrete blocks, beer bottles, milk cartons, plastic bags, pieces of nets and ropes, and the other myriad discards of the consumer age.

The coral reefs at Eilat, while not among the most beautiful or the most extensive in the world, are precious nonetheless. Many of the corals were dying; they were covered by a grey scum, which comes from untreated discharges from the shore, or possibly from the many freighters in the bay. Many corals were smashed and in a deplorable condition. Since I had first dived at Eilat, there had been a huge increase in the populations of both Eilat and Aqaba, with a corresponding huge rise in the number of pleasure boats and commercial shipping. Each time a small boat or a huge ship dropped its anchor, another coral head was damaged beyond redemption.

The two city's ports are separated only by a narrow stretch of water. The Bay at the top of the Gulf of Aqaba, is almost a closed environment. It is very narrow and very deep, and the sea floor drops rapidly from the shore. Because there is little tidal movement in the Gulf, there is not a natural cleansing of the shallows and the shores, such as we have in Ireland. To be fair, the authorities have introduced regulations to prevent the 'boat people' dropping their anchors when and where they pleased. There are now large fixed multiple mooring points in the more popular diving and swimming locations, and the authorities have presumably reduced or treated the discharges into the Bay. But no matter what the Israelis and the Jordanians do to improve the situation, the damage has already been done. The corals cannot recover, as they require the kind of sea conditions that can never again be found at that end of the Gulf. It is entirely too late for the corals, they will be seen again only in photos or movie films taken at least thirty years ago.

Aside from the negative effects of mankind on the coral reefs in the warm waters of the world, we have our own problems here at home too. There are many old-fashioned fishing methods still in vogue, but one of the most damaging must surely be the trawling for bottom living fish. Long before the arrival of Fungie, I made some dives at Dingle and was delighted at the wonderful spread and diversity of marine life on the sandy/muddy bottom on the Birnam side of the inner harbour. However, when local fishermen discovered that there were good quantities of scallops on the harbour floor, they trawled as much of the harbour as they could reach.

I happened to dive there again soon after they had trawled the harbour bottom and I was shocked at what I saw. The tracks of the trawls ran across the muddy sand like railway lines, leaving a trail of broken shells and uprooted seaweeds. The surface had been destroyed and the fragile environment on which so many species of marine life depended had been ruined. The sea bottom presumably recovered in time, but it would have taken a long time, while some species may never again be found in that location. Trawling is a very old and traditional method of fishing but it causes great damage. Because they cannot see the damage they are doing, the fishermen persist with a very inefficient and harmful method of fishing instead of looking to science and technology to give them a better alternative.

What is needed to protect the oceans is a kind of 'Prime Directive' as depicted in the science-fiction series 'Star Trek', where no interference whatsoever would be permitted in the affairs of the denizens of the deep and in their conditions of life. Clearly, this would be impracticable. What could help though, would be to select designated bays, river estuaries or even stretches of the coastline and declare them to be areas of conservation, where no fishing or development whatsoever is permitted, either permanently or for a given number of years. It would not be enough to make a declaration of intent, it would be necessary to supervise and patrol the zone to ensure compliance. There are several such conservation zones in countries in the Far East, and the results are already very impressive. One reason why they are succeeding is that from the beginning the local fishermen have been involved in every aspect of the planning. As fishing was their only means of making a living, their full support was essential from the outset. As a result of the evident success of the projects, the fishermen are now the most enthusiastic exponents of the plan. They have been able to see for themselves that the conserved zones actually supply replacement fish stocks to the unprotected zones nearby.

In 1974, the committee of CFT proposed to the Government that Kilkee Bay be designated as an under water Conservation Zone or Nature Reserve, but nothing was done. Nobody at official level was sufficiently interested and the officials of the young CFT were too busy. The motion from CFT read in part as follows:-

'Comhairle Fo-Thuinn, the Irish Underwater Council represents the organised sport of diving - - - consequently wishes to have the following points discussed and investigated;

* The formulation of legislation to create and control areas of conservation in inshore waters and at offshore islands.

* The use of these areas for the furthering of studies of marine flora and fauna and related subjects.

* To see the authority to govern these areas vested in a national or government agency.

* The feasibility of controlling the use and sale of spear-guns, harpoons etc, and their use with self-contained underwater breathing apparatus '.

I feel that this proposal by CFT, or a similar one, needs to be resurrected and the necessary legislation introduced. As has been demonstrated in Thailand, the results would be very beneficial.

While all cetaceans were protected under the Wildlife Act of 1976, this country took an honourable stance in 1991 by designating the waters of the Irish Economic Exclusion Zone (EEZ) a cetacean sanctuary. Across the world's oceans, the numbers of whales, porpoises and dolphins have been declining over the years as a result of the activities of the whaling and fishing fleets. Also in 1971, the Irish Whale and Dolphin Group, a voluntary group, was formed with the intention of educating the public while at the same time learning more about the distribution, status and seasonal occurrence of the mammals in Irish waters. There is a Seal Sanctuary based at Garristown, Co. Dublin. It is a voluntary organisation and it attempts to influence the Irish public into taking a more tolerant view of seals.

In 1984, two divers of Tralee Sub Aqua Club, John O'Connor and his daughter Deirdre, were diving near the mouth of Dingle Harbour. They were startled to see a dolphin moving around them and apparently having a good look at them. This was not an unusual event, divers often meet up with dolphins, but this one proved to be very special. Because seventeen years later that same dolphin is still living in the waters of Dingle Bay, attracting worldwide attention. A mini-industry has grown up around Fungie, where some of the fishermen have given up fishing, finding it more lucrative to take out tourists to meet or to dive with the dolphin. The realisation that a large pod of dolphins have been living in the Shannon estuary for very many years has also generated considerable tourism in that area.

It is alleged, without conclusive proof, that dolphins are possessed of special therapeutic powers and that contact with, or proximity to, dolphins is beneficial for people suffering from depression or certain other disorders or handicaps. It is accepted that they are among the most intelligent animals in the oceans and appear to have a well-developed 'language' of their own. In 1990, a film called 'The Dolphin's Gift' was made in Dingle by a group from London. John Hurt did the narration; the director was Kim Kindersley, and the producer was Victoria Cotton. The film was given its premiere in Dublin on 29th of May 1991 and the profits were donated to the new Whale and Dolphin Group.

*   *   *   *   *   *   *   *

In October 1962, I attended the 2nd World Congress of Underwater Activities in London and heard Jacques Cousteau deliver his famous 'Homo Aquaticus' speech in which he made two predictions. He said that as the world became more and more populated, the pressure on the available space would eventually lead to the construction of whole towns and even cities under the water. He also said that medical science would develop a form of regenerating 'gill' to be implanted under the arm of a diver so that he could live and work underwater indefinitely, drawing on the available dissolved oxygen in the water as do fish. To achieve this, the diver's lungs would have to be filled with a special enriched fluid. This technique was simulated very many years later in the film 'The Abyss'. Cousteau's first prediction made an impact in Japan where it resulted in a serious study of the possibility of constructing an underwater town in a country where land is a scarce resource. However, the plan never left the drawing boards, possibly because much of Japan lies in an earthquake zone. The second prediction has yet to be realised, although there is some progress in the development of a suitable liquid, where small rodents have been able to survive while immersed in a heavily oxygenated fluid.

At that same Congress in London, Sir Alistair Hardy, Professor of Zoological Field Studies at Oxford University, and author of many books on the sea and fish, spoke about the probability of having to farm the sea at some time in the future. He claimed that many regions of the sea were already over-fished and that the sea would have to be treated like the land in order to provide for the rapidly increasing world population. He believed that, in the past, man may have been much more aquatic, living on the shore and swimming for a great deal of his food. He also said that he believed that the 'sub aqua movement', as he described it, would lead the way to a really big revolution in our fishing methods that will in turn lead to a future farming of the sea. He has been proved right in this prediction, but perhaps not quite in the way that he described.

While the predictions of Cousteau were received at the time with reactions varying from ridicule to enthusiastic support, I personally believe that there is one serious drawback to mankind ever taking permanently to the underwater life. It is simply the need for humans to be able to see their way, to make maximum use of the gift of sight. Even with the most powerful of lights, the ability of a diver to see around him is extremely limited. Without lights, and in shallow clear water, he can see at most for about thirty metres around him, while in very deep water he will see nothing whatever. I believe that the greater scientific efforts will always be devoted to the exploration of outer space. In space, an astronaut, looking out of his porthole, can 'see for ever'.

Before the exploration of space became a practicable reality, technology had developed sufficiently to support a number of initiatives to explore the ocean depths, sometimes called 'inner space' as opposed to 'outer space'. They can be divided into three general categories: craft lowered from the surface carrying observers, habitats, where groups attempted to live under water for prolonged periods, and finally, the many varieties of craft, both manned and unmanned, that were independent of the surface or were controlled remotely.

The modern technological era of ocean research can be said to have started when two Americans, William Beebe and Otis Barton, developed a diving 'vehicle' in 1930 which Barton called the bathyscaphe. It was a steel sphere, only 4 feet 9 inches in its inner diameter, designed to be lowered on a chain from a surface ship. In the bathyscaphe, the daring duo made several 'dives', culminating in a dive to 3,000 feet in 1934. The evident risks and the poor returns made this method an unpopular means of exploring the depths.

After World War 2, the Swiss professor, Auguste Piccard, known to the world for his record-breaking ascents in a balloon in the 1930s, turned his attention to the oceans. Spotting the flaw in the efforts of Barton and Beebe, Piccard designed a new craft able to move freely and independently of a surface support ship. The crew of two were placed in a metal sphere, similar to that of Beebe, except that it was suspended under a large tank filled with petrol, which, being lighter than water, provided the buoyancy. He also called his craft a bathyscaphe but christened it FNRS 2 (Fonds National de la Recherche Scientifique) after the Belgian foundation that supported his efforts. The first trials were unsatisfactory and he moved to Italy, where he built a new vehicle that he named the 'Trieste'. At the same time, the French Navy, proceeded to build the FRNS 3 to the same general plans as the original. After many attempts, the French Navy crew of Huout and Willm reached a maximum depth of 4,000m, (13,000 feet), in the Senegal Deep off Dakar. The American Navy eventually took over the 'Trieste' and in January 1960, the crew of Dr. Jacques Piccard and Lieut. Donald Walsh achieved the 'Everest' of the underwater world, when they touched down at 11,000m, (36,000 feet), in the Marianas Trench off Guam. However, like the bathyscaphe of Beebe, this means of exploring the depths also proved to be hazardous and unrewarding and was abandoned.

The 1960s saw a great movement to establish 'underwater habitats' in a bid to demonstrate that humans could live and work at depth. This movement was aided at the time by the international discussion about the need for farming the oceans and mining the seabed. Cousteau organised a number of projects under the name 'Conshelf'. Conshelf 1 took place in 1962 off Marseilles where two divers remained at 10 metres for eight days. Conshelf 2 featured divers living at 25 metres for up to 30 days in the Red Sea in 1963. The final Conshelf 3 took place at Cap Ferrat in 1965 where six divers lived at 100m for three weeks. The Americans also placed dwellings underwater in Californian waters under the 'Sealab' programme that was partly intended to assist the space programme. Even amateur groups in different parts of the world constructed their own 'houses'. While it was proved that men could live and work without any great difficulty underwater for months at a time, the 'habitats' were mostly in shallow water, down to 10 metres. The projects were generally under-funded and the habitats proved to have little long-term usefulness, and were eventually abandoned.

Although interest in the exploration of the oceans through the use of bathyscaphes, free or tethered, had waned, a new generation of vehicles appeared as a result of the development of new technologies, particularly electronics. These vehicles were designed for such practical uses as deepwater recovery, repair and inspection of oil wellheads as well as a myriad of scientific tasks. Projects such as 'Denise', the ' flying saucer' of Cousteau; 'Deepstar', the two-chamber submarine of Ed Link; the scientific recovery vehicle 'Alvin'; or the DSRVs (Deep Submergence Rescue Vehicles), designed for the rescue of submarine crews, all proved to be extremely successful. In a most unusual experiment, Dr Jacques Piccard and five scientists spent 31 days in the 'Ben Franklin' research vessel, drifting underwater with the Gulf Stream from Palm Beach to near Halifax, covering 1,500 miles.

Due to the inherent hazards and costs associated with sending down manned vessels, and with the rapid advances in technology, a new generation of small, unmanned robots called ROVs (Remote Operated Vehicles), came into general service. The ROVs came in many sizes; they carry cameras and a variable range of scientific instruments and they can be sent into situations considered too hazardous for divers. They are in widespread use now for a multitude of purposes and have vastly extended man's ability to investigate the oceans of the world.

*    *    *    *    *    *    *    *

It is obvious that the exploration of the sea has come a long way in a very short time, due mainly to the advances in technology. Some of the predictions of Hass, Cousteau, Hardy, and other scientists have been confirmed, even though there is still a very long way to go. Diving in all its forms, even sport diving, has contributed to this in a substantial way. It seems to me that globally there is more interest than ever in the sea, caused in part by concerns about global warming and climate change and in part by the realisation of the true importance of the oceans in our lives. I believe that we are in at the beginning of yet another and more productive 'wave' in the exploration and development of the resources of the great oceans that can only have lasting benefits for mankind.

At long last, here in Ireland too, there appears to be a realisation that we really do live on an island. Following the neglect of many years, we are slowly starting to re-discover our real heritage, the sea. The Maritime Institute of Ireland, an entirely voluntary body of men and women, has been ploughing a lonely furrow over the years. The National Maritime Museum that they have established at Dun Laoghaire, with little or no help from the State, is probably better known outside Ireland than within. It should be visited by anyone who has an interest in the sea. These dedicated men and women have been trying to show a largely indifferent public the true worth and potential of the seas around us. Perhaps at last their efforts may well be coming to fruition. Greater numbers of Irish people than ever before are enjoying the seas, the rivers and the lakes of Ireland. These include the yachtsmen, sea scouts, the sports fishermen, those who use canoes, sail boards, surfers, oarsmen, and the whale and dolphin watchers, not to mention the many thousands of divers.

Consider the many events and disparate initiatives that we have witnessed in Ireland of recent years. Events such as the Brendan Voyage by Tim Severin, the offshore oil and gas discoveries, or the establishment, in 1994, of a long-overdue Marine Institute, and the establishment of independent harbour authorities for all our major ports. The State has displayed increased and greatly over-due concern for the small, isolated offshore island populations as evidenced in the construction of piers, and the provision of electricity, telephones, cable cars, ferries and airstrips to improve the quality of life of the inhabitants. A major new seven-year programme of research in our coastal waters and seabed has been announced, costing £21m. The Naval Service is being re-equipped and improved, and a new Coast Guard Service has been formed. The Coast Rescue Service is being modernised and there are significant improvements in the helicopter-based rescue service, where the true value and expertise of the Air Corps is finally being recognised in the purchase of large helicopters for rescue. The Royal National Lifeboat Institution is being recognised by the state for its value to all who go to sea. A new Maritime College is under construction in Cork to provide for both Naval and Merchant training at the most modern level.

New and more versatile vessels have been put into service recently, such as the new research vessel - the 'Celtic Explorer', with another larger one, 'The Celtic Voyager' to be launched later on. Irish Lights has recently introduced a very impressive navigation lights tender, the "Gránuaile". The Gárda Diving Unit has become the Gárda Maritime Section and has taken delivery of its first Inland Patrol vessel, 'Colm na Cora' on the Shannon, with another due soon for the Liffey. Island Ferries Teo. has put into service its biggest and fastest ferry to date, 'Draoícht na Mara', able to carry 272 passengers between Rossaveal and the Aran Islands. Bigger and more powerful fishing vessels are going into service, including the dubious purchase of the world's biggest fishing vessel, 'Atlantic Dawn', so big that it is doomed to fish permanently outside European waters. As a result of the revival of interest in the tragedy of the mass emigration following the Great Famine, two replica Famine Emigrant ships, the Jeannie Johnston and the Dunbrody, have been built and launched, to serve as realistic reminders of those grim times and events.

Consider the following facts:

It is generally accepted that the human species developed from primitive organisms that crawled out from primordial seas.

There is a striking similarity between the composition of seawater and human blood.

All human beings spend the first nine months of their lives totally and happily immersed in an amniotic fluid.

Life as we know it could not exist without a plentiful supply of fresh water.

Water makes up approximately 70% of the composition of our bodies.

Approximately 70% of the planet is covered by water.

From a particular point in space over the Pacific Ocean, the earth appears to be a water world, with only islands and the merest suggestion of land on the peripheries.

In the words of the famous writer, underwater explorer and maker of TV films, Dr Hans Hass of Austria, "70% of our world is covered by water, 70% of our world is unexplored".

"How inappropriate to call our planet Earth when clearly it is Ocean", Arthur C. Clarke, science-fiction writer and diver.

Is it any wonder then that from our earliest days, we are fascinated by water in its many and varied forms? When we go to the beach, we stare at the sea all the time, and not at the land. How many of us love to sit for ages on a beach or on a cliff top, gazing out over an expanse of water, drawing contentment and relaxation from the sound, the motion and the changing colours. We are inspired to dream, to write poems or to paint pictures of the ever-restless, ever-fascinating sea.

The sports diving movement of the last 45 years has introduced tens of thousands of Irish people to the wonders around our coasts. These people now share in the greater realisation, understanding, and concern for all the oceans of the planet. Ever since Jacques-Yves Cousteau and his associates liberated us from the clumsy diving suits of the helmet diver by inventing the demand valve in 1943, the seas have been invaded by millions of happy humans who may be reverting, without ever being conscious of it, to their own far distant primal origins.

# Appendix "A"

## Comhairle Fó Thuinn

### THE IRISH UNDERWATER COUNCIL

Inaugurated: 23 September 1963

CFT is the officially recognised national body representing the sport of diving in Ireland. Composed of 83 affiliate clubs and 2,700 divers for the year 2000, it is affiliated to CMAS, the World Underwater Federation in Rome, and to CCEAS, the European Underwater Federation.

Headquarters Building : 78A Patrick Street, Dun Laoghaire, Co Dublin.

Phone:  01- 284 4601    Fax:  01- 284 4602

Web Site:  http://www.ScubaIreland.com    E-Mail:  scubaireland@eircom.ie

\*    \*    \*    \*    \*    \*    \*    \*

## PRESIDENTS AND NATIONAL DIVING OFFICERS

### Presidents

| | | |
|---|---|---|
| 1963: Shane O'Connor | 1975: Ted Spendlove | 1990: Ronnie Fitzgibbon |
| 1964: Hugh Hennessy | 1976: Nigel Mathers | 1991: Paul Ryan |
| 1966: Hugh Quigley | 1977: John Hailes | 1992: John O'Connor |
| 1968: Ronnie Hurley | 1978: Gerry Stokes | 1994: Stewart Clarke |
| 1969: Jim Whelan | 1981: Brian McGuinness | 1997: Peter Brady |
| 1971: Jim Sweetman | 1983: Bart McMullin | 1999: Gearoid Murphy |
| 1973: Mick Moriarty | 1984: Billy Nott | |
| 1974: Jim Sweetman | 1988: Pat Bergin | |

### National Diving Officers

| | | |
|---|---|---|
| 1971: Brian Cusack | 1981: Pat Bergin | 1994: Irene Harrison |
| 1972: John Hailes | 1984: Bart McMullin | 1997: Don McGlinchy |
| 1975: Tom Mason | 1985: Gerry Stokes | 2000: Kevin O'Shaughnessy |
| 1976: Billy Nott | 1990: Dave Jackson | |
| 1979: Brian McGuinness | 1992: George Malone | |

## Editors of Subsea

| | |
|---|---|
| 1973 to 1982 | Hugh Hennessy |
| 1982 to 1985 | Ronan Quinlan |
| 1985 to 1988 | Harry Smith |
| 1988 to 1992 | Billy Nott |
| 1992 to 1995 | Pat Dillane |
| 1995 to 1998 | Eddie Bourke |
| 1999 - | Polly Dolan |

## CFT Yearbooks

| | |
|---|---|
| 1967 | Hugh Hennesssy |
| 1968 | Mick Moriarty |
| 1969 | Hugh Hennessy |
| 1974 | Hugh Hennessy |
| 1975 | Hugh Hennessy |
| 1976 | Hugh Hennessy |
| 1978 | Hugh Hennessy |
| 1979 | Hugh Hennessy |

## List of CFT Publications

Subsea - Quarterly magazine, Editor Polly Dolan, address as above
ISSN 0791 – 475X . Printed by W&G Baird, Ltd, Antrim, Northern Ireland.
Annual subscription, IR£12.50 (issued free to all registered divers).
Underwater Ireland Guide to Irish Dive Sites, 1994, IR£10.00
Underwater Ireland Guide to Irish Dive Sites, Vol. 2, 1999 IR£15.00

## Other Relevant Publications available from CFT Head Office

Ireland's Seashore, Sherkin Island Marine Station
Ireland's Marine Life, Matt Murphy
Shipwrecks of the Irish Coast, E.Bourke
Shipwrecks of the Irish Coast, Part. 2, E Bourke
Shipwrecks of the Irish Coast , Part 3, E.Bourke
The Harsh Winds of Rathlin, T. Cecil
Sealife of Britain and Ireland

## Further Reading

| | |
|---|---|
| Fungie, The Dingle Dolphin | Ronnie Fitzgibbon |
| The Skeilig Story | Des Lavelle |
| Death in the Irish Sea, the sinking of the RMS Leinster | Roy Stokes |
| Donegal Shipwrecks | Ian Wilson |
| The Lusitania – Unravelling the Mysteries | Patrick O'Sullivan |
| Ireland's Armada Legacy | Laurence Flanagan |
| Historic Hook Head, Co Wexford | Billy Colfer |
| We Own the Laurentic | Jack Scoltock and Ray Cossum |

## Other References

**BIOMAR Biotope Viewer,**

CD published by the Environmental Sciences Trinity College, Dublin.
ISBN 0 9526 735 4 1, Version 2.0, a map-linked database of information
on marine sites, habitats and species on the sea shore and seabed.
From Ecoserve, 17 Rathfarnham Rd, D6W.
01- 492 5694, ecoserve@ecoserve.ie

**The National Coastline Survey,**

7,000 digital pictures on CD, available from the Marine Institute,
80 Harcourt Street, D2. IR£25.00 per CD.

**The Irish Maritime Archaeological Society, (IMAS),** a CFT subsidiary,

Membership to: 29 Castlelands, Hyde Road, Dalkey, Co Dublin
or: dtully@eircom.net

**The Ocean: Our Future**

Published by the Independent World Commission on the Oceans, Geneva.
E-mail: secretariat@world-oceans.org

## Useful Addresses

**The Department of the Marine and Natural Resources**,

Roinn na Mara agus Acmhainní Nádurtha,
Helpline: 1850 392 392

**The Marine Institute**, 80 Harcourt Street, D2,

Tel: 01- 478 0333 Fax: 01- 478 4988 Web Site: www.marine.ie/qsr

**The Maritime Institute of Ireland**, Haig Terrace, Dun Laoghaire, Dublin.

Tel: 01-280 0969 Website: www.mii.connect.ie

**The Maritime Museum**, Haig Terrace, Dun Laoghaire, Dublin.

Tel: 01- 280 0969

**The Heritage Council**, Kilkenny

responsible, amongst other matters for marine archaeology.
Tel: 056 70777, Fax: 056 70788

**The Environmental Agency**, St Martins House, Waterloo Road, D4.

Responsible for the licensing regulating and controlling activities for the
purpose of the protection of the environment.
Tel: 01 667 4474, Fax: 01 660 5848.

**The National Safety Council,** 4 Northbrook Road, D6.

Responsible amongst other matters for water safety
Tel: 01 496 3422, Fax: 01 496 3422
Web: http://www.national-safety-council.ie

# Appendix "B"

## Confederation Mondiales des Activités Subaquatiques (CMAS)

### THE WORLD UNDERWATER FEDERATION

Founded at Monaco - 1958

CMAS is the world body representing 20,000,000 recreational divers in 83 countries throughout the world.

Address:  The Secretary-General,   Pierre Dernier,
Viale Tiziano, 74 – 00196  Rome, Italy

Phone:  (39 06) 36 85 84 80     Fax:  (39 06) 36 85 84 90

Web Site: http://www.cmas.org   E-Mail: cmasmond@tin.it

\*   \*   \*   \*   \*   \*   \*   \*

## Conseil Communauté Européen des Activités Subaquatiques (CCEAS)

### THE EUROPEAN UNDERWATER FEDERATION (EUF)

CCEAS is the official organisation representing recreational divers in Europe. It has the affiliation of  2,000,000 divers in 5,000 clubs, with 1,000 instructors and 1,000 diving schools.  It is affiliated to CMAS, the World Underwater Federation.

It principal aim is to promote underwater sport, exploration and science, and related studies within the European Union.

President:  Derrick Ellerby,  BSAC,

Secretary:  Poul Jensen     DSF

Address:    18 Leen Valley Drive, Shirebrook, Mansfield, NG20 8BJ

# Appendix C

# BIBLIOGRAPHY
## (From my own collection)

**The Silent World**
Cousteau, Dumas          The Reprint Society, London 1954

**Man and the Underwater World**
de Latil and Rivoire     Jarrolds, London 1956

**Free Diving**
Dimitri Rebikoff,        Sedgwick and Jackson, London, 1955

**The Complete Manual of Free Diving**
Taillez, Dumas, Cousteau,  Putnam, New York, 1957

**The Undersea Challenge**
Bernard Eaton, Editor,   The British Sub Aqua Club, 1963

**World Beneath the Sea**
James Dugan              The National Geographic Society, 1963

**The Sea**
Leonard Engel            The National Geographic Society, 1969

**The Sea Around Us**
Rachel Carson            Staples Press, London 1951

**The Edge of the Sea**
Rachel Carson            Staples Press, London 1952

**The Last Resource**
Tony Loftus              Hamish Hamilton, London 1969

**Archaeology Under Water**
George F. Bass           Thames and Hudson, London 1966

**Under the Red Sea**
Hans Hass                Jarrolds, London

**Ordeal by Water**
Peter Keeble             Longmans, Green, London, 1957

**Underwater Saboteur**
Max Manus                    William Kimber, Great Britain 1953

**Sea Devils**
J. Valerio Borghese          Arrow Books, 1956

**The Frogmen**
Waldron and Gleeson          Evans Brothers, London, 1950

**The Silent Adventure**
Peter L. Dixon               Ballantine Books, New York, 1968

**Undersea Exploration**
Ken Roscoe                   Hamlyn. London, 1971

**Collins Guide to the Sea Shore**
Barrat and Younge            Collins, London, 1972

**Ireland's Marine Life**
Matt and Susan Murphy        Sherkin Island Station, 1992

**A Beginner's Guide to Ireland's Seashore**
Challinor et al.             Sherkin Island Station 1999

**The Open Sea, Its Natural History, Parts 1 and 2**
Sir Alistair Hardy           Collins, London 1959

**The Wrecks of Scapa Flow**
David M. Ferguson            The Orkney Press, 1985

**Guide to Irish Dive Sites**
John Hailes, Editor          Comhairle Fó-Thuinn The Irish Underwater Council, 1994

**Guide to Irish Dive Sites, Second edition**
John Hailes, Editor          CFT/IUC 1999

**The Brendan Voyage**
Tim Severin                  Hutchinson and Co. 1978

**Stars Beneath the Sea**
Trevor Norton                Arrow Books, 2000

**The Shores of Connemara**
Séamus Mac an Iomaire        Tír Eolas, 2000

# Appendix D

# GLOSSARY OF TERMS

ABLJ:          Adjustable Buoyancy Life Jacket

ADC:          Aide de Camp

AFAS:          The Association for Adventure Sports

ASAG:          Army Sub Aqua Group (now the Army Diving Group, ADG).

BSAC:          The British Sub Aqua Club

CCEAS:          Conseil Communauté Européen des Activités Subaquatiques

CFT:          Comhairle Fó -Thuinn - The Irish Underwater Council

Clearance Diver:          A Naval diver who is qualified to dive to depths of 50 metres, on air or mixed gases and to deal with welding and other work as well as demolitions, setting or disarming mines and other explosive devices.

Club Diver:          The minimum CFT grade of sports diver (CMAS 2 Star) qualified to lead another diver on an open water dive.

CMAS:          Confederation Mondiale des Activités Subaquatiques – The World Underwater Federation

Cox'n:          Abreviation for Coxswain, one who steers a boat

CPR:          Cardio-Pulmonary Resuscitation

DFCAT:          Defence Forces Council for Adventure Training

DSRV:          Deep Submergence Rescue Vessel, designed to carry out rescue of submarine crews at great depths.

DV:          Demand valve

EUF:          The European Underwater Federation

FFESSM:          Fédération Français d'Études et de Sports Sous-Marins.

Inflatable:          A rubber boat with inflatable pontoons and keel

| | |
|---|---|
| ISAC: | The Irish Sub Aqua Club |
| Moana: | A Polyansian word describing the length, breath or the vastness of the ocean. |
| Moniteur: | An international diving instructor/examiner of either One, Two or Three Stars. Three Star being the highest grade. |
| Narcosis: | Nitrogen narcosis, the 'narks', a condition affecting the air-breathing diver as he reaches certain depths. |
| NCO: | National Competitions Officer |
| NDO: | National Diving Officer |
| NSO: | National Snorkelling Officer |
| Oakum: | Hemp rope soaked in tar, used for caulking seams or stopping leaks |
| O.Rs: | Other Ranks, a military term describing all those soldiers who are not of commissioned officer rank. |
| RDO: | Regional Diving Officer |
| RIB: | A Rigid Inflatable Boat, combining the attributes of an inflatable boat superstructure with those of a rigid fibreglass hull |
| ROV: | Remote Operated Vehicle, carrying cameras and scientific instruments, controlled from on board a surface ship. |
| SCUBA: | Self Contained Underwater Breathing Apparatus |
| Ships Diver: | A Naval diver qualified to dive to 30 metres and who is normally employed to carry out searches and inspections. |
| Shot Line: | A buoyed and weighted line placed on the bottom or attached to a wreck or other object to facilitate a diving exercise |
| UPSI: | The Underwater Photographic Society of Ireland. |